Regional Development Strategy in Southeast Europe

George W. Hoffman

Regional Development Strategy in Southeast Europe

A Comparative Analysis of Albania, Bulgaria, Greece, Romania and Yugoslavia

PRAEGER SPECIAL STUDIES IN INTERNATIONAL ECONOMICS AND DEVELOPMENT

Praeger Publishers   New York   Washington   London

PRAEGER PUBLISHERS
111 Fourth Avenue, New York, N.Y. 10003, U.S.A.
5, Cromwell Place, London S.W.7, England

Published in the United States of America in 1972
by Praeger Publishers, Inc.

© 1972 by Praeger Publishers, Inc.

Library of Congress Catalog Card Number: 75-181696

Printed in the United States of America

For Viola

This book is the result of many years of research, including numerous field observations first in Yugoslavia and then expanded to include Bulgaria, Greece, and Romania. The great spatial contrasts in this region, the continuous interaction of natural and social forces, the relationship between national and regional interests, and the rapid socioeconomic changes in the postwar period have convinced me that a study of the broad outline of the changing economic activities within the context of the development strategy is essential not only for an understanding of changes in Southeast Europe, but of equal importance as a model for societies that have similar problems. Because so many social and economic problems in this area have developed because of similar historical experiences, the changes resulting from World War II can be observed both in the study of developments within each individual country, but also by comparing developments of the five countries.*

My interest in the area goes back almost forty years to my first visits to Yugoslavia, Bulgaria, and Greece. During the better part of the 1960s I was concerned with the problems of economic growth and the development strategy of the countries of this region. But it may well be useful to the reader to say a few words about how this study evolved, to point out what I hope to convey, and at the same time to caution the reader about important aspects not treated. In its inception, research on this project centered around the pattern of economic activities with exphasis on their regional distribution and a comparison of some of the activities of the five countries of Southeast Europe. During the initial research, and especially the fieldwork in Romania and Bulgaria and to a lesser degree in Greece, it became clear that insufficient economic data emphasizing regional distribution were available in each country and that comparatively few indexes were usable for a meaningful comparative analysis of these countries (that data for Albania would be insufficient was obvious from the outset). Even though comparative data have become more plentiful during the last few years, for prewar years and until the mid-1960s they were totally inadequate. This holds even more true for regional data. Together

---

*Albania, Bulgaria, Greece, Romania, and Yugoslavia. See page 3 for a specific definition of Southeast Europe.

with these conclusions it also became clear that a field of study given thus far only limited attention by social scientists was one that explained economic activities from the point of view of decision-making in the development strategy of the countries of Southeast Europe, and further related the decision process in spatial context. To the political geographer such a study of the over-all development strategy, with special emphasis on its regional aspects, seemed to offer a fruitful field for investigation and was especially well suited to emphasizing the comparative nature of the socioeconomic developments in the area. Such an approach also lessened the emphasis on often questionable statistical data and laid stress on the behavioral aspects of both socialist and nonsocialist societies. It offered especially an opportunity to stress the regional implications of the development strategy, including regional behavioral attitudes. This book, however, is concerned primarily with one very basic aspect of economic development; its development strategy and especially its spatial applications. It is not a broadly based regional study, nor a study of all socioeconomic activities with their regional ramifications. There exist a number of good country studies where such information is available. They are pointed out to the interested reader in the footnotes and the selected bibliography.

The discussions emphasize the processes, results, and implications of the development strategy including its regional impact since the conclusion of World War II in countries with different political ideologies. In addition, the discussions offer some thoughts on possible future developments, including the constraints imposed by their strategic location. Owing to my long-term research interest in Yugoslavia, the problems created by its multi-ethnic societies, and the greater accessibility of all sorts of material, greater attention is given to developments in this country.

It is also clear to me that in spite of an abundance of certain data being available in the different social sciences, certain information was not available with the result that an unevenness exists in the material covered. I am also fully aware, and this question was weighed both by myself and the publishers, that some of the background discussions in Part I are too detailed and perhaps of little interest to many scholars. However, it was felt that the great spatial variety of the physical environment together with long-time historical processes could best explain the rapid socioeconomic changes to a variety of interested readers. The greatest problem faced during the research for this book was that of explaining the rapidly changing political scene and of assessing its impact on economic policies in light of the changes. The conclusions drawn from this study, therefore,

must be of a temporary nature since I could not know fully the constraints imposed on the decision-making structure of the countries by
outside (nonregional) forces.

The book is divided into three parts and nine chapters. Part I,
"The Roots of the Problem," lays the background—on cultural and
physical environment, the formation of states, and the regional structure prior to World War II.

Part II discusses the postwar development strategy, while Part
III covers regional development processes.

A series of appendix tables giving comparative data and comparing socioeconomic developments between the countries of the
region will help to satisfy the reader interested in statistics. Tables
referring to specific points mentioned in the text are printed in the
appropriate places. Comparing developments of individual countries
is not always easy owing to the use of a different base. Statistical
information came both from official yearbooks and other compilations
and from special scholarly publications. Mention was made earlier
of the problem of collecting pertinent statistical data for comparative
purposes. Some countries, Bulgaria and Albania especially, publish
only meager data for the country as a whole and hardly any for individual regions. Romania has greatly increased national data, but
its regional data are meager. In addition, it increased the number of
its regions in 1968 from 18 to 39 and comparison of many indexes is
an impossible task. The number of communes in Yugoslavia has
rapidly decreased and districts have been completely abolished during
the last ten years. Opinion polls have been taken on many different
subjects in Yugoslavia, but they are scanty or completely lacking in
all other countries of the area.

In the text and the figures (maps) names are generally rendered
in the original transliteration from Cyrillic letters into Latin alphabet
in Serbian, Macedonian, Bulgarian, and Greek. Basically this follows
the transliteration system of the Library of Congress. Place names
generally follow those published by the Board of Geographic Names
and the National Geographic maps. If an accepted English-usage
form exists, it replaces the usages of local names, e.g., Belgrade
for Beograd, Bucharest for Bucuresti.

As a whole, the discussions in this book, the theories and their
practical application, together with the supporting statistical data and
maps aim to show the development strategy as it evolved during the
postwar period and its impact on the spatial organization of various

socioeconomic activities in Southeast Europe. Stress is laid through-out the discussions on the importance of a comprehensive and integrated regional development policy, of special importance for countries with great spatial disparity and those with multinational societies. The broad long-term aims of such policies in all countries of Southeast Europe are strikingly similar, though their specific policies differ markedly. The conclusions reached from this analysis stress the need for a full integration of sectoral and regional policies—something either not reached at the present time or in many cases not even attempted.

Hopefully these discussions will shed new light on the many developmental problems facing both socialist and nonsocialist societies, thus permitting some deductions as to the future socioeconomic changes in the region. The discussions obviously are of an interdisciplinary nature since the study of the behavior of societies must deal with all facets of the environment—physical, cultural, and political.

ACKNOWLEDGMENTS

Many people in Europe and the United States have answered requests for materials and given numerous interviews which have been vital in providing me with an insight into the workings of the countries herein discussed. Space does not permit the listing of all the individuals who have assisted me. Many top officials in the countries of Southeast Europe, directors and staff members of numerous research institutes and enterprises, members of university departments, of Academies of Science, and editors of journals have made this volume possible. Therefore, my debt is great to many individuals in many countries.

Most of all I must acknowlege with gratitude the many research grants I have received from foundations and the University of Texas at Austin over a period of two decades that made it possible for me to travel numerous times in the area. Albania is the only country not visited. Yugoslavia is best known to me and I have recently visited that country for the twelfth time since World War II. The opportunity to travel in Southeast Europe and other countries of Europe was vital for developing a feel for the region. Research grants are gratefully acknowledged from the National Science Foundation, the American Philosophical Society, the American Council of Learned Societies, and the Social Science Foundation of the University of Denver. My own university, the University of Texas at Austin, awarded me several grants through the University Research Institute, grants used for research assistants, cartographical aids, and miscellaneous items.

Two people in the United States and two in Yugoslavia have been untiring in their encouragement of my work and giving of their time to discuss problems under consideration, reading and criticizing drafts, and assisting me with many vital contacts: Chauncy D. Harris, Samuel N. Harper Professor of Geography at the University of Chicago, a friend and colleague from my wartime services at the Research and Analysis Branch of the Office of Strategic Services, introduced me first to my Yugoslav colleague, Josip Roglić, Senior Professor of Geography at the University of Zagreb. My colleague Donald D. Brand, with his tremendous knowledge of historical processes in nearly every part of the world and with an unrivaled knowledge of bibliographical material, has never failed to answer my questions and has consistently encouraged me to aim at becoming a "regional geographer" in its truest sense. Special appreciation is given to the late Professor Rudolf Bićanić, Professor of Economics at the School of Law, University of Zagreb. His knowledge of the various social sciences, his strong belief in the viability and future of his country, and his willingness to discuss all key issues and to read and criticize various draft sections of this book before his untimely death in 1968 will always be gratefully remembered. I also wish to recognize an outstanding scholar, teacher, and personal friend, the late Professor Philip E. Mosely, who through his profound knowledge and belief in the cooperation of the peoples of Southeast Europe with those of America encouraged me to pursue studies in the area since my service with the OSS when my interest in the area began.

The assistance of numerous officials of U.S. government agencies—the Department of State and its officers both in Washington and the countries of Southeast Europe as well as other government agencies—was most helpful. The same goes for the many government and Party officials and heads of semi-official organizations in Bulgaria, Greece, Romania, and especially Yugoslavia. Specifically I wish to acknowledge the valuable aid received from the following: The Economic Institutes of Croatia and Serbia under the directorship of Professors Rikard Lang and Kosta Mihailović; the Institute of International Economics and Politics in Belgrade under its directors Janez Stanovnik (at present director of the U.N. Economic Commission for Europe in Geneva) and Leo Matec; the Federal Institute for Statistics and its chief of the International Division, Čed Novković; the Center of Planning and Economic Research in Athens under its former director George Coutsoumaris and its head of the regional planning office George Chiotis (now with the Ministry of Coordination); the Social Sciences Center in Athens under its former director John G. Peristiany; the director of the American Farm School in Thessaloniki, Bruce M. Lansdale; the late Basil Laourdas, formerly director of the Institute of Balkan Studies in Thessaloniki; the Sociological Institute of the Romanian Academy of Sciences under its director Ion Matei; the Economic Institute of the Bulgarian Academy of Sciences and its secretary Professor Ivan Zahariev; the Südost Institute in Munich under the directorship of Mathias Bernath and editor Hans Hartl; the Österreichische Ost and Südost Institute in Vienna under its director Richard Plaschka and its staff members Josef Breu and Robert Schwanke. Also the various offices of the United Nations in Geneva and especially Antoni Kuklinski, former head of the Institute for Social Development; the European Coordinating Center of Social Science Research and Documentation Center in Vienna with Adam Schaff as director; the United Nations Industrial Development Organization (UNIDO) under its Executive Director Ibrahim Helmi

Abdel-Rahman; the International Bank for Reconstruction and Development in Washington with the former Director of Information, Harold Graves.

The list of colleagues in geography and the other social sciences who have assisted me is a lengthy one and only a few can be specifically named. Close contacts have been maintained with geographers at institutes in Ljubljana, Zagreb, Belgrade, Skopje, Sofia, Bucharest, Iasi, Cluj, Budapest, Vienna, Munich (Wirtschaftsgeographisches Institut), the London School of Economics and Political Science, University College, as well as geographers at the various institutes of the academies of science. Here it is with the greatest gratitude that special mention is made of the members of the Institute of Geography and Geology (now Geography only) of the Romanian Academy of Sciences and the "Jovan Cvijić" Institute of Geography of the Serbian Academy of Sciences both with the late Borivoje Ž. Milojević and its succeeding directors. I was made an honorary member of the Academy at the Fiftieth Anniversary of its founding, a recognition that was much appreciated. A few colleagues and assistants must be especially recognized for their continuous personal kindness, professional competence, and willingness to provide me with essential research material: Vladimir Klemencic, Žlatko Pepeonik, Veljiko Rogić, Josip Roglić, Jakov Sirotkovic, and Stanko Zutjie in Zagreb; Metod Vojvode, and Igor Vrišer in Ljubljana; Ljubimir Dinev, Kristo Marinov, and Christo Peev in Sofia; Serban Dragomirescu, Constantin Herbst, Vintiză Milhailesev, and Victor Tufescu from Bucharest; Hermann Gross and Karl Ruppert in Munich; Ian Hamilton and Gordon East in London; and Bernard Kayser and Pierre Yves-Pechoux in Toulouse.

To those of my colleagues in the United States who have given generously of their time to read parts of this manuscript and offer critical comments I feel especially indebted, though they obviously should not be held responsible for my interpretation. Many have already been mentioned in the footnotes as authors of important studies. I am happy to give special recognition also to my colleagues in economics, Niles M. Hansen and Forrest M. Hill, whose willingness to guide me through economic terminology less familiar to me is much appreciated. In addition, Niles Hansen has critically read several chapters. Visiting Professor Paul N. Rosenstein-Rodan's comments on four chapters were most helpful. Others who have read parts of this manuscript were Kingsley Haynes of my own department, George J. Demko of Ohio State University, Charles Jelavich of Indiana University, Thomas Poulsen of Portland State University, Joseph Velikonja of the University of Washington, and M. George Zaninovich of the University of Oregon. In addition to conversations with and the study of published and unpublished materials of the above, I wish to acknowledge the help of Richard Burks, John C. Campbell, Huey Louis Kostanick, Irwin T. Sanders, and Evan Vlachos, to mention only a few who have immeasurably contributed to my understanding of the complex social and political problems of this region. My service on comittees of the American Council of Learned Societies also greatly aided my education, especially in other social sciences and the humanities. I also wish to give special recognition to the research staff of Radio Free Europe in Munich under its director of research John F. Brown whose reports have become an indispensible source for scholarly research in my area of interest.

My gratitude to my various research assistants--Richard Van Steenkiste, Jean T. Hannaford, and Kent Gray-is immeasurable. Appreciation is also extended to William Novak, a graduate student in my department, for his valuable assistance in the final stages of the manuscript. Jean Hannaford also was responsible for all cartographic work and her diligence, perception, and dependability has been essential for my work. Ian Hamilton, Norman Pounds, and Methuen-Praeger Publishers gave permission to use two of their maps published in Eastern Europe: Essays in Geographical Problems with only slight modification. Their kindness is much appreciated.

Words of thanks must also be expressed to my students, as well as to my friends, who very often were on the short end of receiving the expected attention owing to my preoccupation with research while in Austin or to my absence on foreign research leave.

Finally, I cannot conclude this long list of acknowledgements without expressing my overwhelming debt of gratitude to my wife, Viola. As editor, secretary, research assistant and ever-ready critical commentator, as travel companion on my numerous field trips, and sharing my respect and love for the people from all walks of life in the countries visited, she has assumed responsibilities way beyond the call of duty. She has become, in reality, a real co-author of this book.

CONTENTS

LIST OF TABLES

TABLES IN THE APPENDIX

LIST OF FIGURES

1

Few areas in the world show as great regional contrasts in their physical, cultural, and economic diversity as the five countries of Southeast Europe.[1] Historical and physical events are reflected in the landscape, and its people and have had an impact on modern regional and national economic problems. Geography and history have interacted in this area, bringing about a complex cultural land-scape with great regional differences and with a "heterogeneous grouping of cultural variables and a political system that has been in constant flux as a result of external pressures and internal instabil-ity."[2] Historical events have played an important role in this region with its often cited "crossroad" or "bridge" position linking Central Europe with the Near East (Levant).[3] This is usually explained by its easy outer accessibility, which made possible movements by many different people and ideas from neighboring power centers into impor-tant peripheral regions and through its corridor-valleys into the heart of the region. Of even greater importance was the impact of the rugged and diverse relief of large segments of the area that pro-duced great inner fragmentation, encouraging particularism and isolationism and thus impeding important historical processes. As Josip Roglić put it, "it was a region where the strong got lost and the weak survived."*

---

*The use of the term Southeast Europe is in many ways an arbitrary one, though it is possible to make a strong case for the use of this term in view of the locational aspects within the European triangle. The best explanation and strongest argument in the defense of the term Southeast Europe was made by Josip Roglić, "Die Gebirge als die Wiege des Geschichtlichen Geschehens in Südosteuropa," Colloquium Geographicum, Band 12. Argumenta Geographica

The complex relief of the area is mainly responsible for the lack of political cohesion that made unification of the area extremely difficult and left a profound impact on the political and economic geography of the region. But the important role played by the mountains also was responsible for the fact that, in spite of the influx of competing foreign cultural influences, diffusion of these influences is superficial, with the result that Southeast Europe is an area not only in which different cultures are superimposed on each other, but in which people have been able to develop "distinct national personalities and highly articulated national cultures."[4] The struggle against foreign domination was further complicated by ethnic and religious conflict, which resulted in the ardent nationalism for which the people of Southeast Europe are so well known.

The movements of the many people and the constant traffic along certain routeways in the well-marked relief of Southeast Europe is attested to by the many remnants of cultural monuments. They include pagan temples, deteriorated sculptures of bygone leaders, pre-Christian tombstones, remnants of once-prosperous settlements, and well-built fortresses of Greek and Geto-Dacian culture, Thracian tumuli, Roman roads, bridges, forums, palaces, baths (public houses), and old weathered coins. There still remain the famous vineyards of the Fruška Gora between the Sava and the Danube, Byzantine fortress walls, churches with their early frescoes, medieval Bulgarian castles, Serbian monasteries, and Turkish mosques and hans (way stations). The similarity of city layouts, with their white baroque churches, typical of the architecture of the eighteenth and nineteenth centuries along the former Austrian Military Border with the Ottoman Empire, is especially visible in the plains resettled after the Turkish defeat of Slavonia, Vojvodina, and the Banat. Finally, there is the architecture and the legacy of its life expressing the characteristics of

---

(Festzeitschrift Carl Troll, 1970), pp. 225-39. Only its northern limit is really debatable; the question of whether Hungary is part of Southeast Europe or not. The author of this volume has excluded Hungary from his discussions.

A number of ideas expressed and developments discussed in this chapter are based on correspondence, discussions, and the reading of both published and unpublished manuscripts from Josip Roglić, senior professor at the Geographical Institute, University of Zagreb. The author appreciates this opportunity extending over a period of twenty years of close professional relations.

Mediterranean civilization. All of these, plus the Cyrillic alphabet, Orthodox religion, and diverse social customs, testify to the important role played by many invaders, conquerors, and the alien philosophies that tried, though with only limited success, to impose new modes of life on the peasant societies of the region. During the long Turkish occupation, people were forced to flee for protection from the plains into the nearby mountains, the high-level platform, the interior basins, and other less-accessible parts of Southeast Europe. This contributed to the unusual emptiness of the most fertile stretches of land along the main thoroughfares during many periods of the long history of this area.

Movements of the many people of different cultures within Southeast Europe were largely dictated by the relief of the region. The generally mountainous character—the relationship between the mountains and hill lands, depressions, and lowlands—defined the available routes, although obviously the importance of specific routes changed during different historical periods. With some exceptions, such as the inner Dinaric Ranges (central Bosnia, Herzegovina, Montenegro), the northwestern Pindus and Epirus (Greece), the Macedonian-Thracian Massif (Bulgaria), Southeast Europe, in spite of its pronounced mountainous character, is accessible and did not provide an insurmountable obstacle to the movements of its people. The importance of individual routeways varied with the political and economic objectives of the roadbuilders. With the exception of temporary or transitory roads, the major routeways remained important throughout history. Thus, in Southeast Europe men and commerce traveled along well-established routes and crossed rivers at easily fordable sites where bridges later were of importance for the establishment of fairs and crossroads settlements. It was not until the era of modern highways that traffic became independent of the contingencies of topography.[5]

Into this highly complicated and diversified physical environment have come numerous people from many different physical and cultural environments, and they have created a quite extraordinary and complex mixture of peoples. Centuries of invasion by many peoples and a sequence of cultures have left a deep mark on the present landscape. Although most of the original inhabitants of these isolated areas successfully resisted being assimilated into the dominating cultures, they could not avoid being affected by them. Byzantine and Ottoman influence extended for the most part south of the Sava-Danube rivers, except in Old Romania (the Walachian and Moldavian principalities). North of this line and in most parts of Transylvania, German influence via the Austrian Empire reached into northern Moldavia and Venetian

Italy along the Adriatic coast. Due to these various influences, there exists even today a clearly visible threefold cultural division in the region: the Central European influence in northern Yugoslavia and in many parts of Transylvania and Moldavia; the Byzantine Turkish influence in the eastern and southern parts of Romania, Bulgaria, central and southern Yugoslavia, northern Greece, and Albania; and the Mediterranean influence along the Adriatic coast and in central and southern Greece.

The Central European influence extended from both the political and military interests of the Austrian Empire and the many dispersed German settlements, most of which have been abandoned as a result of two world wars in this century but nevertheless leaving a strong cultural impact on a number of noncontiguous areas throughout the region—e.g., Slavonia, Vojvodina, Banat, and inner Transylvania. Byzantine impact was more lasting and today is based on the cultural influence of the Orthodox church and historical ties with both Constantinople (Istanbul) and Greece. Turkish influence has almost disappeared in the last twenty years—a few mosques, old Turkish houses, and shops are all that remain of the 500 years of Turkish occupation. Mediterranean influence, obviously, is strong along the Adriatic coast of Yugoslavia—the centuries of Venetian-Italian influence are expressed in the style of the houses and churches, many of the customs of the people, and the layout of the coastal cities. Another influence that should not be totally disregarded is the intellectual stimulation, especially marked in the field of education, that came from nineteenth-century France, to a lesser degree from Germany and Italy, and more recently from the technological stimulus of industrial Western Europe and the United States.

In writing about past events, it is always easy to stress important dates and the problems of ever-changing boundaries. On the other hand, the processes that conditioned those events are really much more indicative of change; while much geography is imprinted in these past events, historical legacies are evident in all national and regional problems in the countries of Southeast Europe. To enable the reader to better understand these regional contrasts, a brief presentation of the great spatial variety in physical environment and its impact on historical processes and social changes affecting the present-day cultural scene will provide the necessary background for a better understanding of the important social and economic attitudes and activities in Southeast Europe (for details see Figure 1, page 7).

FIGURE 1

SOUTHEAST EUROPE

Elevation over 650 feet (200 meters)

SPATIAL VARIETY IN THE PHYSICAL
ENVIRONMENT

Broad physical divisions are clearly discernable. Considerable contrast is evident in the landscape of Southeast Europe where physiographic conditions, climatic influences, and topographic features clearly indicate the great spatial variety of the environment.[6] Three major mountain ranges characterize the relief of Southeast Europe. Surrounding these mountain ranges, which are broken down into numerous separate folds often following structural contacts, are the economically important and more easily accessible lowlands, hill lands, and depressions.

The structure and relief of the topography is extremely complicated and diverse, and the lithic composition varies from limestone to more-resistant crystalline rock. Volcanic intrusions indicate that instability is a mark of many areas, and the numerous earthquakes in this region throughout history are ample proof of this instability (Skopje, Banja Luka, and Sofia have had moderate to severe earthquakes during the last few years).

There are three major mountain ranges in Southeast Europe. The first is the curving ranges of the Carpathians partially encircling the Pannonian Basin and their extension into northeastern Serbia and northern Bulgaria as the Balkan Mountains (Stara planina or Old Mountains) and their parallel range, the Middle Mountains (Sredna gora). The second is the Dinaric ranges, which trend northwest to southeast from the Eastern Alps (Julian Alps), parallel the Adriatic coast to the mouth of the Drin River, and from there extend inland to the Morava-Vardar depression. The ranges also continue inland through most of Albania (the Prokletije Mountains or North Albanian Alps and in the south as the Albanian Epirus) and continue finally as the Pindus Mountains throughout peninsular Greece. Rugged topography, the deep penetration of the sea inland, and a clear physiographic division between plains, foothills and mountains are characteristic of the relief of Greece. The main mountain ranges are traceable through Crete to Rhodes. The third range, the Macedonian-Thracian Massif, also called Rhodope Massif in Bulgaria, crosses the Morava-Vardar depression in a southeasterly direction, partially enclosing the Maritsa Basin (also called the Thracian or Rumelian Basin).

While the various mountains in Southeast Europe have greatly contributed to the survival of ethnic groups and the development of separate civilizations unimpeded by the various conquerors as well

as serving as a refuge for migrating tribes and for pastoralists, of
much greater importance to the cultural and economic landscape are
the nonmountainous areas, fertile valleys, lowlands, depressions,
and intermontane basins. They are few and far apart, however.

The most extensive of these nonmountainous areas are the
Moldavian Tablelands (or Plateau), the Walachian Plain (the Cimpia
Romana, or Romanian Plain), and the Transylvanian Basin, a part
of the Pannonian Basin (sometimes called the Carpathian Basin), all
within Romania. South of the Walachian Plain and the Danube in
Bulgaria is the fertile Danubian or Bulgarian Plateau, which is covered
with loess and dissected by deep and broad valleys that reach east
to the steppe plateau of Dobruja. Another important nonmountainous
region lies between the Balkan Mountains and the Macedonian-Thracian
Massif, the fertile Maritsa Basin, the most densely settled region of
Bulgaria. One of the most productive agricultural regions of the
whole peninsula is located in northeast Yugoslavia and southwest
Romania. It is part of the Pannonian Basin and is known in Yugoslavia
as the Vojvodina. Its eastern part extends into Romania, as Banat.
This fertile region is covered, for the most part, with loess and
interspersed with limestone and crystalline hills and extends west
into the Slovenian-Croatian Hill Lands along the southern and southwestern margin of the Pannonian Basin. It is largely drained by the
Drava and Sava rivers. Besides being Yugoslavia's most important
cereal-producing region, fruit as well as industrial crops play an
ever-increasing role.

Most extensive and picturesque is the coastal zone, including
the many islands of the Adriatic littoral of Yugoslavia, which stretch
from the Istrian Peninsula to the Albanian border and into Greece.
The width of the Adriatic coastal zone varies from a few hundred
feet to ten miles, and the steep slopes of the High Karst block access
to the interior. This region of Mediterranean crops has recently
become one of the main tourist attractions of Southeast Europe. The
low-lying Albanian coastal plain is broader than the Dalmatian coast
to the north. Roughly midway, the Shkumbi River flows into the
Adriatic, dividing the country into a northern and southern portion,
each with its own cultural tradition, including a separate dialect.
An important agricultural area in a location of physical and cultural
transition is northern Greece and southern Yugoslavia, with a series
of faulted basins separated by mountain zones and extensive coastal
plains. Included in this area are Greek Macedonia and Thrace and
the steppe-like southern part of Yugoslavia's Republic of Macedonia.
The most important of the Greek lowlands is the basin of Thessaly.

Romania

The Carpathian ranges of Romania are heavily forested and are characterized by much fragmentation due to their many intermontane depressions, broad river valleys, and many passes permitting easy circulation between the interior basin and the surrounding plains. All these routes are of longstanding historical importance. The ranges are also characterized by numerous high-level platforms where forests have been removed to provide livestock grazing. They also have served as the seasonal as well as permanent home of many people. As has been often pointed out by Romanian writers, these mountains did not act as a major population divide, as was the case, for example, with the Pyrenees or the Alps. On the contrary, due to the numerous passes and depressions, economic exploitation such as high-altitude agriculture and cattle breeding were made possible by the existence of many mountain platforms. It was here that traditional customs, including the purity of the Romanian language, was preserved. Trans-humance between the mountain pastures and the lower parts of the Transylvanian Basin, until recently, characterized the human life of this region.[7]

The Western Carpathians, a branch of the main Carpathian system, stretch from the Danube River north to the Somes Valley. They have a series of valleys opening to the Great Alföld and its main river, the Tisza. The minerals of the mountains, especially the Transylvanian Alps and the metal-rich Poiana Rusca of the western Carpathians, together with the large forest reserves, were exploited for a long period.[8] The Western part of the Carpathians is Romania's oldest and most valued iron-producing region. Records show that production in this area was of importance as early as the Roman period, as shown by the large archaeological findings, including the remnants of the Geto-Dacian royal city of Sarmizegethusa. Large-scale iron and steel production began as early as 1770 in Resita and in 1895 in Hunedoara. The great hydroelectric-power potential developed in recent years gives the mountainous areas an increased economic importance. With the rich petroleum fields of the Sub-Carpathians (Forelands), the resources of this area are a vital asset to Romania's economic development. A large part of the Forelands is very densely settled and includes important recently developed industries.

The Eastern and Southern Carpathians offer a series of transverse passes and valleys, running east-west between the Moldavian Tablelands and the Transylvanian Basin and north-south from the Transylvanian Basin to the Walachian Plain. Probably the most

important of these roads connected the Transylvanian Basin and the
Walachian Plain via the Prahova Valley and Predeal Pass (3,445 feet),
which today carries the Budapest-Bucharest railway and a modern
highway. The Porta Orientalis connecting the Banat and the Mureş
and Bistra valleys with Orsova near the Iron Gate was already a much-
used north-south routeway during the Dacian and Roman periods.
The north-south road through the Olt Gorge via Turnu Rosu Pass,
connecting Oltenia with Transylvania, also played an important role.
Broad river valleys from the Transylvanian Basin offered easy access
to the Pannonian Basin, the Valley of the Mureş being the most important one. It was this Poiana Rusca region that was the core area of
the original kingdom of Dacia.

In the east and south, the mountains slope toward the Moldavian
Tablelands located between the Prut and Siret rivers, and, with the
exception of a central plateau, the entire region is a hilly steppe.
The hills are loess-covered, with fertile chernosem soils, although
recurrent and disastrous droughts do much damage. The agriculturally
important Walachian Plain extends to the steppe-like plateau of the
Dobruja region, which blocks the straight course of the Danube and
forces it northward. The Walachian Plain is a depression that in the
Tertiary period was a gulf of the Black Sea, but which by now has
been entirely filled by river deposits from the Transylvanian Alps.
The southern part of the Carpathians extends to the Kazan Gorge of
the Danube, the Iron Gate being the narrowest part of the gorge.
Loess covers important parts of the plain, especially east of the Olt
River. The Danube River and the broad floodplain (Balta) on the
Romanian side separates the plain from the Bulgarian Plateau (Platform). Actually, both sides of the Danube are very much alike in
regard to climate, soil, and products, but the river still acts as a
barrier between the two parts located in Romania and Bulgaria. West
of the Olt River (Oltenia), the relief is more varied. There is heavier
rainfall and a more diversified agriculture. Besides producing cereals, the area emphasizes vines, tobacco, sunflower, soya beans, and
so on. Bucharest, the capital of Romania, is located in the most
advantageous part of the Walachian Plain, an area known as Vlasia
(inhabited at an early period by Vlahs, or Aromani), the name often
used for the original settlers of Romania. This region was an important link on the old and most-direct route from Stambul (Constantinople)
to the Transylvanian Basin.

The flat Danube Delta, a nature reserve, is an area of marshes
and floating reed islands, with a great variety of birds and sturgeons,
the latter breeding in the braided water channels of the Danube.
Today, the reeds are locally important for the manufacture of cellulose.

South of the Danube Delta, between the Danube and the Black Sea, are the Dobruja Tablelands, which have two distinct parts: the northern, heavily eroded old mountains; and the southern, lower part, with a more even relief. The steppe plateau is an important agricultural region with a relief of just under 600 feet.

The Danube River was an important route for lengthy periods throughout most recorded history, but its use as a continuous routeway was intermittently blocked by political developments. At important periods in history, trade routes also ran across the river rather than just along the river. The route from Vienna to Semlin (Zemun) and later to Vidin (for trade with Sofia) remained the major section of the Danube used during most of the Ottoman conquests, and only in the latter part of the eighteenth century were measures taken to open the river for trade along its whole length. In 1815, Turkey agreed not to hinder Danubian traffic, and this, in turn, permitted the shipment of goods from Vienna to various Danubian ports, thus reducing the time required for transporting goods on the inferior roads.

The Transylvanian Basin, which reaches an elevation of 2,000 feet, was once a sea basin that had filled with river deposits, but it is now high and hilly, having been uplifted and dissected. It has well-drained soils, but in places is heavily eroded, as seen in the sculptured hills and wide valleys. The basin is transitional with regard to climatic conditions. Precipitation is heavy; most of it falls in the early summer and declines from west to east and also from north to south. Unfortunately, summer rains occur during the period of high temperature and high evaporation, which lessens the effectiveness of the precipitation and at times results in serious droughts. On the other hand, late spring snow in the northern and eastern parts of the Carpathians, together with heavy rains and sudden thawing in the mountains, can also bring disastrous floods in the basin.* The basin is drained largely westward toward the Tisza and Danube. Because of favorable climatic and soil conditions, this region was cleared for cultivation; its rich agricultural lands today produce cereals, potatoes in the north, hemp in the center, sugar beets in the southeast, and fruit,

------

*One of the most disastrous floods in the recorded history of this area occurred in May and June, 1970. It was estimated that close to one-third of the agricultural area of the Basin was one or more times under water, especially in the Mureş and its tributaries and the Someş rivers.

with vineyards especially on the south-facing slopes of the Mures
River. The basin also offers a great variety of resources for industrial development—quantities of natural gas with a high methane
content, salt, some lignite in the southeast, and iron ore in the southwest.

Bulgaria

Bulgaria's relief structure is relatively simple. The two major
mountain ranges of the country, the Balkans and Macedonian-Thracian
Massif, both slope eastward toward the Black Sea. West is the Sofia
Depression, the southern border of which is formed by a branch of
the Balkan Ranges extending in a southeastern direction from the
Pirot Basin in Yugoslavia toward the main range of the Rhodope
Massif near the Rila Plannina. The basin has an elevation of 1,800
feet and is easily accessible through several river valleys.

The Balkan Mountains are about 4000 miles in length, and are
structurally a continuation of the Carpathian Ranges. The latter continue south and southeastward from the Danube as the Northeast
Serbian Mountains; east of the Timok River they are known as Balkan
Ranges. The northern slopes of the ranges descend gradually toward
the Danube, where they fall off rather abruptly about 300 feet in a
wall of limestone and loess. This area is known as the Danube or
Bulgarian Plateau. It is extremely fertile and is covered by loess,
but dissected by deep and broad valleys. The valleys have abundant
water and are protected from the cold, dusty winter winds blowing
across the plateau from the Walachian Plain and have numerous,
relatively small cities. The main ranges gradually become lower
toward the east and, together with the plateau on the north, enclose
the small Varna Basin, which opens toward the Black Sea. South of
the main range of the Balkan Mountains are a number of significant
depressions. The best known is the Tundsha Depression, which
results from a downfaulting of the land and is characterized by
numerous hot springs and the widespread cultivation of roses. The
Balkan Ranges are easily crossed via the Isker Valley to the Sofia
Plateau and the Shipka Pass, connecting Danube ports with the Maritsa
Basin.

The Sofia Plateau (1,800 feet) is surrounded by mountains, but,
due to the special characteristics of the river system radiating from
this structurally complex area, an extremely favorable and unique
nodality of the Sofia area is brought about. Were it not for the small
size of this basin, including the coal-rich neighboring Pernik Basin,

from a purely locational aspect this area could have easily exerted its influence over a much larger region of Southeast Europe. Routes radiate from Sofia in many directions. The main road leaves the Morava Valley, crosses the basin of Nis and reaches the Sofia Basin through the low Dragoman Pass, which forms the watershed between the Morava and Isker rivers. The road continues eastward from the Sofia Basin to the valley of the Maritsa River. It follows the Maritsa to the old Turkish city of Edirne and ends at Istanbul. This was an important artery and was already in use in pre-Roman times. During the Roman period, this routeway, called the Via Singindunum, connected Belgrade and the Lower Morava with the eastern Roman provinces; Serdica (Sofia) and Trimontium (Plovdiv), described by Tacitus in 60 A.D., were the most important way stations. Certain pass crossings of the Stara planina between the Bulgarian Plateau and the Maritsa Basin (e.g., the Shipka Pass) were of lasting importance.

The major north-south route in the eastern half of the peninsula, developed largely during the Turkish period, went from Cracow to Moldavia (which provided a link with the important trade route from the Ukraine) and Gelati, crossed the Danube into eastern Bulgaria either at Ruse or Silistra, and continued thence to Stambul (Istanbul) or Selanik (Thessaloniki).

The Maritsa Basin is drained by the Maritsa River and opens toward the Aegean Sea. The fertile alluvial soil and abundance of water of the basin permit the growing of a great variety of crops, especially cereals, tobacco, rice, vegetables, and fruit. It is Bulgaria's most important agricultural area.

South of the Maritsa Basin is the relatively narrow Macedonian-Thracian Massif, consisting of the Rhodope, Rila and Prim mountains. It broadens southeastward and falls gradually toward the east in a series of uplands and dissected hills, which are broken by the Maritsa River northwest of Edirne. The highest part of the Massif is in the Rila planina (Mount Musala, 9,596 feet), an area of volcanic origin containing the headwaters of the Maritsa River. The Massif consists of a number of fertile river valleys and basins, e.g., the Struma and Mesta valleys and the basins of Samokov, Pernik, and Kjustendil. Passes provide access to the valleys. This zone is rich in brown coal and lignite, and a variety of metals are found (especially in the central and eastern Rhodopes). The rivers of the Massif offer great hydroelectric potential, and the forests of the region make an important contribution to the economy of the country. This region has really just opened up in the postwar period. The mild climate, especially in the valleys that open toward the south and southeast, permit the growing of Mediterranean plants as well as tobacco. Part of the Massif is in eastern Macedonia and Thrace in Greece, a region of faulted basins separated by mountain zones and river deltas. Two areas north of Burgas and Varna along Bulgaria's Black Sea coast offer an unusual attraction for tourists because of their mild climate and sandy coast.

Yugoslavia

The relief of Yugoslavia is characterized by a central mountain core, the Dinaric Ranges, and the closely associated peripheral regions. The mountainous part of Yugoslavia (over 1,500 feet in elevation) comprises 45 percent of the total area, while 29 percent is classified as lowlands (below 600 feet). The parallel ranges of the Dinaric system are of limestone of Cretaceous age and trend southeast from the Julian Alps in the Ljubljana Basin toward the Morava-Vardar Depression in the southeast. As the Prokletije Mountains, they form the Albanian-Yugoslav border, with an elevation of over 7,000 feet, continue in a series of parallel ranges southward to merge with the Epirus Mountains, and finally continue as the Pindus Mountains into southern Greece. Smaller forks leave the main mountain chain and open to the north.

Within Yugoslavia, the ranges are triangular in shape and vary in width from 60 to 150 miles, with an average elevation of 4,000 to 6,000 feet. They extend south to the Ibar Valley of Serbia and the Kosovo-Metohija Basin for approximately 350 miles. Durmitor Mountain in Montenegro is the highest (8,275 feet). The Adriatic littoral forms a sharp boundary toward the west, while the borders toward the east are not always clearly defined. The structure of these highlands is extremely complicated and diverse. Volcanic intrusions indicate that the highlands are an area of instability. Steep mountains and small intermontane basins and heavy erosion, especially in the southern part of the highlands, are common. A large part of these is composed of karst. In Yugoslavia, the Dinaric Ranges form a mountainous core, often referred to as the heartland fortress, which is surrounded by the economically important and culturally diverse peripheral zone with its fertile plains, hill lands, basins, and the Adriatic littoral, all easily passable and connected with interior valleys.

The Dinaric Ranges are characterized by great diversity, ranging from the barren, dissected, and waterless High Karst in the west to a series of parallel forested mountains and hill lands in the north and northeast. The ranges include the narrow coastal zone and the Adriatic littoral, with its many islands and depressions that have been created by the invasion of the sea. The littoral and the terraced hillsides have only a limited amount of fertile soil, and Mediterranean crops, such as olives, vines and figs, limited pasture land, cereal acreage, and fishing are traditionally the important sources of support for the population. The large number of tourists who recently have discovered the beauty of the littoral are adding a new and important source of income to this region and give a new vitality to the life of the people.

Access to the interior is blocked by the High Karst, a barren, mainly Mesozoic limestone zone with numerous underground streams and caverns. The relief gives this region its fortress-like characteristics. The river valleys are very short and widely spaced because precipitation falling upon these limestone rocks sinks underground, where it continues to flow. Rivers flow in dissected valleys or through gorges that are difficult to traverse. They carry varying quantities of water and have considerable gradient differences between source and mouth. Their use for hydroelectric projects is now being developed. The whole region consists of a series of barren, rocky plateaus with a series of flat ridges, the so-called planina. Longitudinal troughs, polja, alternate with synclinal depressions that were formed from subsiding hollows and subsequently were enlarged when rain water and rivers dissolved the calcareous rocks. Dolinas (small, round depressions also formed by the solution of calcareous rocks) and uvale (larger dolina—600 feet in diameter)—both covered with alluvial deposits and/or red earth (terra rosa), a relatively fertile soil formed by the nonsoluble material in the limestone—add to the variety of the relief.

The eastern part of the Dinaric Ranges, inner Bosnia and western Serbia, is less barren and rugged. The crystalline rocks of this part, unlike limestone, retain some surface water, and settlements are more prevalent. Narrow and open valleys are interspersed, and extensive mining and logging activities have been carried on throughout the countryside for many centuries.[9] The slopes toward the Sava lowlands and the Morava Valley are the most densely settled areas.

While the peripheral zone is easily reached from neighboring countries, parts of the mountainous heartland are inaccessible and have been both a fortress and a manpower reservoir. The least-populated and most-inaccessible region is the immediate hinterland of the Adriatic littoral. Scarcity of soil and water discouraged settlement. The rugged terrain made conquest either from the sea (by

Roman legions or Venetians) or from the land (by Byzantines or Turks)
extremely difficult. The only areas economically productive are a
few agriculturally important polja (fields)—Sinjsko, Livanjsko, Duvan-
jsko, Popovo, and so on—and parts of the hinterland of Dubrovnik,
but even here summer droughts and floods at sowing and harvesting
make life difficult. The type of agriculture changes from northeast
to southwest. Barley, oats, rye, and buckwheat are predominant in
the northeast; vineyards, tobacco, almond trees, and maize are found
in the southwest. Stockbreeding played an important role, but has
declined gradually since the interwar period, and, as a result, many
of the isolated settlements have lost their livelihood and their people
have moved to more developed regions. The prohibition of open goat
grazing has further accelerated this decline. There are considerable
forests, and many areas of the Adriatic hinterland are rich in bauxite.

     The southern part of the heartland, a region stretching to the
Drina and Ibar rivers, consists of a series of plateaus interspersed
with deeply cut river valleys. The country is easily passable and
the dolomite lime structure, with impermeable bedrock, in the high
mountains assures a summer water supply and mountain pastures that
provide the basis for a rich stockbreeding economy.[10] Sheep and goats
are the main animals. The Montenegrin Mountains are isolated,
extremely rugged, and have a very harsh climate, restricting stockbreeding.

     Toward the north, east, and south of the mountainous core are
a number of clearly defined regions. They are often the important
centers from which valley routes fan out and where the gentle slopes
of the land and lowlands lend themselves to important agricultural
production. Human activities are to be found on the river plains, on
the higher and drier alluvial terraces, and in the loess regions.

     Northwest of the Dinaric Ranges are the limestone Julian Alps,
which, with the Eastern Alps (Karavanken chain), partly enclose the
Ljubljana Basin. Between the Alps and the Dinaric Ranges, an arm
of the Pannonian Plain approaches the Adriatic to within a distance
of seventy-five miles. Adjoining the Ljubljana Basin on the east are
the Slovenian and Croatian Hill Lands, which lie between the Sava,
Drava, and Danube rivers. These are very fertile, loess-covered
lowlands interspersed with limestone and crystalline hills. This
whole region is an area of dense cultivation.

     Further east, at the confluence of the Drava, Danube, Sava,
and Tisza rivers (part of the Pannonian Basin), lies a region of
alluvial plains, sandy dune areas, and crystalline hills covered with

fertile loess, known in Yugoslavia as the Vojvodina. It extends toward the east to the Transylvanian Alps as the Banat. The landscape of this region is undergoing rapid changes. Irrigation, drainage, and building of embankments and dikes are bringing the rivers under control, reclaiming the land.[11] The areas that were regularly flooded, once usable only for pasture and meadow, are now cultivable and form the basis for large-scale maize and wheat culture. The fertile loess plateaus (northern Bačka and southern Srem), generally below 300 feet in elevation, were turned into valuable arable land. The steep slopes of the Fruška Gora, an isolated low mountain range stretching in an east-west direction for roughly fifty miles between the Danube and the Sava, has vineyards in the southern slopes and forests already planted by the Romans. The lower sections between the slopes and the alluvial plains, with easily accessible drinking water, became the preferred area for settlement. Other areas in the Vojvodina and southeastern Banat are now planted to trees and grass and support vineyards and livestock. A dense network of roads, navigable waterways, and railroads connects all important parts of the Vojvodina and links this vital region with the rest of Yugoslavia.

The climate is characterized by cold winters and hot summers and is typically continental. Precipitation is low. Rainfall averages twenty-seven inches a year and comes in sudden downpours, usually heaviest in late spring and early summer. Since summer showers are often followed by high temperatures, evaporation is excessive and only a small portion of the rain is absorbed by the crops, a serious problem for a reliable crop output. The Vojvodina includes 8.5 percent of the total area of Yugoslavia and has approximately 20 percent of the arable land, producing roughly one third of Yugoslavia's maize harvest, 30 percent of its wheat, and 45 percent of its sugar beets.[12]

Undoubtedly, the most important interior routeway of Southeast Europe is the corridor between the Danube and the Aegean Sea (about 300 miles), affording a relatively easy route to settlers and warriors alike and connecting the Danube Valley with the northern Aegean Sea and its head port, Thessaloniki. The region through which this routeway goes is known as the Transitional and Basin Lands of the Morava and Vardar, or the Morava-Vardar Depression. It is an area of great diversity and includes the Morava-Vardar Depression, with its many tectonic basins alternating with the steep highland belts that lie along the Morava, Ibar, and Vardar rivers. The depression is bounded on the west by the dissected karst of the Dinaric Ranges of detached mountain blocks and basins connected by narrow passages. The region south of the Danube is Central Serbia, which is agriculturally important and also has an old tradition of cattle, sheep, and pig

raising. The southern basins and valleys are also rich in minerals,
some of which have been mined since the twelfth century. To the
east is a somewhat isolated mountainous area, the Northwest Serbian
Mountains mentioned earlier, which structurally form a link between
the Carpathian and the Stara Planina. The lower Morava region shows
continental characteristics, with maize and wheat predominant, while
the upper Morava and Vardar regions show some Mediterranean
climatic influences that permit the growth of wheat, tobacco, rice,
and cotton as the chief crops. Fruits, especially plums, are also
widely distributed.

Belgrade, the capital of Serbia and Yugoslavia, served as a focal
point for roads leading in many directions. The original citadel and
settlement rose on a limestone crag 140 feet above the Danube. At
this strategic spot, the Celtic fort and the Roman city of Singidunum
and the Turkish fortress of Kalemegdan were built, overlooking the
loess plains of the Sava and the Danube and the fertile hills of Central
Serbia. Only a little to the southeast, near the confluence of the
Morava and the Danube, is the medieval fortress of Smederevo, an
important trading center.

South of Central Serbia is a most diverse region, including all
the territory of southeastern Yugoslavia. This includes the basin of
Kosovo-Metohija and the Vardar Depression of Macedonia. This
region consists of a series of basins connected with each other by
low mountain passes and isolated by mountain blocks. The Vardar
Depression in Macedonia consists of a series of very fertile isolated
basins, which were formerly lakes. In Macedonia, only a small
percent of the total area can be cultivated. The original forests
having been destroyed, soil erosion on the hills and sheet erosion in
the basins are widespread. Macedonia is a transitional region, an
area of great instability structurally, climatically, culturally, and
politically. With the partition of the region between Bulgaria, Serbia
and Greece at the end of the Balkan wars in 1913, it lost its inner
unity, which has been aggravated by the artificial division between
the Aegean Sea, with its important head port of Thessaloniki, and
the hinterland. The largest part of this region, the Socialist Republic
of Macedonia, is now part of Yugoslavia.

Extending in an easterly direction from the Transitional and
Basin Lands of the Morava-Vardar Depression is the relatively
narrow Macedonian-Thracian Massif, which broadens southeastward
into Bulgaria. Mention was already made of the importance of the
Morava-Vardar Depression as a routeway connecting the northern
Aegean Sea with the Danube Valley and the connection from the Morava

Valley at the Niš Basin to the Sofia and Maritsa basins and eastward
to Istanbul. The valley of the main Morava River and the Southern
Morava follows a generally southeastern direction until it turns southwest below Grdelica in southern Serbia. Between the Morava and the
Vardar, a low watershed of about 1,500 feet permits easy connections.
This route is also used by the main Belgrade-Skopje-Thessaloniki
railway. A second route runs to Lapovo, located approximately halfway
between Belgrade and Niš, southwest to Kraljevo, through the valley
of the Ibar to Priština, the capital of Kosovo, and then south to Skopje.
A railroad was built through this route after World War II.

    A number of important roads cross the mountainous core of
the country and played important roles at various periods in history.
In the northern part of Yugoslavia, a route connects the Pannonian
Basin with the northern part of the Adriatic and the Po Plains, crossing
from the Sava valley to the Ljubljana Basin and across the Pivka Basin
to Trieste. This link was also important for traffic between the Baltic
and the Mediterranean. It has been used by traders, invaders, and
travelers from the sea as well as from the continental interior for
the movement of Roman armies to the Danube, for defending the
Habsburg Empire, and for connecting the Italian and Turkish battle-
fields. The thoroughfare was defended against Turkish attack by the
so-called Military Frontier.[13] The importance of this gap has by no
means diminished with time. It affords the shortest route between
the ports of Rijeka and Trieste and the Danubian hinterland, with
modern highways today running between the Adriatic ports and the
economically rich interior.

    A number of roads running eastward from the Adriatic played
important roles as trade arteries with the interior. This held true
especially in the important mining areas of the Raša watershed in
the southeastern part of the Dinaric Ranges, a trade that reached its
height during the period of the Serbian Empire in the thirteenth and
fourteenth centuries. Only during the late sixteenth and seventeenth
centuries, when the instability of the Turkish Empire resulted in a
decay of the road system, did trading (including mining) activities
cease. They were not resumed until the nineteenth and early twentieth
centuries. Neither railways nor first-class highways were built along
these routeways until recently. The Bar to Belgrade railway is now
being completed in southern Yugoslavia, closely following the Roman
road from Lissus (Alessio near the mouth of the Drin River).[14]
Modern highways are being built connecting the Adriatic with the
interior, serving both tourism and the people of these mountainous
areas.

The Romans built the important Via Egnatia connecting Dyrrachium (Durres, Albania) on the Adriatic and Thessaloniki, the key city on the crossing with the important road from Singidunum (Belgrade) south through the valleys of the Morava and Vardar. Perinthus (Pekirday, Turkey) on the Propontis and ultimately the new Rome, Constantinople (Istanbul), were the goal of the Via Egnatia. Mention also should be made of a road of considerable importance during the Roman period, though largely discontinued since the twelfth century. This road branched off from the Via Egnatia in a northern direction from Heraclea (Monastir in Turkish, Bitola in Macedonian), crossing the Vardar at the important city of Stobi, and reaching the Serdica (Sofia) Basin by the upper Struma, continuing to Oescus at the Danube and ultimately leading into the Transylvanian Basin via the Olt River Valley. This was primarily a military road, especially important at the height of the Roman activities in the southern part of the peninsula and north of the Danube River.

Albania

Mention has been made that the Dinaric Ranges also continue through most of Albania. The Prokletije Mountains, with deeply cut valleys and jagged ridges, form a high mountain zone with a series of parallel and lower limestone ranges south and southeast of the Drin Valley to the southern end of Lake Prespa. An inner tectonic depression is suitable for intensive agriculture. A central zone is important for forest production and has some mining activity (chrome, copper, and iron ores). The southern part of Albania consists of high mountain ranges trending northwest to southeast into Greek Epirus. Between these mountainous regions are triangular-shaped coastal lowlands facing the Adriatic between the Drin River and the Gulf of Glossa with its apex near Elbasan. Fast-running rivers descend from the mountains, each with its own drainage and often flowing into one another, flooding the river plains.

At one time, a large part of the lowlands was marshy and malaria-infested, but extensive drainage works begun before World War II made most areas suitable for agriculture, especially grains, but also for cotton, tobacco, and citrus fruit. Where the mountains and lowlands meet, there is a narrow region of dry terraced hillsides, a few fertile alluvial fans, and valleys suitable for agriculture. This is also the most densely settled area. Grazing and mountain agriculture were the main occupation of the people until recently. The many small natural regions, at the same time, have isolated the people from each other, retarding the growth of national unity and contributing to the backwardness of the country.

Greece

The southern continuation of the Dinaric Ranges are the Pindus Mountains, extending far into the southern Aegean.[15] These rugged mountains consist of blocks that are separated by narrow depressions that form transverse valleys, some of which are submerged. Regional differences in Greece are accentuated by the contrasts provided between the narrow and widely scattered coastal plains, the relatively few upland basins, and the mountainous regions. The east and south coasts have a very irregular configuration that contributes to the ease of communication between the mainland and the sea.

Three major landform regions can be distinguished in Greece: (1) northern Greece, which includes the Epirus, the central and western Pindus Mountains, the basins and mountains of Thessaly, and the basins and mountains of Macedonia and Thrace; (2) Central Greece and Euboea, with mountains extending in a general east-west direction, forming the border toward the north and serving as a clear divide for the Mediterranean climate—a seventy-foot wide channel separates Euboea, with its mountains reaching 6,000 feet, from the mainland; and (3) southern Greece, consisting of the rugged Peleponnesus Peninsula and the Aegean Islands.

Northern Greece extends from the western coastlands (Epirus) to eastern Thrace. It is a region of great structural and climatic diversity. In the northwest are the folded limestone ridges of the central and western Pindus Ranges (6,700 to 8,600 feet). The ranges are characterized by heavily eroded soils and a total lack of minerals. This region is among the most isolated and unproductive of the country. Transhumance is still widespread. The Epirus, consisting of limestone ridges that continue from Albania, has offered people no great obstacles in their movement, and as a result there has been intermingling of population and unavoidable boundary disputes. The Epirus runs parallel to the western coast and terminates at the Gulf of Arta (Amvrakokos), though some of its ridges are terminated in the mountains in the south bordering the Gulf of Corinth. Rainfall is ample and vegetation is dense; deciduous forests above the Mediterranean vegetation, if not cleared for cultivation and pasture, are substantial. Vineyards and large olive and orange groves, especially in the deltaic plain north of the Gulf of Arta, are widespread in the coastlands. The Ionian islands, including Corfu, Levkas, Zante, and

others, are structurally similar to neighboring Epirus. The islands
have good soil, are densely populated, and, due to their westerly location, have ample rainfall.

The basin of Thessaly with its two tectonic basins, those of
Larissa and Trikkala, is one of the largest lowland areas of Greece.
The Pindus Mountains form a major divide and communication obstacle
between the eastern and western portions of northern Greece. The
only route runs between Trikkala and Ioannina. Oceanic influences
are largely excluded from the Thessaly lowlands by the surrounding
mountains. As a result, rainfall is very low, but with the introduction
of modern agrotechnics the plains produce a rich harvest of wheat
and tobacco. Still, additional irrigation would offer greater return,
including a greater diversification of crops. Thessaly's only harbor
of any importance is Volo, which is also the largest city.

Northern Greece also includes Greek Macedonia, which extends
from the Pindus Range in the west to the Nestos River in the east.
The lower Vardar, or the Axios, as it is called in Greece, is Macedonia's main river. It enters Greece from Yugoslav Macedonia at
Ciganska Gorge and flows south a short distance into the Gulf of
Thermaikos near Thessaloniki. This is a rich agricultural region,
which was only recently drained and is now producing a great variety
of Mediterranean crops. Thessaloniki itself was founded in 316 B.C.
to exploit its geographic location at the southern end of the easily
accessible Axios, which in turn offered access to a large hinterland,
extending at various periods north to the Danube, west to the Adriatic,
and east to the Sea of Marmara and the Black Sea.[16] The city is
located at the head of the Thermakos Gulf where important trade
routes from the hinterland converge between the sea and the steep
scarp of the Chortiatis Mountains. However, this hinterland has
largely lost its importance to the city's trade due to its political
boundaries. The port of Thessaloniki, in effect, is today without a
hinterland.

Eastern Macedonia and the neighboring area of Thrace is a
region of faulted basins separated by mountain zones and river deltas,
most of which belong structurally to the Macedonian-Thracian Massif,
an ancient crystalline block. The coastal plains are often flooded
in the late winter and spring and are generally wider than those found
in most of peninsular Greece. These lowlands and plains lie in
tectonic basins that were arms of the sea and have been partially
filled by a change in the sea level and by silt that has been deposited
in the delta by the Vardar, Struma, Nestos, Maritsa, and other rivers.
Rising from the alluvial plains are the rounded, maquis-covered

foothills of the Macedonian-Thracian Massif. The more-elevated parts of the lowlands have been agriculturally important for centuries. The Drama Plains, for example, specialize in world-famous tobacco cultivation and are one of Greece's most densely populated regions. Thrace and Macedonia are among the important agricultural areas of Greece, accounting together for more than one third of the country's cropped area. Tobacco, cotton, wheat, fodder, and rice are the most important crops. This is an important region for its convergence of routes, its provision of essential livelihood, and its role as a meeting place for people from many different countries.

The contrast between northern and central Greece is quite marked. Besides feeling the full influence of the Mediterranean climate, marked by insufficient rainfall resulting in mostly maquis vegetation, central Greece is the typical Greek landscape of small arable plains, always close to the sea, from which arid foothills covered with chaparral rise and give way to towering mountains with scant vegetation affording pasture only for sheep and goats. Even in the greater heights, trees are rare and only few mountains have a winter snow cover, notably Mount Parnassus, east of central Greece, on a small coastal plain between barren heights and the sea.

Southern Greece, the peninsula of Peleponnesus, can also be looked upon as an island since the completion of the Corinth Ship Canal in 1893. Its rugged mountains rise more than 6,000 feet, and the contrasts between the barren, east-south exposed slopes and the more rainy and wooded west and northwest exposed slopes are striking. The plains of Messina in the west are the most productive and most densely populated; that of Laconia is the longest. Typical Mediterranean products of the peninsula are wine, olives, sheep, and, of special importance in southern Greece, sun-dried raisins (currants). Included within southern Greece are the many islands in the southern Aegean Sea. For the most part, these are remnants of the Pindus Range that have been partially submerged.

CULTURAL ENVIRONMENT

Until very recently, basic economic activity in the mountainous areas, with some exceptions such as mining, was related to pastoral activities based on transhumance. This provided for a very modest and hard life, which in turn had to be adapted to the seasonal migrations of the livestock. Small herds of cattle and sheep predominated and were grazed on mountain pastures, wintering in the milder lower regions. Livestock breeders played a great role in establishing caravan routes across mountains, and, as Roglić pointed out, "this livestock-breeding hinterland was, for example, the basis for the extensive commercial development of medieval Dubrovnik."[17] The caravan routes extended all the way from Dubrovnik to the Thracian Plains. The richest pastures not only provided a larger population with its livelihood but also served as nuclei of the Slavic medieval states of Bulgaria and Serbia. Some areas served as fortresses in the later period of the Turkish invasions, e.g., the high Dinaric plateau of central Herzegovina and south to the mountains of Montenegro (Serbian name, Crna Gora, meaning Black Mountain). A number of well protected polja (fields) in the mountains of the central Dinaric Ranges played important roles as places of refuge.

Many conflicts among the pastoralists were caused by the ever-occuring problem of concern for better summer and winter pastures and the vital movements of flocks and man. Constant dangers loomed in connection with severe winters or summer drought. Poverty was widespread and often generated disregard for others. Relations between peoples were unstable, and only the strongest survived. Contacts with the outside world rapidly decreased with the Turkish invasions. The invasions of the mountainous areas succeeded rapidly (at least in the heartland of the Dinaric region), in part because they followed the old, established caravan routes over the mountains. As Roglić pointed out, the pugnacious Turkish livestock breeders were successful because they were able to make the necessary contacts and were able to understand the local people, who were engaged in the same occupation as themselves. Even the Turkish invasion finally became bogged down and failed in this natural and social labyrinth.

Backwardness and lawlessness provided fertile fields for rebellion. The conflict between the demoralized Turkish rulers and the dissatisfied and exploited people created opportunities for intervention by the great powers. The term "Balkan" acquired a specific connotation for its political and cultural disorganization and unrest, and when it became popular it had tragic significance for the region itself.[18] Even when strongest, the Ottoman Empire was unable to completely control some of the mountainous regions or even some of the lands beyond the Danube in the Romanian provinces of Walachia and Moldavia. While it is true that the Turks controlled most of the Danubian routes across the plain, the local rulers (the nuclei of the Romanian state established in 1859), in spite of their being named by the Sultan, often resisted any control and ruled with almost complete independence.

The impact of the crop-farming economy and manufacturing that was spreading from Western Europe made itself felt in the backward Ottoman Empire by the end of the seventeenth and the beginning of the eighteenth centuries. The borders between the Ottoman Empire and the West, along the Sava and Danube rivers and the Carpathian Mountains, divided political units as well as different civilizations, a division that even now leaves its impact on the people and important economic activities. Abandonment of the protectionist policies of the Ottoman Empire coincided with the stagnation and decline of the Empire, and an inadequate urban market for farm products of the regions controlled by the Empire forced landowners to sell their surpluses in foreign markets. Southeast Europe therefore became a natural source of food supplies for Western and Central Europe, whose cities, population, and industry rapidly expanded and made great demands on the products produced by these areas. Large quantities of grain, cattle, meat, oil, leather, silk, wool, cotton, tobacco, and timber were exported from various regions of Southeast Europe.[19]

Goods went through the port of Thessaloniki; a smaller percentage went by caravan to the Danube ports and on to Vienna and Western Europe. Other routes carried this trade on the Danube to Galati and via Moldavia to Poland or Russia. Only warfare and the paralyzing plague retarded this trade. Greeks, Albanians, and Vlachs served as forwarding agents for Macedonia, Thessaly, and Epirus; Thracian merchants, Armenians from Bulgaria, and later Serbian pig merchants of the Šumadije and agents from Bosnia set up business in the border towns of the Turkish Empire, as well as in some of the great trading towns of Central and Southern Europe. Stoianovich credits these small groups of Balkan merchants, mostly Orthodox, with serving as the "human catalyst which joined the Balkan peoples to Europe, both by their commerce and ideas.[20]

Increased trade with the West brought about an increased agrarian colonization and the establishment of numerous communications by the early eighteenth century. The colonization of the central Danubian Plain after the Ottomans were forced to retreat south of the Danube was accomplished with great material and human effort, and the results even today are impressive. Settlers from all over Europe brought new techniques and new crops such as potatoes and tobacco. The farmsteads along the Turkish border were large, laid out by surveyors along geometrically regular lines. Houses duplicated the architecture of many parts of Western Europe, and even today the settlements in the southern and southwestern part of the Pennonian Plains (Vojvodina and Banat) are clearly distinguishable from those of the neighboring regions. The plains of eastern Walachia and north of the lower Danube (Moldavia) and adjacent to the Ottoman frontier were still largely uninhabited during the eighteenth century. Austrian authorities initiated settlement of this area in part to provide agricultural supplies for their armies. Agrarian colonization was encouraged and people from Walachia, Serbia, and the Transylvanian Mountains provided a substantial proportion, having migrated, in part at least, to avoid the heavy taxation and oppressive rule of the Phanariot regimes.[21]

According to McNeill, "it seems highly likely that the spread of maize cultivation was primarily responsible for this phenomenon. By the nineteenth century it had become customary for the peasants of Walachia and Moldavia to make cornmeal mush the staple of their diet, while consigning practically all of the wheat they raised to export."[22] Peasants raised maize for themselves, and this reduced the amount going to tax and rent collectors who were not interested in this new crop, which for a long time was rejected by the urban population of the Ottoman Empire. The suddenly expanded source of food supply also contributed to a great expansion of the agricultural population in the hitherto sparsely settled plains. Settlers came from the overpopulated, poverty-stricken mountainous parts of Southeast Europe in an ever-quickening pace. Suddenly, the plains became a great source of internal conflict within the Ottoman Empire. The open frontier of the Walachian and Moldavian provinces quickly disappeared and was "in the process of an awkward transition from Ottoman-Byzantine to Russo-Western cultural affiliations. But the only effective choice lay between two foreign models."[23]

Maize also played an important and similar role in many other sections of Southeast Europe, where its cultivation was a part of the emergence of agriculture as a commercial venture beginning in the seventeenth century.[24] But the introduction of the new agrarian economy moved extremely slowly in the Ottoman Empire. What made colonization and agricultural advance so successful in the Austrian and Russian border areas was "an economically self-sustained operation, the fiscally self-sustaining character of the process, a hardworking, submissive peasantry, tax collectors under enough discipline to make them channel resources as directed to central authorities, and central authorites interested in using their power to forward settlement."[25]

On the other hand, the Ottoman Empire, in the last 150 years of its existence, or roughly after the middle of the eighteenth century, completely lacked most of the requirements mentioned above. The Sultan's authority often reached only to those provinces close to Istanbul. While armies played a decisive role in the agricultural

progress of both Austrian and Russian open lands, they usually personi-
fied the power of the state and at first administered the new settlements
and laws to which the new settlers had to conform. But many of these
settlers were military men, and thus there was established a very
close collaboration between the settlers and the military. This was
completely different in the border territory under the Ottoman Empire,
where the army considered itself quite separate from the peasant
settlers, whom they despised. It was not unusual in this period for
peasants to flee from areas where Turkish army posts were prevalent,
thus leaving an agricultural vacuum. Within the core lands of the
Ottoman Empire, the situation was not much different. Some of the
most fertile agricultural areas were devoid of settlements, and their
riches were not exploited.

Pressures exerted by more-advanced Western economic activities, together with the political pressures of the great powers, certainly contributed to the breakup of the European part of the Ottoman
Empire, but it was the internal processes—discord within and independence of the bureaucratic society, including important army units,
from the central authorities—that were decisive. A rapidly disintegra-
ting Turkey was forced to make a number of trade concessions.[26]
In 1815, Turkey agreed not to hinder Danubian traffic, and this, in
turn, permitted the shipment of goods from Austria to various Danubian ports, thereby reducing the time for transporting goods. Most
of the great powers received various trading privileges during the
first part of the nineteenth century. Passage was made easier on
the Danube River, and a number of rivers of the region were made
navigable. The coming of the railway put an end to the old caravan
trade. A line connecting the ports of Ruse and Varna in Bulgaria
was built in 1867. The line from Constantinople to Adrianople (Edirne)
and Sarambey was completed in 1875. It was part of the main line
to Niš and on to Belgrade. The line from Bucharest to the Danube
port of Giurgiu was completed in 1869. The line from Saloniki
(Thessaloniki) to Üsküb (Skopje) and Mitrovitza (Kosovaska Mitrovica)
was completed in 1875 and extended to Belgrade by 1888, at the same
time of the completion of the line from Constantinople to Belgrade.
All these lines were built largely with foreign capital.[27]

Various economic pressures, internal political weaknesses,
and pressures exerted by the great powers contributed to the establishment of a nucleus of national states in the remnants of the European
part of the Ottoman Empire during the nineteenth century. This
drastically changed the conditions of the habitat and left their impact
on the economic activities of most of the people of Southeast Europe.
The Romanians, who had survived centuries of invasion and foreign

rule, after considerable struggle united the principalities of Moldavia
and Walachia in 1859 under a native aristocrat (boyar), Alexander
Crza.[28] The Bulgarian people, who were the first to succumb to the
Ottoman-Turkish invaders, benefited from the revolutionary fever
in Southeast Europe. As a result of the Russo-Turkish war in 1877-78,
Bulgaria gained status as an autonomous principality with an elected
prince. Though the Treaty of San Stefano of March, 1878, signed by
Russia and Turkey, provided for a Bulgarian territory between the
Danube in the north, the Black Sea in the east, the Aegean Sea in
the south, and the land west to Lake Ohrid, the strong opposition of
numerous European powers forced a compromise on the territorial
extent of Bulgaria in the subsequent Treaty of Berlin of June, 1878.

This treaty also had important repercussions on other countries
of Southeast Europe. Bulgaria north of the Balkan Mountains became
autonomous and elected its own rulers; Eastern Rumelia, south of
the Balkan Mountains, received a Christian ruler appointed by the
Sultan, but approved by the Great Powers, though this arrangement
was short lived. Access to the Aegean Sea and the incorporation of
Macedonia from the Turkish Empire, promised by the Russians to
Bulgaria in the Treaty of San Stefano, was withdrawn. The results of
these promises, spelled out in the Treaty of San Stefano and never implemented, left a lasting impact on the political life of Bulgaria as well
as on its relations with the other countries of Southeast Europe. The
Treaty of Berlin also brought about independence for Serbia, Montenegro, and Romania. Bosnia and Herzegovina were assigned to Austria-
Hungary for administrative purposes. A few years later, in 1886,
Eastern Rumelia, which included the fertile Maritsa Basin, was united
with the principality of Bulgaria. A portion of the Turkish population
fled, and with it the hated landowners, bays, and pashas, and the whole
Turkish bureaucratic system collapsed. Whole villages suddenly
were depopulated, and the hated Tartars and Circassians left, never
to return. People from the overpopulated mountainous areas moved
with amazing speed into the fertile lowlands. The cities and settlements
quickly lost their Oriental character. The hated chifliks* were rapidly

---

*The chiflik is the successor to the Turkish timar, land given
as a fief to a deserving warrior. But unlike the timars, which were
under strict control of the central government, chifliks were a result
of its declining power, were never really recognized, and were held
by their owners as fully heritable property. Peasants working on the
chifliks were tenant farmers, easily evicted, and their freedom was
often restricted. For details, see L. S. Stavrianos, The Balkans
Since 1453 (New York: Rinehart and Co., 1959), pp. 138-41.

transferred to small peasant ownership and Bulgarians who had fled
to Walachia, Moldavia, Macedonia, and the Vojvodina returned and
were quickly absorbed into the many partly settled villages, especially
in the eastern part of the country. By 1890, all Turkish property was
again in Bulgarian hands.

Macedonia was divided at the end of the Second Balkan War of
1913, with the southern plains (now northern Greece) and its important
city of Saloniki (Thessaloniki) being incorporated into Greece. The
largest part was assigned to Serbia and, until 1944, was called Southern
Serbia (including today's autonomous province of Kosovo), and a small
part centered in the Struma River Valley was assigned to Bulgaria.
The political settlements culminated in the withdrawal of Turkey from
most of Southeast Europe. This accelerated the migration from the
mountainous regions, home for many of the indigenous people for
many years, and is still going on. After World War II, the farmsteads
in the Vojvodina, left empty by the departing German settlers, were
occupied by people coming from the central and southern Dinaric
Ranges. The movement from rural and especially mountainous regions
to the constantly growing urban concentrations, with their new manufacturing activities, is a process still continuing in all the lands of
Southeast Europe.

The movement of settlers to the plains meant a move to a
better life, a new way of life for people traditionally tied to livestock
and permanent insecurity. The trend toward the plains and a stable,
crop-farming life, though in the beginning based on extensive subsistence farming, was a strong stimulus in the struggle for liberation
from Turkish rule. According to Josip Roglić, liberation from the
Turks, the creation of independent states, and structural changes
in the agrarian economy were part of a wider complex process.
Acquisition of arable land was not always an easy task, however,
and the struggle for rapidly diminishing arable land often based on
the "right of forefathers" frequently led to conflicts, with a corresponding foreign intervention. The animosities that followed have been
slow to disappear.

The preservation of national personalities, including peculiar
social customs, was greatly influenced by the relief of the region,
which contributed to seclusion, separation, and isolation of the
numerous cultural characteristics so typical of Southeast Europe.
While there obviously existed considerable diffusion of foreign
influence, at the same time preservation of the unique and peculiar
social customs of ancient nomadic and peasant cultures in close
proximity with various advanced cultures contributed to the unique

FIGURE 2

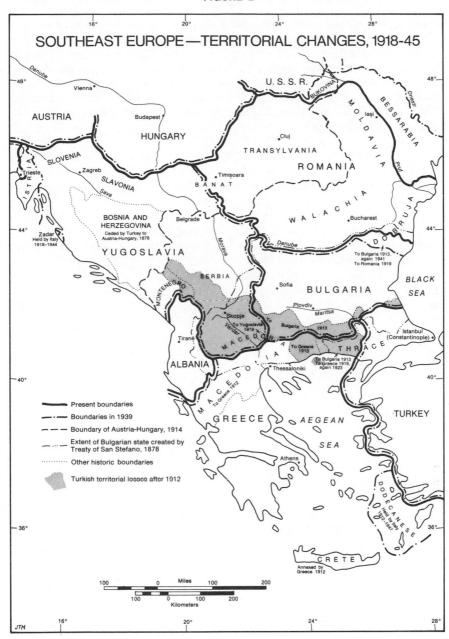

SOUTHEAST EUROPE—TERRITORIAL CHANGES, 1918-45

31

cultural characteristics. Though it must immediately be stressed
that these traditional social forms and societies have steadily declined
since the establishment of national states during the nineteenth century,
the impact of Western ideas and economic changes, including industrialization, and political and social changes in the area generally have
left obvious repercussions on the cultural environment of the region.
Completely new conditions in the life of the people of Southeast
Europe have emerged.

This complex geographical and social transition, together with
the internal disorganization and upheavals in the countries of Southeast Europe, was in large part responsible for the breakup of the
Ottoman Empire. It contributed to World War I and left its impact
on the political changes as a result of World War II (See Figure 2).
The transition of the social processes and economic adjustments is
still incomplete and continues at the present time. Details will be
discussed in the following chapters.

2

The agrarian economy and society, characteristic of the countries of Southeast Europe, was a product of the nineteenth century, when Austria-Hungary was the main source of wheat for Europe. This left an important impact on the regional structure of the whole area and influenced the developmental strategy through the whole period prior to World War II. Political history also left its mark on the location and spread of industrialization before 1939. Certain regions under the Dual Monarchy, such as Slovenia and the Banat, and important regional capitals made a start in industrialization during the late nineteenth and the beginning of the twentieth centuries. The industries, especially those located in regional capitals, acted with varying intensity as growth poles during the interwar period and played an important role in the early postwar development strategy.* Industrialization spread through the countryside slowly and thus did not change substantially the basic regional structure of the area. Only in the larger regional urban agglomerations did "the well-known cumulative process, in which industry and the super-structure mutually incite each other, resulting in concentration and at times even in a super-concentration of economic activities and population" leave an important impact.[1]

It must also be remembered that most of Southeast Europe was opened to outside contacts only after 1830, and autonomous economic policies were not possible until the end of the nineteenth century. Nicholas Spulber made it clear that

_____

*For a discussion of the theory and concepts of regional development, see Chapter 6.

> it was the decay of the Turkish Empire, not their political
> status, which set for all of them the benchmarks at which
> they could enter into economic contact with foreign coun-
> tries, engaged in <u>de facto</u> autonomous economic policies,
> and enact integrated domestic economic measures. . . .
> truly enough, the secession from the Ottoman Empire
> opened the door to the spreading influence of other great
> powers.[2]

Even then, the economic and political initiative of these countries was
severely limited due to the interests and influences of the great
powers, though, as Spulber indicated, "these influences remained
diverse in nature and different in scope and often neutralized each
other."[3] In an effort to attain national, including economic, independence, the countries of Southeast Europe had a common social and
economic base and a common identity of purpose when their hard-won
autonomy within the Ottoman Empire, and later their independence,
began.

This identity of purpose was largely confined to the fulfillment
of "national aspirations" of the newly independent countries, which,
in practical terms, meant the creation of

> modern armies and administrations . . . which, alas, often
> meant the acquisition of the same pieces of territory—and
> to become integrated into the broad currents of capitalist
> growth and industrialization embracing western and cen-
> tral Europe. To encourage industrialization they resorted
> to tariffs, subsidies, state purchases of products of do-
> mestic industry; moreover they facilitated the growth of
> an integrated banking system and created favorable con-
> ditions for foreign investments.[4]

All this meant for the newly founded national states an ever-increasing
foreign indebtedness, with exploited minerals usually shipped to
industries in foreign countries for payments of these debts or in
exchange for needed manufactured goods. Efforts to modernize and
integrate these countries with the economic expansion of Western
and Central Europe were made under extremely difficult conditions,
considering the paralyzing effect of the many years of Ottoman domination. The inefficient agriculture that suddenly had to compete on
world markets, the absence of any large-scale industrialization that
could serve as a recipient for the rapidly increasing population, and
the large number of artisans living in the towns that suffered the
loss of Turkish markets raised serious obstacles in modernizing
the social and economic base of the countries of Southeast Europe.

The problems involved in changing the regional structure of these countries while modernizing their socioeconomic structure became even more urgent as a result of World War I, with the acquisition of both backward and advanced territorial units by Romania and Yugoslavia. But in spite of considerable regional diversity among the countries of Southeast Europe, key socioeconomic indices showed similar characteristics before the outbreak of World War II. Peasants produced crops mainly for home consumption, and even the more-fertile regions could not easily distribute their surpluses to other parts of the same country because of the deplorable condition of transportation. The considerable forest and mineral wealth, especially in Serbia, already exploited in the prehistoric Iron Age, the Roman era, and the early Ottoman period, was largely neglected during the later Ottoman period. The reserves in the western Carpathians in Transylvania were exploited during the Dacian and Roman period and again after the fourteenth century. But generally, large-scale exploitation did not commence until the interwar years, when foreign capital, enticed by high returns, made this possible. The amount of Greek, Albanian, and Bulgarian metallic and nonmetallic minerals was small compared with that of Serbia and, later, Yugoslavia and Romania especially, but mineral-starved Europe was willing to invest under conditions of high profit. The results were not always wholly beneficial to the countries whose minerals were exploited, and the impact on the labor market and national income was very minor indeed (in Yugoslavia, mining in the interwar years contributed only 2 percent of the national income). Refining and processing was usually done outside the country.

It is clear that, in view of the retarding impact of the Turkish occupation of large parts of Southeast Europe, independence per se did not and certainly could not bring sudden changes to the backwardness of wide areas of the peninsula, but only to a few more-privileged centers. State intervention, especially during the interwar years, became widespread, and, while some economic advances were obvious, the effects of the legacy of the Ottoman Empire and the depressions of the late 1800s and again in the 1930s had serious effects. In addition, the nationalist barriers, which made fruitful cooperation among the countries of the area impossible, still have not been completely overcome, even within individual countries, as the developments within Yugoslavia clearly show. The barriers are visible also in the relationship between the so-called developed and underdeveloped territories.

As mentioned earlier, the regional structure of all of these countries to a great extent was influenced by economic developments during the nineteenth century, but, after wheat exports lost their importance, the traditional social and economic structure of the region simply was never able to adjust to the processes of modernization. The agricultural crisis affected the whole of economic development, which was clearly expressed by the lack of domestic investment capital, so desperately needed in the development of a broadly based industry. Economic development within the countries of Southeast Europe had become more and more dependent upon foreign capital and initiatives. The absence of a modern infrastructure, or often of any infrastructure at all, such as utilities, transportation, and sewage, in turn had a stagnating influence on the important aspects of economic development in every country. Kosta Mihailović even spoke of a collision of two types of society—a countrywide viewpoint connected with a cash economy and a modern civilization vs. a regional point of view characterized by an attitude to modern development largely based on one's own poverty and "pre-occupied with short-range direct interests and the desire to make the maximum use of local possibilities."[5]

The specific development processes and strategy of the countries of Southeast Europe obviously differ, though, as the discussion in the following chapters will show, the achievement of basic structural changes—the transition from a traditional agrarian economy to a modern industrial or mixed economy—was not achieved by 1939. A base had been laid, however, from which to proceed after the destruction caused by World War II had been repaired. The lack of a balance between a rapidly increasing population and the accumulation of capital, of vital importance in modernizing a country, was not solved at the outbreak of World War II. Regional differences between the few so-called advanced regions and developing urban centers and the large underdeveloped regions were even sharpened, in part due to political conditions. Still, some progress was made on the long and hard road toward economic and social modernization. This transformation and especially the development after World War II cannot be understood without an analysis of the regional structure and spatial distribution of economic activities in the whole area since the time independence was gained in the nineteenth century. The following analysis, together with the preceeding regional synthesis, will illustrate the major cultural and economic problems of this region; it thus presents the "roots of the problems" as they affected the development strategy of the countries of Southeast Europe in the post-World War II period.

THE FORMATIVE YEARS

The task of building a viable economy which would develop the agricultural and manufacturing resources of the newly independent Southeast European countries was a difficult one in the face of the general backwardness of the area and other obstacles.[6] The limited quantities of productive soil, the structure of landownership, the rapidly increasing population, the deplorable or nonexistent infrastructure, the absence of easily accessible resources, and the small urban concentrations made economic development and the integration of these new, highly independent nationalist countries into the broad currents of the Western and Central European development difficult.

The basic motives in the economic development of all Southeast European countries before 1939 were remarkably similar. By emphasizing a market economy and encouraging production of domestic goods, it was hoped that the value of this production and of exports could be increased and that this, in turn, would lead to an increased national income and thus to funds available to the state. By creating working places in the industries, it was reasoned that the surplus agricultural population would find sufficient employment opportunities. In addition, with each country building a domestic industry, it was hoped that each country would become largely self-sufficient in the production of most foreign industrial goods, thus gaining economic independence and securing at the same time political independence. The state in the pursuance of such policies had to assume a special promotional and usually protective role, e.g., by guaranteeing purchase of the goods produced, by instituting fiscal monopolies and thus guaranteeing repayment of foreign loans, and by a variety of protective measures.

Agriculture remained, until the late 1950s, the main occupation of most of the people of Southeast Europe (See Figure 3). Throughout the nineteenth century, large reserves of fertile land were available for the gradual ploughing of the cultivable area. The economy was mainly of self-sufficient agrarian character as late as the middle of the nineteenth century, and not until the onset of rapid population growth and the various land reforms were small-scale holdings to become predominant. As late as the 1890s, agricultural labor was insufficient in the fertile lowlands of the region. Taxation, the tenure

FIGURE 3

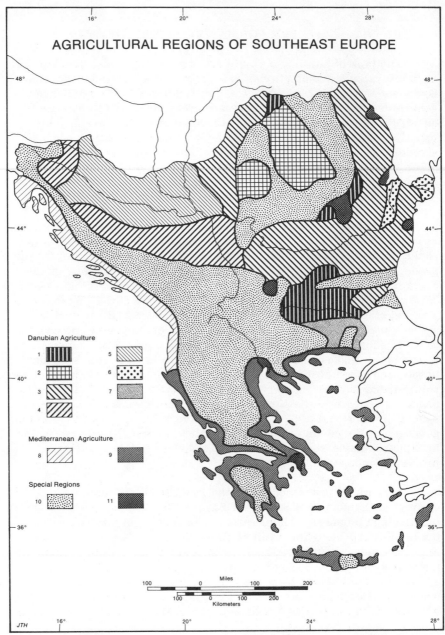

AGRICULTURAL REGIONS OF SOUTHEAST EUROPE

Danubian Agriculture

1
2
3
4
5
6
7

Mediterranean Agriculture

8
9

Special Regions

10
11

1. Vineyards, orchards, vegetables
2. Corn and wheat, potatoes, dairy beef
3. Wheat and corn, sugar beets, beef
4. Vineyards, orchards, vegetables, animal husbandry
5. Wheat and corn, sugar beets, animal husbandry
6. Beef cattle, fisheries

7. Wheat, tobacco
8. Mediterranean marginal (vines, some olives)
9. True Mediterranean (vines, olives, citrus fruits)
10. Forests, grazing, pockets of cultivation
11. Suburban, vegetables, dairying

After Jacek I. Romanovski, "Geographic Research and Methodology on East Central and Southeast European Agriculture," in George W. Hoffman, ed., Eastern Europe: Essays in Geographical Problems (London and New York: Methuen and Praeger Publishers, 1971), pp. 34-35.

system, insecurity, and plain ignorance contributed to the neglect of agricultural potential. Efficient rotation practices were unknown, manure was frequently burned as fuel, and the ox-drawn plow was the most advanced agricultural implement. Even after large tracts of cultivable lands were ploughed, peasant life in the area was characterized by a low level of consumption, wretched working conditions, and taxation imposed by the state and owners of large estates (latifundia in Romania and Greece).

David Mitrany called the exploitation of the peasants "Raubwirtschaft" and it brought about considerable social upheaval.[7] It was mostly the fertile soil of the plains that kept peasants from starvation. The mass of peasant holdings as early as the beginning of the twentieth century were below five hectares (and a large percentage below three hectares), with low yields per acre and per capita. Even on the large estates, obsolete methods of cultivating grain were usual. Maize was the predominant cereal crop of the dry regions, and wheat and potatoes were introduced in the middle of the nineteenth century in the more moist hill lands. The custom of transhumance had rapidly declined by the latter part of the nineteenth century in the more fertile lowlands of Southeast Europe due to the extension of intensive crop farming into areas that formerly had provided only winter grazing. In Romania, for example, the area of ploughed land increased from one to six million hectares between 1837 and 1916.

The modernization of the economy and the broadening of the economic basis of the various regions of Southeast Europe were closely connected with the opening of the Ottoman Empire to foreign influences and the independence movements and subsequent establishment of the Southeast European states of Serbia, Greece, Bulgaria, and Romania. Economic contacts with the West began around 1860, and by the late 1880s a considerable amount of economic independence was reached. The need for capital for the economic expansion of these newly independent countries resulted in a slowly increasing foreign influence over all aspects of the economy and, at times, of the political life. Austria-Hungary's influence was paramount in Serbia until 1903, as was Russian influence in Bulgaria from the eighteenth century to 1886 and after 1896. German influence is questionable, except for the peculiarities of 1914-18 and 1939-45.

Emphasis on economic development ever since the independence of these countries had been on direct state investments and inducements offered to both domestic and foreign entrepreneurs. Direct state investments were responsible for the building of a diversified economy with investment priorities given to building industries related to military needs, by participation in the development of an infrastructure—a basic network of railway lines,* utilities, public education—and by encouragement of agricultural exports. To accomplish these goals, all the countries of the area saw a constantly increasing amount of state involvement in the economy. This state involvement grew in scope and intensity as a result of the world depression of the 1930s and as the danger of World War II arose. Pressure for state intervention and involvement came both from external sources (the demand by the foreign investors to have the state guarantee their investment) and from various domestic economic pressure groups such as bankers, industrialists, landowners, peasants, and the military.

The expansion of the economic activities thus was made possible by heavy borrowing from abroad, and this in turn resulted in an increasing public indebtedness that necessitated an increasing taxation burden. These forced an increased reliance on exports of agricultural products, especially from Romania, Bulgaria, and Serbia, with the result of further depressing the rural standard of living. Because of insufficient diversification in economic production, exports were limited to a small number of products. Protectionist measures included laws "encouraging domestic industries" and a variety of tariff measures that were enacted in all countries of the area between the 1880s and the outbreak of World War II.** With the demand for foreign credits rising, partly due to the need for military expenditures, the governments were forced by the foreign investors and lenders to guarantee repayment by organizing so-called financial monopolies for certain products such as tobacco, sugar, salt, and matches, the income from which was used to amortize the foreign debt.

Promoting industrial production was largely centered in the commercial banking system that was established after 1880 (in Greece

---

*These lines soon connected Vienna and Budapest with Zagreb, Sarajevo, and the Adriatic, Vienna and Budapest through Serbia with Salanika (Thessaloniki), and through Bulgaria with Istanbul.

**Hungary was the first country to pass a law encouraging the building of industries by instituting administrative protectionist measures; Romania and Serbia followed in the early 1890s, Bulgaria in 1894, and Greece in 1910.

in the 1840s), but foreign control of most commercial banks and even national banks slowly increased. Spulber came to the conclusion that

> the role of the state in the development of a banking system, the railroads, and manufacturing was overwhelming during all these years. Direct participation of foreign capital became in its turn decisive in banking, mining and manufacturing around 1900. The participation of private capital remained very limited.[8]

Foreign credits, in spite of the high costs of repayment, contributed to some notable economic progress before the two Balkan wars (1912-13) and World War I. These loans served for the construction of a variety of industries and laid the foundation for an essential infrastructure by furnishing funds for the building of bridges, ports, and railroads, though many of the new railroads were foreign-owned. At first, handicrafts and a few industries were confined to the territories under Austro-Hungarian rule, especially in Slovenia and Transylvania. Industrial enterprises hardly existed in the newly independent countries—Greece, Romania, Serbia, and Bulgaria—though handicrafts were quite well developed. This was especially true of Bulgaria at the time of independence in 1878. Industries were non-existent in Montenegro.

Greek economic activities were only intensified after the late 1880s. As late as the 1870s, only about half of its potential arable land was cultivated. Roads and railways hardly existed until the turn of the century. The Greek merchant marine grew rapidly after 1880, and the opening of the Corinth Canal (1893) was an important event for the country. Mineral wealth remained untapped until the early twentieth century, and the exploitation of the country's agricultural resources remained inefficient, in part due to the tenure relationships. Huge foreign loans, especially after 1880, and the remittances by increased numbers of emigrants and shipping earnings did little to improve the economic situation. As a matter of fact, most of this income was dissipated by costly wars and an inefficient and corrupt administration. Industrial progress was slow, but at the outbreak of World War I Greece counted over one hundred factories that employed over twenty-five people, largely in food processing, shipbuilding, and various repairs.

Romania, with its rich agricultural lands, permitting sizable grain exports from its large estates, and considerable petroleum reserves (the first refinery was built near Ploieşti in 1857) was the best endowed of the four countries. Its relatively large domestic market, an elaborate system of tariffs and laws encouraging the establishment of industries, and a sizable foreign trade contributed to more rapid economic growth than in the other independent Southeast European countries. The number of industrial plants employing 25 workers or more increased between 1886 and 1910 from 83 to 847, giving the country a total industrial labor force of 8 percent of the working population. Its oil output reached 100,000 tons in 1897 and had climbed to 2 million at the outbreak of World War I. Many of the smaller plants were flour mills, saw mills, and food, textile, or leather plants, but the number of so-called big industries also grew rapidly between 1902 and 1914. Romania's rail network grew slowly and reached only 3,500 kilometers by 1913.

Serbia's economic growth was at first rather significant. Grain production on the sparse agricultural land available rose rather rapidly between 1890 and 1910, and livestock breeding played a rather important role, especially with its exports of pigs to Austria before the so-called pig war in 1906. The number of industries had reached 75 factories in 1903, for the most part small in size, but by 1910 their number had grown to 170. These industries were mostly agriculturally oriented, whereas the country's varied minerals were shipped outside for processing. Railway building advanced slowly, reaching 976 kilometers in 1913.

Bulgaria's economic development before 1879 closely resembled that of Serbia. Agriculture was characterized by the monoculture of grains, by the great variability of crop yields, and by archaic livestock raising. With the departure of the Turks, whole villages suddenly became depopulated, and people from the overpopulated mountainous areas and Bulgarians who had fled to other areas of Southeast Europe moved into the fertile lowlands, a process duplicated in Serbia and Romania. Chifliks were rapidly transferred to small peasant ownership.[9] By 1890, all Turkish property was again in Bulgarian hands, but thereafter the need for additional land was soon felt. Industries developed slowly from 20 in 1879 to 345 by 1910, but they employed under 16,000 workers, providing approximately 8 percent of Bulgaria's labor force. At the same time, a railway network was built. It had already been started during the Turkish reign, with the important line from Belgrade to Istanbul completed in 1888. By 1913, over 2,000 kilometers had been completed, mostly serving military needs.

Concerning those lands of Southeast Europe under the control of Austria-Hungary, such as Slovenia, Croatia (including Slavonia and Dalmatia), Vojvodina, and Transylvania, the most advanced territory

in terms of a balanced economic development was without doubt
Transylvania, with its 60 big mining and metallurgical enterprises
and a labor force of nearly 20,000, as well as 322 big industries
employing 33,000 people. An important and rapidly growing iron and
steel industry had developed since the eighteenth century in southwest
Transylvania and the Banat, using local iron ore and charcoal-fired
furnaces. The first blast furnace was started in Reşiţa in the Banat
in 1771 and in Hunedoara in southwestern Transylvania in 1882. The
production at Reşiţa of the number of steel varieties was expanded
in the second half of the nineteenth century with the introduction of
coke. By 1938, 66 percent of Romania's pig iron and 74 percent of
the steel came from this region. Even today, a considerable part of
Romania's pig iron and steel output comes from this concentration
of plants in southwest Romania near the major bituminous coal fields
and iron-ore deposits. Slovenia counted 367 factories by 1908,
Croatia-Slavonia 322, Dalmatia 49, and Vojvodina 277.[10] Most of
the production served the domestic market only. Industries engaged
largely in the production of agricultural products, lumber, textiles,
and some raw-material processing. Most other necessary industrial
products were imported from other parts of the Austro-Hungarian
Empire. Industrialization and the processing of minerals was largely
financed by Austrian and, to a lesser degree, Hungarian capital.
Railway building progressed rapidly, but was largely influenced by
military strategic needs. There is no question that the agricultural
and industrial products of these areas greatly benefited from the
large market provided by the Dual Monarchy.

Albania, whose nominal independence was declared only in 1913,
Macedonia, part of the Ottoman Empire until 1913, and independent
Montenegro were among the most backward areas of Southeast Europe.
Albania did not open its first primary school until 1887 and did not
introduce a common orthography until 1908. Its one-time rich grain
fields of the littoral had long since become malarious marshes.
Before World War I, there existed in the whole country only 185
kilometers of disconnected, generally unasphalted roads. Montenegro
was the first country in Southeast Europe whose formal independence
was recognized by the sultan (1799), though it had a long history of
de facto independence.[11] Its population was estimated at 80,000 in
1855, and its "national wealth" consisted largely of livestock, over
315,000 sheep and goats alone and 37,000 head of cattle.

Many of the twentieth-century problems of the countries of
Southeast Europe must be related directly to the period of nation-
building in the preceding century and were mostly a legacy of the
Ottoman Empire. This legacy of insuperable backwardness among

the poverty-striken peasantry created a serious problem of economic development and contributed to the great spatial differences and internal political problems, especially in today's Yugoslavia. The efforts made by the four countries* to establish a modern and often oversized bureaucracy, modern armies, a variety of mostly duplicating industries, and a transportation and public-utility network and the constant dream of its leaders of acquiring additional territories from its neighbors, creating unbridgeable rivalries among these countries, left an impact on their economic development. It is obvious from the preceding discussion that most of these agrarian societies had an extremely low standard of living, and the building of modern armies as well as modern economies had to be done largely with borrowed foreign funds, especially after the 1880s.

It is therefore surprising how much progress had been made by 1912—the outbreak of the First Balkan War—though a good part of the progress achieved, especially in Romania, was accomplished by a merciless squeeze of the peasants. The Balkan wars of 1912-13 and shortly thereafter World War I largely destroyed this progress. While a political union of these countries never was within the realm of possibility, an economic union or at least a more sensible use of resources would have made economic progress much easier. Instead of cooperating, the so-called competitive independence of the four Southeast European countries resulted in constantly increasing barriers, bringing about several wars for the purpose of small territorial gains and the rekindling of centuries old dreams of bygone empires. These wars resulted in the squandering of whatever economic progress had been made since independence, perpetuating the poverty and misery in which a substantial part of their people lived. Finally, it must be pointed out that much of the foreign borrowing came either from international speculators exerting outrageous interests or from foreign countries with political interests. These foreign loans often brought about control of important budgetary revenues and expenditures. Greece, for example, had foreign debts as early as 1893 comparable to 35 percent of its foreign receipts.

THE INTERWAR YEARS

World War I had a profound political and economic impact on Southeast Europe: Albania (population 800,000) received a government,

---

*Bulgaria, Greece, Romania, and Yugoslavia; Albania was not founded until 1920.

the war created a united south Slav state (the Kingdom of the Serbs, Croats, and Slovenes, later renamed Yugoslavia), and Bulgaria lost valuable territory to Greece and Romania. Romania nearly doubled the size of its former territory and population, mainly by the acquisition of Transylvania. Greece soon became involved in another war with Turkey in 1921 that ended in Greece's smashing defeat and caused a great population upheaval—1,350,000 refugees entered Greece between 1922 and 1928 and 434,000 Turks departed. Bulgaria and Greece exchanged some 54,000 Bulgarians for 46,000 Greeks. On the whole, the Southeast European region was economically disorganized, but the various population transfers at least reduced the size of the many minority groups. It was hoped that this reduction would contribute to greater political transquility in the area. Unfortunately, this hope remained unfulfilled throughout the interwar years. The most serious problem was to be found in the south Slav state, Yugoslavia. The many centrifugal forces—religious, national, as well as economic—provided little cohesion for the newly organized state. The addition of the more advanced territories of Slovenia and Croatia only added to the already serious national situation. Italy's territorial claims over parts of Dalmatia, as well as its growing influence in Albania, also contributed to the political instability of the region.

The socioeconomic structure of the five Southeast European countries in the interwar years was quite similar, though they differed in size and population. The economic development of the whole region, in spite of the addition of new territories, was characterized as being overwhelmingly agrarian, with a large population surplus. Industrialization was slow in coming, and as a result the primary sector of the economy dominated all economic activities. The tertiary, and to a lesser extent the secondary, sector was largely underdeveloped. Every country depended heavily upon foreign capital for the development of industries, mining, and basic infrastructure.

The main structural characteristics were changed little from the formative years and can be summarized as follows: a large labor force engaged in agriculture, with a high percentage of underemployed (Greece was an exception, being heavily dependent upon the trade using its large ocean shipping fleet); extremely backward farming methods; a high rate of illiteracy among the masses, especially in those territories longest under Ottoman control; the continuation of an irrevocable trend toward further fragmentation of landholdings in agriculture,*

---

*Croatia (Yugoslavia) serves as a good example. In all, it witnessed five land reforms, two of which came after World War II:

further aggravated by post-World War I land reforms aimed at providing farmland to the landless and underemployed, but failing to accomplish this goal because of a constantly increasing population. The enactment of several land reforms in the interwar years in every one of the Southeast European countries, contributed to the similarities of the structure of landownership, but did little toward solving the problem of the poverty and backwardness of a large surplus agricultural labor force.

State assistance for agriculture was small, but of importance to the other branches of the economy, especially in the emphasis on industrialization, state monopolies, and autarky. The protectionist policies of the pre-World War I period (quotas and tariffs) were further expanded during the interwar years by the enactment of laws encouraging large and national industries that restricted the free exchange of trade and thus contributed to the economic disintegration in the 1930s.* Behind this protective curtain, the state expanded its domestic industries and its control of mines, transportation, banking, and foreign trade. The resultant economic benefits did not materialize, and additional foreign borrowing, simply to sustain the ever-growing state holdings, became a necessity, doubling or even tripling their indebtedness by the onset of the world depression in 1930. In addition, the repayment of prewar foreign loans, reparation payments for some countries, and military outlays (absorbing between 25 and 35 percent

---

1755-80, 1848, 1918, 1948, and 1953. All these land reforms had certain similarities, but none really solved the basic agricultural problem of the country, the question of sufficient land for the people living off the land. Rudolf Bićanić, "Five Land Reforms in Croatia (Yugoslavia) 1755-1953" (unpublished manuscript, 1955).

*Pasvolsky, Economic Nationalism of the Danubian States (Washington, D.C.: The Brookings Institution, 1928), discusses in some detail the impact of these policies, enunciated under the slogan "nostrification" and directed mostly against the earlier dominant nationalities and old and new minorities. The results of such policies by the nationalist leaders of Serbia and Romania were that valuable economic contacts with Vienna and Budapest business houses and especially banks with their former partners in Zagreb and Cluj were cut off and ruined in this process. See also the discussion in Frederick Herz, The Economic Problem of the Danubian States (London: Victor Gallancz, 1947).

of the budget) forced a continued reliance on foreign borrowing. The
depression in the 1930s thus found the Southeast European countries
already in a precarious position largely of their own making. Protectionist measures, often with a purely nationalistic aim, had restricted trade, but these measures were further expanded in the 1930s
to protect the national industry. A cut in vital expenditures affected
the social and economic life of the population, but did little to improve
the over-all economic situation. By building additional military production capabilities, the state expanded its sphere of operation, but this
had little impact on the over-all economic and social situation or
even on the ultimate military situation.

A mass of national and international statistics has been published—
with much contradictory data—analyzing the economic and social
developments in the interwar period. All came to the general conclusion that the structure of national income had changed only very
little, the labor force absorbed in agriculture had hardly changed at
all, and, though industry doubled its employment, its contributions
to the national income increased only slightly. Statistics for the population dependent on agriculture as the main livelihood are extremely
difficult to establish due to the "prevalence of the family type of peasant economy in agriculture," but here, too, hardly anything changed
in the interwar years.[12] Figures for the agricultural surplus population vary, but for the agricultural populations in 1937 there is general
agreement that the range for the countries of Southeast Europe was
between 24 and 35 percent. The retarding impact on agricultural
production was obvious.[13] Total trade turnover of manufactured
goods in the mid-1930s was sharply reduced from the late 1920s.
Per capita income showed some increase in the period 1929-39, from
2 percent in Yugoslavia to 8 percent in Romania, 11 percent in Greece,
and 35 percent in Bulgaria, but, as Nicolas Spulber estimates, per
capita income amounted to only $100 to $130 at the end of the 1930s.
Other published estimates run even lower: for Romania and Greece
between $60 and $70, and for Yugoslavia and Bulgaria from $55 to
$65. Table 1 indicates some of these developments.

Earlier, the fundamental importance of agriculture for the whole
economic development of all the Southeast European countries was
cited, including its contribution as a major source of livelihood for
the majority of the population. Three major characteristics hold true
for all these countries during the entire interwar period: the prevalence of small to dwarf holdings producing largely for their needs,
with some exceptions in Romania and Yugoslavia; the absence of

TABLE 1

Selected Social and Economic Data for the Interwar Period

Item	Albania	Bulgaria		Greece		Romania		Yugoslavia	
Structure of national income (percent of total); figures for 1926 and 1938[a]									
Industry		14.8	20.2		20.0	21.1	25.5	17.4	20.3
Construction		0.8	1.7		0.8	3.1	2.9	1.6	1.8
Agriculture		71.4	63.1		40.8	60.2	53.2	53.4	52.2
Transport		2.2	2.9		6.0	3.6	5.4	4.8	5.5
Trade		10.8	12.1		11.9	12.0	13.0	12.5	11.8
Others		—	—		21.3	—	—	10.3	8.4
Structure of labor force; figures for 1936 and 1939 if not otherwise indicated[b]									
Agriculture	90[c]	82.4	80.0	49.6[d]	55.6	79.5[e]	80.0	78.9	76.3
Mining and Industry		8.1	8.0	16.2	16.1	8.0	9.1	9.9	10.0
Trade		2.7	3.1	8.1	9.0	2.7	2.9	4.3	4.2
Other		6.8	8.9	26.1	19.3	9.8	8.0	6.9	9.5
Industrial manpower (in thousands) for 1920 and 1938[f]		20.0	103			157	373	174	301
Ratio of industrial manpower to total population[g]		0.4	1.7			1.0	1.9	1.4	1.9
Percent of population dependent on agriculture as main livelihood, 1938[h]		72		46.4		68.4		70	
Agricultural population per 100 hectares of agricultural area, 1938[h]	107	100		91		74		76	
Total trade turnover (in million dollars) for late 1920s and 1934[i]		105	34	260	80	350	154	270	85

[a]Nicholas Spulber, "Changes in the Economic Structures of the Balkans, 1860-1960," in Charles and Barbara Jelavich, eds., The Balkans in Transition (Berkeley and Los Angeles: University of California Press, 1963), p. 366, Table 4.

[b]Ibid., p. 367, Table 5.

[c]The Royal Institute of International Affairs, Committee on Reconstruction, "Agricultural Surplus Population in Eastern and Southeastern Europe" paper presented to Economic and Statistical Seminar, London, July, 1943, p. 14, Table II (unpublished).

[d]Figures for Greece are for 1920 and 1951.

[e]Figures for Romania are for 1913 (old Romania and therefore not quite comparable).

[f] Nicolas Spulber, The State and Economic Development in Eastern Europe (New York: Random House, 1966), p. 57, Table I.3.

[g]Ibid.

[h]Economic Development in Southeast Europe (London: P E P Political and Economic Planning, Oxford University Press, January 1945), p. 26.

[i] Spulber, Economic Development, pp. 74-75.

modern technologies, including improved farming and livestock methods such as crop rotation, fertilization, and type of seeds, not to speak of mechanization, resulting in low productivity and yields per capita; and the reliance on grains and tobacco as cash crops, the latter especially in Bulgaria, Greece, and Yugoslavia. This poverty and backwardness of a large proportion of the peasants arose precisely from the divided and dwarf landholdings that made it simply impossible to increase productivity by using improved techniques. With only a slow increase in industrialization, new labor input had little choice other than internal (seasonal workers) or external emigration, or an increase in the number of unemployed or underemployed. Even though various governments devised some policies that were to assist agriculture, such as land reforms, including consolidation of scattered holdings, some price support, especially after falling demands in the world markets, and the organization of agricultural credit facilities, most of these policies, in the opinion of experts, were either wrongly conceived, too little, came too late, or contradicted each other.[14] In addition, the tax structure, limited educational facilities, and the allocation of an increasing share of the gross national product (GNP) to defense left agriculture in a deplorable condition throughout the interwar years, something that affected the standard of living of a majority of the population.

Land reforms of varied impact were enacted throughout the area after World War I, but these reforms contributed to a continuing rise in subsistence farming and an even further increase in the agrarian surplus population. The comparisons that follow will illustrate the structural weaknesses in the agriculture of the area.

By the end of the 1920s, 63 percent of Bulgaria's farms were in holdings of less than five hectares. The average-size holding declined between 1900 and 1940 from seven to four hectares, and each farm consisted, on an average, of ten strips, often some distance apart. In Yugoslavia, 68 percent of the farms were in holdings of less than five hectares, occupying roughly one third of its arable land (34 percent of the holdings were less than two hectares). The figures for Romania and Greece were 75 and 85 percent, respectively; most of the holdings in Albania were under five hectares, but it must be born in mind that only 16 percent of the total area of Albania was arable. Efforts to increase the cultivated area and yields in the countries of Southeast Europe were only partly successful. Generally speaking, the area devoted to cereal crops increased slightly in the interwar years, e.g., by around 10 percent in Yugoslavia and Romania, but productivity remained low. The countries of Southeast Europe had the poorest ratio between agricultural population and arable land.

In Greece, a special case, the cultivable area was expanded by nearly 70 percent as a consequence of the influx of 1.3 million refugees. Agricultural improvements in Greece went further than in any other country of the area, but much of the land was marginal. Between 1921 and 1940, it was estimated that a total of over 1,125,000 acres, were added to the cultivable land through irrigation projects, drainage, and flood control. In addition, over a million acres of low-grade, including slope, land were brought under cultivation.[15] Over-protectionist policies that created a high cost structure in agriculture became a heavy burden for the consumers. The structure of agricultural exports changed little, and the relationship of the major crops to the cultivated area, with the exception of vegetable and truck products, which doubled between 1924 and 1938, saw few basic changes.

In Romania, 90 percent of the arable land in the 1930s was devoted to grain (corn slowly began to take the place of wheat in many parts of the country), but in spite of some increase in the total area available for cereal crops, the harvest in 1934 was only 60 percent of that of 1914. Nevertheless, these exports remained the major foreign-trade item. The continued land fragmentation (low crop yields and low productivity per capita) only made matters worse. Over 4 million hectares were obtained by the state through confiscated land of absentee and foreign landowners and were further subdivided and distributed to the landless peasants. Also, in spite of the various land reforms, a considerable amount of arable land remained in the hands of medium and large landowners, while about 700,000 peasants remained landless in the 1930s. In the early 1930s, 75 percent of all landholdings were less than five hectares, but occupied only 28 percent of all agricultural land. On the other hand, 2.5 percent of the holdings were twenty hectares or more, but they occupied 40 percent of all agricultural land. It was clear that such a situation created a serious social and economic problem for the country.

One of the really serious problems closely connected with the backwardness of agriculture in the interwar period was the rapid rate of population increase and the large labor force, the distribution of which had hardly changed and whose livelihood was drawn from agriculture, a considerable part of which was considered surplus— partially or wholly unemployed, though usually "disguised." The actual number of the surplus population has been theoretically defined "as the number of people engaged in agriculture (active or dependent) who, in any given condition of agricultural production, could be removed from the land without reducing agricultural output.[16] According to the previously cited study by the Royal Institute of International Affairs, compiled by Paul N. Rosenstein-Rodan, the figures for actual surplus

agricultural population in 1937 for the countries of Southeast Europe
were estimated (surplus as percent of agricultural population) as
follows: Greece, 24.3 percent; Bulgaria, 28 percent; Romania, 20
percent; and Yugoslavia, 35 percent. The seriousness of this siutation
was obvious, and it must be remembered that every one of the Southeast European countries had a very limited capacity to employ additional labor in industry. All the governments in the area were concerned with the problems caused by the large surplus population, and
the answer they found pointed toward greater state intervention in the
economy, increased industrialization, and heavy reliance upon foreign
capital, induced and protected by a variety of protectionist policies.
Differences arose among various political parties about the best way
to proceed and about the direction industrialization should take, but
not about the basic policy to industrialize.

        The drive toward industrialization actually already had begun
in the late nineteenth century, as seen from the earlier discussion.
The formation of Yugoslavia from its nucleus in Serbia with the
inclusion of economically advanced Slovenia and the formation of
Greater Romania including Transylvania,* both having important
industries acted as an incentive for further industrialization in the
respective countries. Throughout the interwar period, industrialization was the key facet of the policies of all countries of the region,
and, considering over-all economic growth by individual countries,
the net output of industrial products (based on 1938 prices) increased
32 percent in Yugoslavia, 143 percent in Bulgaria, 50 percent in
Albania, 43 percent in Romania, and 75 percent in Greece between
the late 1920s and 1939.[17] In his analysis, Spulber comes to the conclusion that increased industrial plant capacity was difficult to ascer-
tain, but industry proper doubled its employment capacity during the
interwar years.

        The measures taken to encourage domestic industries (1931) in
Yugoslavia expanded the production base of a variety of industries.
At the end of the 1930s most of the consumer goods required could
be produced in the country, a good beginning was made in the building
of capital-goods industries such as iron, steel, and cement; and the
foundation was laid for chemical and wood-processing industries.
Unfortunately, due to the greater availability of skilled labor, a
better-developed infrastructure, and increasing purchasing power,

----

*The number of Romanian industries increased 225 percent as
a result of territorial acquisitions.

a considerable proportion of the new industries were established in the northern part of the country (north of the rivers Kupa and Sava), close to a few urban centers, further accelerating the already existing polarization and spatial differentiation in the economic and social structure of the country.

Yugoslavia's foreign trade structure reflected this limited diversification. Exports consisted of ores, concentrates, timber, and foodstuffs, but 52 percent of all exports was comprised of five products: lumber, corn, wheat, iron, and copper ores. Eighty percent of the imports consisted of semifinished and finished products. Important industries were state owned; iron and steel, lumber mills, coal and iron mines, and some small processing facilities, in addition to river and maritime shipping. Important mining production was controlled by foreign investors: 35 percent of the bituminous coal production value, 55 percent of the lignite value, 100 percent of the bauxite, copper, antimony, lead, and zinc value, and 98 percent of the chrome ore value (all are 1938 figures).[18] The participation of foreign investors in Yugoslavia's industrial production amounted to an over-all 46 percent.[19] It is clear from this picture that foreign capital had a major control averaging nearly half of the total industrial production of Yugoslavia in 1939, e.g., "75-90 percent of all mining, metallurgy and chemicals, 50-75 percent of all metal working, timber and textile industries and 25-50 percent of all ceramics, glass, food, leather, and electrical production."[20] Based on a careful study of foreign capital in the Yugoslav economy by Sergije Dimitrijević, the conclusion was drawn that the percentages for the major participants was as follows: Switzerland, 20 percent; United Kingdom, 16.5 percent; Germany-Austria, 15.6 percent; France, 12.8 percent; Czechoslovakia, 9.6 percent; and United States, 6.7 percent. Altogether, eighteen countries participated as lenders and investors of foreign capital in Yugoslavia.[21] While foreign capital contributed, without doubt, to the industrialization of the country, reliance on such a high percentage of foreign capital, especially in minerals, meant emphasis on the exploitation of those minerals that were in great demand in foreign countries. But the financing of domestic processing facilities using the local metals was not in the interest of the foreign investors. This heavy reliance on foreign capital also had a retarding influence on more broadly based industrial production, industries perhaps better suited to the total needs of the population.

All in all, Yugoslav economic development during the interwar years was not more rapid because of a lack of capital, the deplorable condition of transportation, which often prevented the exploitation of important mineral deposits or broadening the basis of agricultural exports, the general backwardness of agriculture, nationalistic economic policies, and faulty economic decisions. But considering the over-all situation, both domestic and external, including the impact of the world depression, economic progress was made.

Basically, the problems in Romania were not unlike those of Yugoslavia. Industrial development began before World War I, but was of little importance in the total economy in the early 1920s. Over three fourths of Romania's exports consisted of agricultural products, with the remainder consisting of petroleum and timber. Foreign capital and technicians developed the petroleum industry. Laws to encourage and to protect industries were passed in 1912 and were modified and extended in 1921 and 1936. The addition of Transylvania after World War I, with its well-known iron and steel, textile, and various light industries and important coal mines, was a valuable acquisition and contributed to the greatly expanding industrial base of the country. On the other hand, lack of capital and the small domestic purchasing power acted as a brake in the development of the economy. In addition, the nationalistic economic policies of most governments limited foreign investment in a Romanian enterprise to 40 percent of the capital (the majority of the employees had to be Romanian); the petroleum fields, mines, and some of the largest metallurgical plants in Transylvania were taken over as state property, while the use of the petroleum fields was granted to companies as state concessions. Industrialization was encouraged by means of export taxes on agricultural products, and high tariffs and other protectionist measures were part of government policies; but the mining and construction industry contributed only 28.4 percent to the national income in 1938, employing only 9 percent of the labor force. The state sector in the economy, with its large property holdings, exerted a dominant influence on the economic development of the country.

The over-all volume of industrial production rose in Romania by over 50 percent between 1929 and 1938, with the food-processing and light industries (mainly leather and textiles) accounting for half of all production. A special financial Institute for Industrial Credits was established in the early 1920s, with 60 percent of its capital contributed by the state. It played an important role in encouraging and financing industrial development by extending cheap credits. On the whole, industry still played a relatively small part in the total economy in 1938; 95 percent of the needed machinery and equipment had to be imported. Production of agricultural machinery, of much importance in a predominantly agricultural economy, provided only 16 percent of the country's needs.

Economic and social developments in many ways can be more easily compared in Bulgaria and Greece. Both countries are much smaller in population than Yugoslavia and Romania, both are relatively poor in minerals, and in addition both were engaged in a series of wars after their independence that gravely affected their economic development and growth. While Greece was on the winning side at the end of World War I, its ill-conceived war with Turkey a few years later left a devastating impact on its economy, in addition to the impact of absorbing 1.3 million refuges.

Throughout the interwar period, protectionist policies encouraging autarky and industrialization were an important facet for Bulgaria and Greece. In both countries, stress was placed on the development of light industry, largely producing for home consumption. A law governing the "encouragement of domestic industry" was passed as early as 1894 in Bulgaria, which extended to industry such privileges as land grants, custom exemptions, and reduced freight charges on state-owned railways. The great depression of the early 1930s, with its flight of foreign capital, the catastrophic fall of agricultural prices, and numerous other factors, brought a momentary halt to the industrial expansion of the 1920s in both countries. Because of the systematic encouragement of the building of a domestic industry by the state in both Bulgaria and Greece, the impact of the depression on the development of those relatively protected industries was more easily overcome. As a matter of fact, it must be made clear that before World War II the state, more in Bulgaria than in Greece, played an important role in the control and even outright ownership of numerous enterprises, including all important mines, railroads, public utilities, and, in Bulgaria only, river and maritime shipping. But in spite of these changes, the structure of the industrial labor force (including handicrafts) hardly changed in the twenty years of the interwar period. It remained at 16 percent for Greece and 8 percent for Bulgaria. The previously mentioned lack of domestic capital in Bulgaria necessitated an intensive effort for foreign investments, which contributed 43 percent of all corporate capital, 60 percent of the capital for power generation, 46 percent of the capital in the paper industries, 43 percent of the capital in food and tobacco industries, and 24 percent of the capital in metal and chemical industries. Twenty-four percent of the foreign capital was invested in mining industries.

Industrial development in Bulgaria and Greece was heavily protected by tariffs. This had an adverse long-term effect on the economic development of the countries. High tariffs protected domestic production and produced inefficiency and in both countries acted as a barrier to a greater regional dispersion of industrial production. As a result, a relatively heavy concentration of industrial production developed in the two capitals—Sofia and Athens. Industry in both countries relied heavily on the domestic resources produced by agriculture and this, too, was protected. In part, this development was shown in the composition of foreign trade, which was typical of an underdeveloped economy. In Greece, throughout the interwar years, foreign trade was dominated by three commodities: tobacco, raisins, and currant products, which accounted for 61 percent of the total value of commodity exports in 1937. Receipt of invisibles (emigrant remittances and shipping income), accounting for two thirds of the value of commodity exports, covered the trade balance.[22] Bulgaria also relied heavily on agricultural exports during the interwar years; 54 percent of the total export income was derived from tobacco, wheat, and eggs. Imports were largely industrial goods. The large balance of payments deficit was covered in part by foreign loans. Throughout the interwar years, the two countries made a great effort in their economic development. With the enactment of land reforms and a policy of autarchy and industrialization, the social and economic structure of both Bulgaria and Greece had become quite similar by the outbreak of World War II.

The developments in these two countries before World War II can be briefly summarized to serve as a focus for a better understanding of the postwar changes. Most of the points raised in this summary also hold true for the other countries of Southeast Europe:

1. A backward agriculture based on subsistence farming lacking technical improvements and using outmoded methods of animal husbandry
2. Heavy demographic pressures that combined with land fragmentation; some effort to expand land by reclamation, with greater success in Greece due to massive infusion of funds both from the Greek government and international agencies needed because of the larger influx of refugees than in Bulgaria
3. A domestic industrial expansion largely of light industries heavily dependent upon agricultural resources supported by protectionist policies and a nearly complete lack of heavy industries; the majority of the labor force employed in extremely small-scale, low-productivity plants*

---

*In 1939 industrial production of textiles, food and tobacco industries comprised 70 percent of the industrial production in Bulgaria.

4. A heavy reliance on foreign capital for the development of industries and an infrastructure that resulted
in large indebtedness
5. Heavy military outlays absorbing between one fourth
and one third of the budget*
6. State involvement in various spheres of the economy,
including ownership of most public transportation
and utilities and industries for the development of
national military capabilities
7. Concentration of industrial expansion in a few urban
centers—Athens, and to a much lesser extent
Thessaloniki in Greece and Sofia, and to a lesser
extent Plovdiv and Varna, in Bulgaria—that resulted
in their rapid growth, but hardly any changes in the
traditional countryside.[23]

Greece's whole economic development was much affected, more than
that of Bulgaria, by the permanent or temporary emigration of its
citizens. Close to 2.5 million people had left Greece by 1940, and
some of the most active age groups thus were removed from the economic development processes. On the other hand, the remittances
in foreign currencies of these emigrants were of importance to Greece's
economy. Unfortunately, their value was largely lost by the poor
management of Greece's economic and political affairs.

Before World War II, Albania was entirely an agricultural country;
over 80 percent of its labor force was engaged in agriculture. The
Albanian establishment of a National Bank (Italian controlled) in 1926
and a national currency were the first steps in developing an economic
infrastructure. Because of a small domestic market, and acute
shortage of capital, the poverty of the country, a legacy of four and
one-half centuries of Turkish domination, and encirclement by jealous
neighbors, economic progress obviously was limited. A few light industries (mostly food and textiles), some handicraft, several saw mills,
cigarette manufacturing plants, a brewery, a cement factory, two
modern olive-oil-extracting plants, and several small plants manufacturing soap, furniture, and handmade tools and carts comprised
the industrial inventory in 1940.

---

*In Greece between 1894 and 1922 a large part of her foreign
loans went to support her wars. The situation for Bulgaria was not
much different.

The picture was more hopeful relative to minerals, and the first concession (1875) given to a foreign mining concern (British) was the Selenice bitumen mine. This concession was bought in 1918 by an Italian concern. Italian occupation forces successfully drilled oil in 1918 and also developed coal mining. While other foreign developers were actively seeking concessions from newly independent Albania, actual production proved to be so small and uneconomical that most of the foreign concessions were sold during the 1930s, largely to Italian concerns. Production, with the exception of oil, coal, chromium, copper, and bitumen, was discontinued. All in all, industrial and mining development in the interwar years was of minor significance. Nearly half of all exports consisted of the entire output of chrome ore, crude oil, and some timber; the rest was agricultural produce. A large trade deficit was met by emigrant remittances and Italian loans. The economic structure of Albania by 1939 had hardly changed since its liberation. It was, in effect, the most backward of the Southeast European countries.

3

CHARACTER AND LEVEL
OF THE REGIONAL STRUCTURE
AT THE OUTBREAK
OF WORLD WAR II

The lack of over-all economic and social progress in the countries of Southeast Europe, including the difficulties of changing the inherited regional structure, was characteristic of the socioeconomic development between the establishment of the new national states in the nineteenth century and the beginning of World War II*. The difficulty in changing the basic regional structure resulted largely from a variety of historical conditions in the various units of the new national states and was further influenced by specific governmental policies or the lack thereof. The economic activities of the newly independent countries and their various regional units showed only slight changes during the whole period, and existing regional differences were actually widened by economic and political developments during the interwar period.

The discussions thus far have clearly shown that the economic and social progress of the five countries of Southeast Europe, after their independence, pointed toward the creation of modern capitalist states, but progress was so slow that in many ways these countries in 1938 were still considered the most backward parts of Europe. The reasons for this are many: the numerous involvement in costly wars; a huge, inefficient, and often corrupt bureaucracy; a large, dissatisfied population that, especially in Yugoslavia, produced internal rivalries based on ethnic allegiances; a rural backwardness, indicated in much of the area by low levels of literacy; inadequate educational opportunities;

---

*For comparative statistical data, see the various compilations in Appendix Table A.1 - A.8.

and great demographic pressure, resulting in large agrarian surplus populations and huge foreign indebtedness.[1] Of importance also were regional socioeconomic differences, especially accentuated in Yugoslavia by ethnic sentiments and barriers and also found to a lesser degree in Romania, between the more-advanced territorial units, formerly part of the Austro-Hungarian monarchy, and the backward, underdeveloped regions comprising most of the other territories.

The preceding discussions clearly demonstrate that all countries of Southeast Europe had reached a similar social and economic development at the outbreak of World War II. The basic economic and social problem affecting every country of Southeast Europe must be related to the large agrarian population, the increasing demographic pressures, and the slow development of industrialization, resulting in an ever-increasing landless surplus labor and serious social problems. The rapidly increasing population was forced to move into the limited agricultural areas due to the lack of alternative working possibilities. As a result, large numbers of peasants lived on the arable land that had been subdivided numerous times to provide working places for the landless peasant labor; this resulted in underemployment and low productivity and thus contributed to the low per capita income. The lack of capital retarded growth of industrialization and limited alternative employment opportunities for the nonagrarian population.

The previously cited study by Rosenstein-Rodan clearly showed that population densities per hundred hectares of arable land, the population dependent upon income derived from agriculture, and the agricultural surplus population, in spite of several land reforms having broken up large landed estates, direct government financial aid, and other government measures, had had little impact during the interwar years. The level of living of the population as expressed in available housing facilities and medical services, was extremely low. A high illiteracy rate of considerable regional fluctuation—from 80 percent of those over ten years of age in some areas of southern Yugoslavia and Bulgaria, northern Greece, most of Albania, and prewar Romania, to as low as 10 percent in other regions of these countries, with the exception of Albania—slowed the building of a modern society. Peasants produced mainly cereal crops and even the more-fertile regions could not distribute their surplus easily to other parts of the same country because of the deplorable condition of transportation. Over-all, real income per person in terms of purchasing power was perhaps one fourth to one fifth of that of France or the United Kingdom. Peasants were frequently caught in the price squeeze between industrial and agricultural prices, and competition from overseas often resulted in large surpluses. Industrialization was just beginning to leave its impact in some of these countries, although it was confined largely to those parts formerly under Austro-Hungarian control in Yugoslavia and to concentrations in western Romania. Exceptions were the development in Ploiesti and Bucharest in Romania and the primate cities of Sofia and Athens. For the most part, economic growth was government induced and controlled, with much foreign capital invested. Domestic private entrepreneurship for the most part was absent.

The slow development of industrialization can also be seen in the fact that those employed in handicrafts outnumbered the workers in industry. The small number of nonagrarian workers also left a great impact on the level of urban development. The countries of Southeast Europe were among the least-urbanized areas of Europe (between 10 and 30 percent of the population was urban, with the exception of Greece). Though it must be stated that there existed numerous medium-size towns of 10,000 to 50,000 population (this was especially true in the Pannonian Basin), their essential agrarian character was never questioned. Thus one can see that the limited supply of capital, the low productivity of labor, and small domestic markets had an adverse effect on the general economic activities as well as on their spatial distribution. The depression of the 1930s added to this dismal picture.

The character and level of the socioeconomic changes in the regional structure within each one of the countries of Southeast Europe show clearly the important influence of historic conditions. These conditions had left an impact on the uneven socioeconomic developments ever since the countries of Southeast Europe became independent in the nineteenth century. In some countries, they are even more pronounced today. The acquisition of more-advanced territories, as a result of the dismemberment of the Austro-Hungarian monarchy containing various elements of a modern society, and its impact on the older territories raised serious socioeconomic and political problems for the new states.

It has repeatedly been stated that "societies in transition abound in social phenomena";[2] the societies in Southeast Europe were no exception. The very slowly changing economic structure left its impact on the social structure, though the latter underwent changes much faster than the economic structure. As a matter of fact, long before the emphasis on industrialization made itself felt, especially in the interwar years, the traditional societies underwent rapid transformation. The main reasons were the great demographic pressures, starting with the turn of the twentieth century and the scarcity of agricultural land, which could absorb neither the new population nor those migrating from the protection offered by mountainous regions once the danger of foreign occupation had receded. The resultant landless or under-employed population became the greatest threat to the traditional societies and their social structure. It was obvious that the change of the traditional social structure was inevitable. But that these pressures came at a time of economic stagnation or during periods of very slow change while industrialization, the main source offering diversified employment opportunities, was not yet ready to play this important role in the general social and political changes of the period was of profound impact.

In all the years since the independence of these countries, this conflict between two types of societies—the traditional one, receding from the scene, and the new one, not able to be absorbed fast enough— was a recurrent theme in the slowly moving socioeconomic relationships of Southeast Europe. The lack of economic opportunities left those anxious to change only a narrow choice of opportunities— emigration, mostly permanent, to foreign countries, or domestic migration to a few urban concentrations or to the already overpopulated fertile agricultural areas. The pressures exerted by the agrarian overpopulation and the changing societies were responsible for the continuous division of landholdings, the destruction of forested areas, the extension of soil erosion, the high cost of farmland and even upland areas, regardless of their quality, the decline in labor productivity and per capita agricultural output, the inability or unwillingness to experiment with new farm techniques, and the huge debts carried by the peasants.

These are all characteristics of an underdeveloped and backward society, and most areas of Southeast Europe fell into this category at the outbreak of World War II. Space does not allow a discussion in detail of the characteristics of these poverty-stricken societies and their attitudes and behavior with regard to change, but historical, social, and religious influences, together with the absence of economic opportunities, exerted much influence on the behavioral pattern of the people.[3] The money- and market-oriented economy was encroaching and demanding a rapid restructuring of the traditional economic activities and of the archaeic social structure, but a rapid change simply was not in sight due to the lack of a modern, industrial-type social organization, a basic infrastructure, and an efficient administration. In addition, and an important fact, was that the perception of a large majority of the people did not reach beyond their immediate environment, thus showing little understanding of the many problems faced by the society as a whole.

Though most of Southeast Europe was considered underdeveloped at the outbreak of World War II, certain basic changes already were clearly noticeable. Most of these transformations at first were confined to territorial units added to the nineteenth-century national states after World War I. A few larger market and administrative centers showed marked regional variations in the degree of manufacturing activities developed."[4] In Yugoslavia, for example, the distribution of industries showed a strong concentration north of the Kupa-Sava line, with an employment capacity of 77 percent of the country's total, including the administrative districts of Belgrade, with 11 percent, and Zagreb, with 7.4 percent.[5] Industrial development south of this line was very limited and was concentrated in the central regions of Bosnia (10.8 percent of the country's employment capacity), Serbia (7.4), and Dalmatia (3.8). South Serbia (including today's Macedonia and Kosovo) and Montenegro were among the least developed and together accounted for only a little more than 1 percent of the Yugoslavian industry's employment capacity. These are precisely the territories that, since World War II, have been designated as "underdeveloped regions," and for this reason received special consideration. Based on a study of addresses of industrial plants in 1938, Hamilton comes to the conclusion that approximately 40 percent of the Yugoslavian industrial concentration was located in Slovenia, Western Croatia and Eastern Slavonia, Vojvodina, and the Belgrade district.

Differences in the developmental level of individual regions were also marked in Romania.[6] Industrial production was concentrated in six centers, which accounted for 70 percent of the industrial production and comprised 60 percent of the industrial labor forces: the capital of Bucharest (30 percent of the total value of production and 20 percent of the industrial employment capacity), southwestern Transylvania, with its old iron and steel works and supporting industries in Hunedoara-Deva, Reşiţa and Timişoara, Braşov and the Prahova Valley with Ploiesti as its center. The historic provinces of Dobruja (Dobrogea), Moldavia, and Oltenia, which are very rich in natural resources, contributed only 12 percent to the prewar industrial production, though they had 38 percent of the country's total population.

Manufacturing activities in Greece and Bulgaria, with the exceptions of the concentration in Athens and its surrounding territory, Sofia, and smaller concentrations in Thessaloniki and Plovdiv, were only of minor importance. Handicraft employment still far outweighed industrial employment. The many advantages of Athens, with its dominant economic position in nearly every branch of the economy, adversely affected economic development in all other parts of the country. In the late 1920s, nearly one half of the manufacturing industries of the country were located in Athens and Piraeus, and in Bulgaria over one third were in Sofia. Industrial concentrations in Albania were nonexistent.

The cumulative processes brought about by manufacturing activities contributed to a more rapid economic advance in Southeast Europe; they also contributed to basic socioeconomic changes, but the statistical impact was slow to show. Industrialization also expanded in the more important towns of certain agricultural regions, especially those of Slavonia, and Vojvodina of Yugoslavia, and the Banat of Romania. Even though the agricultural population was dominant in these towns, many had become important regional markets and administrative centers with a core of small industries. These areas had a very good basic infrastructure, mostly completed during the Austro-Hungarian period, when the surplus wheat of these areas was shipped to various parts of the Dual Monarchy, though, with the changing political history of the area, connections with its new hinterland were often nonexistent, greatly hampering its economic activities making this region a prime example of a lagging area. Consumer-oriented industries—flour mills, potteries, cement, food, and so on—were established for the most part when these territories became part of Yugoslavia and greater Romania, though the loss of large markets brought stagnation to these areas with their many village towns.

Throughout the interwar years, the most-advanced agricultural regions of Yugoslavia and Romania were among the most-depressed areas. Agrarian-industrial structures in the rich agricultural regions had emerged relatively easily, but, due to new political conditions, stagnated and could make little contribution toward advancing the socioeconomic structure of their respective countries. The brief post-World War I period of prosperity of the 1920s quickly changed to the most devastating depression this area had known since the Turkish wars. The towns of the region stood as monuments to past economic growth; the huge peasant and village indebtedness, the structure of agricultural production, and overpopulation, in part due to the division of the large pre-World War I estates, all contributed to the stagnation of this important agricultural region.

The regional development at the outbreak of World War II showed a contradictory picture. Large areas were backward and underdeveloped, though the impact of a slowly emerging modern industrial civilization had left its mark on the traditional societies. Potential growth areas were largely confined to former territorial units under the Dual Monarchy and to a few of the more-important administrative capitals, including the primate cities of all the countries of Southeast Europe, Albania being a somewhat special case. Slovenia, Slavonia, Vojvodina, the Banat, the central Maritsa Valley, and central Greece with Athens had the basis for the modern infrastructure needed for manufacturing activities and a market-oriented agriculture, though the impact of the political changes after World War I, especially in the most-fertile regions of Yugoslavia and Romania, together with the depression of the 1930s, left these economically important regions in a state of stagnation and depression.

A few urban concentrations where industrialization was beginning showed some dynamic advances. They were the potential growth poles and centers, and it was hoped that they would lead to "spread" effects of modern economic development. Mihailović, using the example of the East European countries and especially Yugoslavia, pointed out that polarization is to be expected at a low level of development simply because the volume of manufacturing is not great enough to spread over the whole territory.[7] Industry is of necessity concentrated in regions where a superstructure, a skilled labor force, and a market exists. There are few such areas in underdeveloped countries, and for this reason a certain amount of polarization in regional development is inevitable. In Mihailović's opinion, socialist writers omitted the fact "that the socio-economic conditions under which the inherited structure of regions and settlements was for the most part established were such as to make it impossible for that structure to meet the requirements of an industrial type of contemporary economy and civilization."[8] The original urban concentrations already acted as zones of gravitation for people from backward areas and for the building of manufacturing activities, but their "spread effect" had to await events after World War II. Still, these developments often served to accentuate regional differences instead of ameliorating them. The traditional countryside was little affected by industrialization. The few urban concentrations and the building of an infrastructure, tying together the various regions of the individual countries, was at best in its infancy. Many regions in 1940 were still without a unified or even a simple transportation network.

Thus, it can easily be seen that the level and distribution of all economic activities in Southeast Europe before 1939 was affected by the inherited and dominant position of agriculture and by the rapid increase and impoverishment of the agrarian population. A strong regional, social, and political consciousness and tradition exerted its influence on every aspect of the social, economic, and political life throughout the formative and interwar years. Basically, then, the emphasis in the development strategy pursued by all countries of Southeast Europe before 1939 was on changing the socioeconomic structure by industrialization, largely relying on foreign sources for the needed capital. It must be emphasized, however, that none of the countries had anything resembling, even in the slightest, sectoral and/ or regional development plans. Progress was extremely slow and at

times, such as in the 1930s, nonexistent or even regressed. A few
larger industries located in potential growth centers, while on the
increase, simply were unable to absorb the huge agrarian surplus
population, and hung like an albatross around the countries of Southeast
Europe. The great spatial differences within the individual countries
remained unchanged and were often actually accentuated during the
interwar years. There was no doubt that the traditional economic and
social structure was slowly changing, but what was really needed was
a thorough reconstruction. The aftermath of World War II brought this
thorough reconstruction, faster than anyone thought possible.

Since World War II, few countries in the world have experienced such far-reaching basic structural changes in their cultural, economic, and political life as the four socialist countries of Southeast Europe—Albania, Bulgaria, Romania, and Yugoslavia. Only Greece has used a more traditional approach in its development strategy, though changes there also have been considerable. Broadly speaking, all the countries of Southeast Europe followed three closely related development aims throughout the postwar period: a rapid economic development with major emphasis on industrialization, the greatest possible use of domestic resources, and an ultimate goal of "equality"* for their regions.

To accomplish these aims, the whole development strategy of the postwar period emphasized rapid industrialization, especially in the socialist countries, which were to accomplish basic structural socioeconomic changes in the shortest possible time. Industrialization as the main vector of change was intended to absorb rural surplus labor in the increasing number of new industries and also to provide a rapidly growing number of secondary and tertiary employment opportunities. Industrialization meant an increasing mechanization of agriculture that in turn would permit accelerated transfer of underemployed rural labor. Such a strategy, it was hoped, would bring about greater economic and ultimately political independence for each country by producing an ever-increasing number of semifinished and finished manufactured products and thus would participate in the international division of labor by increasing emphasis on multilateral foreign trade. Emphasizing industrialization as the vector of economic development also created increased demands for domestic natural resources, many of which were exported in raw form before the war. Finally, it provided an opportunity, by the use of planned investments, to influence the location of new industries, thus contributing to a wider regional distribution and spread of economic activities. In the socialist countries, agriculture in such development schemes received low priority and generally stagnated until the 1960s.

---

*Equality in the Marxian approach is understood as multidimensional, implying social equality in terms of work for everyone, with the emphasis on equal conditions of production and the abolition of class differences.

With the exception of Yugoslavia, after 1952 the socialist countries followed the Soviet model of a "centrally directed and comprehensive system of management of the economy," accomplishing their goal of basic structural changes by shifting from a market to a centrally planned economy, by widespread nationalization, and by the channeling of all available savings according to specifically planned targets. Restrictions placed on consumption, as well as the rapid increase of capital formation, permitted sustained economic growth, at least throughout most of the 1950s, though the established investment priorities created numerous imbalances in production. With increasing diversification of production and a greater sophistication of processes, as well as increased foreign (especially Western) trade, a serious problem of managing the centrally planned economies arose in the late 1950s bringing internal pressures for economic reform. Yugoslavia, as a result of its expulsion from the Cominform, gradually initiated basic changes in its economic system, including institutional changes in the management of its socialist enterprises, changes that also left their impact on the political scene. Throughout the postwar years, Greece pursued a development strategy modeled after that of the Western European countries and thus differed radically in its development strategy from all other Southeast European countries.

The discussions of the postwar development strategy in Chapters 4 and 5 are divided between those of the immediate postwar period and those of the period of the 1950s and 1960s, though such a division is less meaningful in the case of Yugoslavia and Greece. The development strategy of the socialist countries for the 1950s emphasized the creation of equal conditions (implying social equality), to be brought about by a rapid social and economic change, industrialization and collectivization being the main agents. In addition, for the 1960s, this strategy was characterized by the emphasis on economic reform, which aimed at restructuring the planning and management apparatus of the centrally planned economies. This emphasis on reform was brought about largely by the demands of a more sophisticated economy, increased foreign trade (with the exception of Albania), especially with Western countries and its impact on domestic production, including the need for greater efficiency and initiative. Over-all, the policies in the postwar period were thought by all the countries to be a contribution to the development of a rational spatial distribution of all economic activities. Albania only recently has begun to emphasize a limited reform of its management apparatus. Yugoslavia continued its economic reform throughout all the postwar years. This reform was accelerated in the latter part of the 1960s, partly due to pressures exerted by the people of this ethnically diverse and often discordant society, but the results and impact of this reform constantly collided with both the economic and political expectations of the people and the ideological basis of a socialist society. Thus a constantly increasing rift among the people of Yugoslavia developed, which, in 1972, raised some serious questions about the future of the Yugoslav state. Both internal and external constraints influenced the development strategy, especially in the 1960s, with the Czech crisis of 1968 generally having a regressive impact on the reform movement in Bulgaria and, to a lesser extent, in Romania.

Finally, it should be stressed here that no attempt is made at an exhaustive analysis of specific aspects of economic activities and specifically of their regional variations. Specific developments in individual countries are presented under separate headings, but here, too, major trends and patterns are stressed, together with the broad impact of Soviet bloc policies as they affect the socialist countries of Southeast Europe. The analysis of the regional impact of the development strategy is carried out in Part III.

CHAPTER

4

**FRAMEWORK
FOR CHANGE:
THE AFTERMATH
OF WORLD WAR II**

World War II left a deep impact on the whole social and political life of all Southeast European countries, evidenced in population displacements and in the tremendous physical damage to production facilities, transportation, utilities, and urban centers. While the economic base in several countries was actually broadened during the German occupation, through the building of new industrial plants or the expansion of existing ones, the basic structure and distribution pattern of economic activity, including the large surplus agricultural population, remained unchanged. The wartime and immediate postwar years saw many adjustments in the area in the form of boundary shifts and changes in the political and economic institutions and property relationships. Romania, Yugoslavia, Bulgaria, and Albania each went through a political revolution that brought about basic social changes. Old institutions were transformed, and the static society, with its traditional social structure, was radically changed as new generations became indoctrinated in the philosophy of socialism. Greece took a more evolutionary path after suppressing a bloody rebellion that destroyed much human and material resources. Some modernization of its institutions took place along traditional democratic lines until 1967, when a group of military officers replaced a weak and disorganized civilian royal government.

Vast population movements between 1940 and 1946 affected every one of the countries of Southeast Europe, resulting in severe disruption of economic activity.[1] The postwar map for the region showed Romania as having lost 20 percent of its interwar territories—Bucovina and Bessarabia going to the Soviet Union and the southern part of the Dobruja reverting back to Bulgaria (along with 15 percent of its population). Bulgaria was forced out of the territories of Thrace (Greece) and Macedonia (Yugoslavia), which it had occupied during

the war, but it gained the southern Dobruja from Romania. Greece
gained some of the Aegean Islands from Italy, and Yugoslavia acquired
areas of Croatian and Slovenian populations along the Adriatic littoral,
including much-disputed Istria from Italy.

   The immediate emphasis by all postwar governments was to
overcome the war destruction, which varied considerably among and
within the individual countries. Of the socialist countries of Southeast
Europe, without doubt Yugoslavia was in the most serious condition.
Greece, especially after the civil war, suffered enormously. Huge
efforts, often assisted by international organizations (United Nations
Relief and Rehabilitation Administration) or, in the case of Greece,
by additional aid from the United States and the United Kingdom, went
toward recovery of the war-damaged economies. At the same time,
the social and political transformation affecting the socialist countries
was begun by the enactment of wide nationalization measures in key
sectors of the economy, i.e., banking, trade, transportation, and
industry. Private ownership also was sharply curtailed in agriculture,
with the first steps being taken for a complete takeover by the state.
All medium-size and large farmholdings were broken up and either
distributed to the landless peasants or taken over by the state and
administered as machine-tractor or peasant cooperative farms in
preparation for subsequent collectivization. By 1950, the agricultural
area in the socialist sector varied from 15 to 24 percent of the total.
Nationalization by 1948 encompassed most of the nonagricultural
sectors; in industry, it "accounted for 92 percent of the gross industrial output, 100 percent of bank turnover, 80 percent of wholesale
trade turnover, and 50-100 percent of retail trade turnover."[2] From
the policies enacted between the end of the war and the first long-term
plans in 1948, it became clear that the example of the Soviet Union,
as well as its historical experience, had become the model after
which the four socialist countries of Southeast Europe were patterning
their socioeconomic transformation.

   A number of limited options at first were available in planning
the development strategy of the socialist countries for transforming
their social and political life in the postwar period. These options
centered on the organization of the economy—specifically on the
relationship between the state, the cooperative, and the private sector,
on the extent of the nationalization of the productive branches, on the
priorities in industrialization, especially its emphasis on heavy
industry to the exclusion of other branches of the economy, and on
the type and power of the central planning apparatus. In those countries occupied by Soviet troops—Romania and Bulgaria—the large
number of Party members trained in the Soviet Union and returned

with the Soviet army and placed in key governmental and Party positions, with their ideological training and close Soviet ties, were in the vanguard of those urging a strategy of rapid transformation of the social and political life, including complete nationalization of all productive branches of their respective economies and a copying of the Soviet model of economic growth. Pressures were also strong in Yugoslavia and Albania, where imitation of the Soviet model was at first thought to be the only possible choice.

THE SOVIET MODEL

The countries of Southeast Europe, with the exception of Greece, all adopted the Soviet model of socioeconomic planning.[3] But, as Charles Wilber stressed, "the term 'model' does not mean a detailing of every strategy, correct and incorrect, that was used by the Soviet Union. Rather it is an abstraction of the essentials from the Soviet experience modified by the later experience of the various socialist countries."[4] The Soviet model of organization should not be looked upon as a direct application of Marxian theory nor as a system of management carefully designed by social scientists. In essence, it was a system of ad hoc practices that emerged during Bolshevik rule over the previous quarter-century, as well as from standard operating procedures. The value of the model "lies in the establishment of a framework which gives interpretation and meaning to the facts and descriptions assembled by quantitative research."[5]

The prerevolutionary market economy was replaced with the Soviet-type centrally planned economy under a bureaucracy organized in a series of parallel functional hierarchies. The huge bureaucratic apparatus was "coordinated by being fitted into identical administrative-region molds, each of which was supervised by communist party officials controlled through the separate hierarchy of the party secretariat."[6] Through such central control, the socialist countries of Southeast Europe hoped to achieve very rapid sectoral growth in the production of key industrial products, while at the same time achieving a sustained increase in both total and per capita product.[7] Industry received the highest possible priority in investment planning and, as Ian Hamilton, George Hoffman, and Fred Warner Neal in their detailed studies on East-Central and Southeast Europe and Yugoslavia have stressed, became the prime vector of change in the spatial economic structure. Location decisions for investments in industry became an important part of state and Party policy-making.[8] These decisions were made

within a framework of collective ownership and management of most capital infrastructure, production, resources,
and services . . . embodying coordination between economic
sectors and regions and are incorporated in medium- and
long-term plans which are executed through state controlled
allocation of fixed capital investment and circulating cash.
Decisions are intended to fulfill socialist ideals, fundamentally the deliberate maximum economic and cultural
development for the maximum and equalized benefit of
every member of a society.[9]

Important to Soviet-type planning "is the definition of objectives
by the top political authority."[10] The various targets and their priorities are formulated in considerable detail, with the planning directives
based on studies prepared by the National Planning Board. Before the
plan is submitted to the government, considerable communication with
technical ministries and enterprises takes place, and once all adjustments have been made the plan is submitted to the government to be
put into law. Planning authorities also prepare income and expenditure
accounts and formulate the aggregate national product. Nicolas Spulber
pointed out that "Soviet planning proceeds first from a definition of
objectives in aggregate terms to plan elaboration involving a great
deal of disaggregation. Then this process is reversed with the consolidation of specific detailed accounts into a new set of national
accounts."[11]

It is clear that the example and experience of the Soviet Union
gave the socialist countries of Southeast Europe very little choice
between the operating Soviet model and possible experimentation
with new models of their own. Yugoslavia stepped out on its own
only after the Cominform expulsion, and throughout a long period
evolved its own model of economic development, a continuing and
danger-fraught experiment as anyone following Yugoslav internal
discussions can readily testify.

SOCIOECONOMIC TRANSFORMATION

As an immediate first step in this process of socioeconomic
(and political) transformation and closely connected with the introduction of a collective socialist economy, centralized planning, including
the establishment of branches of planning authorities at various
regional levels, became part of the postwar changes in the socialist
countries of Southeast Europe. Clearly, the policy of nationalization
and the practice of channeling all savings according to planned targets

placed powerful resources and tools in the hands of the state. This enabled the state to initiate forcefully a complete restructuring of the economic and social life by a policy of allocating investments, thus influencing the location of new economic activities or the expansion of existing ones.

To accomplish this, investments in the socialist countries received about 20 percent of the total national income during the recovery period, and from 20 to 25 percent during the long-term plans after 1947 or 1948, roughly four times the prewar level. Between 32 and 47 percent of the total investments were allocated to industry and construction during the recovery period and between 40 and 53 percent during the long-term plans, with the largest share going to capital-goods industries. The smallest share of the total investments went to agriculture, between 6 and 13 percent in the recovery period and between 8 and 15 percent in the long-term plans. Personal consumption was drastically curtailed.[12] At the same time, a major effort was initiated to educate potential and existing industrial manpower and to absorb an ever-increasing amount of agricultural surplus labor in the newly established or enlarged industries. The results of such an emphasis on the creation of a heavy industrial base resulted in an increased production of steel, iron, and cement, but the immediate impact of such policies in some countries caused considerable social and economic dislocation, a stagnant agricultural economy, and, in the long run, serious imbalances in industrial production.

Planned investment allocations in Yugoslavia, Bulgaria, and Romania, in the early postwar period, had already spread industrial-ization to an increasing number of regions and communities (see Figure 4). Excluding Greece and the insignificant developments in Albania, employment in industry increased between 1938-39 and 1950 from 650,000 to 1,750,000. This rapid growth was made possible by large numbers of surplus agrarian laborers being absorbed into existing manufacturing industries—by the introduction of shifts and the use of labor for capital—and by the rapidly expanding minerals and energy production. It also must be pointed out that the predomi-nance of small industries in the countries of Southeast Europe made recovery from war damages much easier and facilitated a much quicker return to production and expansion. Within a short period after the end of World War II, all four socialist countries had opted for the Soviet type of centrally planned economy. As part of this decision, a very high proportion of their national product was allocated to investment and a very large proportion to heavy industry. With the recovery generally completed by the end of 1948, the first long-term plans were launched.[13]

FIGURE 4

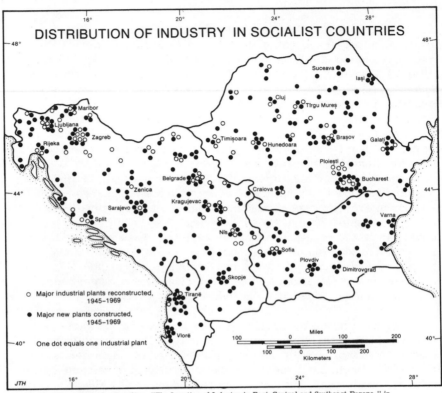

DISTRIBUTION OF INDUSTRY IN SOCIALIST COUNTRIES

○ Major industrial plants reconstructed, 1945–1969

● Major new plants constructed, 1945–1969

One dot equals one industrial plant

Modified from F. E. Ian Hamilton, "The Location of Industry in East-Central and Southeast Europe," in George W. Hoffman, ed., Eastern Europe: Essays in Geographical Problems (London and New York: Methuen and Praeger Publishers, 1971), pp. 180–81.

APPROACHES TO DEVELOPMENT

Broadly speaking, the long-term economic aims of all Southeast European countries were not unalike. The most-pressing problems for the socialist and capitalistic countries were always their need for basic, far-reaching structural changes in their economy. The paramount question was how to reach their desired goals. Two fundamentally different development approaches were available to the socialist countries at the end of World War II. These approaches to economic development, and specifically to the problem of industrialization, were discussed during World War II in an article by Paul N. Rosenstein-Rodan.

> (i) That Eastern and South-Eastern Europe should industrialize on its own, on the "Russian model" (by which we do not mean communism), aiming at self-sufficiency, without international investment. That would imply the construction of all stages of industry, heavy industry, machine industry, as well as light industry, with the final result of a national economy built like a vertical industrial concern. This way presents several grave disadvantages: (a) It can only proceed slowly, because capital must be supplied internally at the expense of a standard of life and consumption which are already at a very low level. It implies, therefore, a heavy and, in our opinion, unnecessary sacrifice. (b) It will lead finally, since there are appropriate natural resources in the area, to an independent unit in the world economy implying a reduction in the international division of labour, i.e., the output of the world as a whole would be less than it might be, the world would be poorer in material goods . . .

> (ii) The alternative way of industrialisation would fit Eastern and South-Eastern Europe into the world economy, which would preserve the advantages of an international division of labour, and would therefore in the end produce more wealth for everybody. It would be based on substantial international investment or capital lending. This way presents several advantages: (a) It could proceed more quickly and at a small sacrifice of consumption of this area . . . (b) The sound principles of international division of labour postulate labour-intensive—i.e., light industries in overpopulated areas. (c) Even for the purpose of an expanding world economy, the existing heavy industries

in U.S.A., Great Britain, Germany, France, and Switzerland
could certainly supply all the needs of the international
depressed areas.[14]

As the developments in the postwar period have shown, industrialization along the Soviet model became the guiding motive in all
socialist countries of East-Central and Southeast Europe. Emphasis
was placed on heavy industries, especially at first on metal-working
industries, which received priority over consumer-goods industries
and, over light industries, generally. In addition, the developmental
strategy emphasized a goal of maximum degree of self-sufficiency in
each country and reliance largely on internal sources of capital accumulation. Rosenstein-Rodan's remarkable analysis—largely of historical interest today—discarded the whole Soviet philosophy that aimed
at self-sufficiency without international investment, that brought about
much individual sacrifice and disregarded the principle of international
division of labor. His analysis is for all the countries of East-Central
and Southeast Europe, and it is therefore difficult to extract detailed
figures for the four countries of Southeast Europe alone (Albania is
excluded in his analysis). Rosenstein-Rodan's assumptions were
based on an agrarian excess population* in 1937 of over nine million
people, or close to 20 percent of the total population, for whom jobs
had to be found by industrialization.[15] He stressed an approach for
the whole region "in order to reach an 'optimum size' of the industrial
enterprises" and advocated the establishment of various industries on
a broad front to create a large and varied internal market. He emphasized light industries to avoid excessive heavy industrial capacity
throughout the world and to "generate" export surpluses that in turn
would contribute toward payment of the foreign debt.

While the model actually followed in the socialist countries of
Southeast Europe was radically different from that proposed by
Rosenstein-Rodan, his analysis of the forces of external economics
and balanced growth, of the key role of government in promoting
growth, of the role of international investment units or even foreign
aid made important long-term contributions to understanding the
development processes. Some of the policies advocated by Rosenstein-
Rodan are certainly controversial. His advocacy, for example, of a
"balanced growth" position in economic development is opposed by a

---

*Totally or partially unemployed, although the unemployment is
usually disguised.

school of thought favoring "unbalanced growth."* The allocation of
investments in the prewar Soviet Union and in the first postwar period
in most of the socialist countries of Southeast Europe is a good example
of the "unbalanced growth strategy." The argument by those expounding
the principles of unbalanced growth in cases in which a development
strategy emphasizing industrialization is stressed is directed toward
concentrating on a few key objectives that will, in the long run, contribute to transforming the economy. A real danger exists here, according
to this argument, that in advancing on too many fronts, available
resources can easily be dissipated.

It is clear that the socialist countries, already in the initial
period of recovery and reconstruction, had abandoned the possibility
of alternate strategies in their development policy, and there is some
doubt if they ever seriously considered them at all. Reliance on
Soviet-style institutions, emphasis on industrialization as the main
agent of change in the spatial economic structure, and the correspondingly low priority given to agriculture became universally accepted
policies by 1948 and, with the exception of Yugoslavia after the Cominform break in 1950, generally have been followed by all socialist countries throughout most of the postwar period. The planned economy
replaced the market economy, and important decisions were highly
centralized. Specific regional planning policies, with the exception
of those of Yugoslavia, did not exist.

Another policy initiated by the Soviet government and forced on
all the socialist countries was the so-called joint partnerships or
mixed cooperations.[16] Though their existence was short-lived, their
operations were a further indication of how Stalinist economic policies
and economic integration in the socialist countries under Soviet leadership was implemented. For the most part, they were based on the
former German assets and they were largest in the former "ex-enemy
countries.[17] Romania, besides being forced at the end of the war to
pay reparations in the form of goods to the Soviet Union from its
current production for a period of six years (later extended to eight),
was also forced to accede to the formation of numerous Soviet-
Romanian companies. Most of these joint companies were based on

---

*Albert O. Hirschman is the strongest exponent of the unbalanced
growth strategy. His book is something of a classic: The Strategy of
Economic Development (New Haven: Yale University Press, 1959),
esp. Ch. 4, pp. 62-75. See also the theoretical discussions in Chapter
6.

former German assets. They penetrated into every aspect of Romanian
economic activity. There were only a few joint partnerships between
the Soviet Union and Bulgaria. In Yugoslavia, there existed only two
joint Yugoslav-Soviet companies, but they were the source of unending
controversy in the short time they existed (between early 1947 and
mid-1949). All the joint partnerships were liquidated by 1954, but
from the various records presently available, they clearly were established to control vital parts of the economy of the individual "brother"
socialist countries.

LONG-TERM PLANNING

The period discussed in this section extended through the recovery
and reconstruction period in the individual countries. This period was
generally concluded in 1947 in Yugoslavia, in 1948 in Bulgaria, and in
1950 in Romania and Albania. It was then that every one of the socialist
countries developed their first long-term national development plans
(see the discussion in Chapter 5). Because of the break between the
Cominform and Yugoslavia, developments in the latter country assumed
a character quite different from that of other socialist countries. In
Greece, developmental processes obviously were greatly affected by
the civil war. The level of the prewar GNP per capita, for example,
was not reached until 1956. In Bulgaria, it was realized in 1950.
When long-term planning was introduced, the private sector, with the
exception of farming, was all but extinguished. Institutional reforms
reproduced in miniature the developments in the Soviet economy.
This was true for the whole cumbersome planning apparatus, including
agrarian reforms, with their forced collectivization and nationalization
of every branch of economic activity.

Romania and Bulgaria at first developed a "three-sector economy,"
but by 1948 had turned completely to the state sector only. Spulber
argues that the social structures in these two countries were better
preserved at the end of the war, and this necessitated a somewhat
slower development. Also, because of their intention to "return to
the international scene under the best possible conditions [they] did
not feel free in their movements, at least up to the signing of the peace
treaty in 1947."[18] Romania emphasized first expansion of existing
manufacturing industries, and Bulgaria, beginning in the 1950s, emphasized the dispersion of new industries throughout various regions of
the country. Albania and Yugoslavia opted at an early stage for the
Soviet-type economies of complete nationalization and centralized
sector and branch planning and consolidated state influence in all
sections of their respective economies.

Yugoslavia

The outstanding feature of the Yugoslav First Five-Year Plan
(1947-51) was its extreme centralization and its complex planning
hierarchy. The plan was supported by sweeping laws on nationalization
enacted in July, 1946, and affecting retail trade, cultural and health
institutions, and also often only formalizing the status quo, especially
the many confiscations of the early postwar years. During this so-
called administrative planning period, the state had become the manager
of the whole economy, with individual enterprises as economic organs
of the state. State organs fixed prices for all services. Farmers were
compelled to sell their crops to state enterprises at fixed prices, and
the market as an indicator of production costs and prices was, in effect,
eliminated. The practices in Yugoslavia were basically no different
from any of the other socialist countries after 1948, though they were
enunciated much more rapidly. This was especially true in nationalization measures and in the early collectivization efforts.

Yugoslav development differed markedly in one way from the
other socialist countries—in the locational decisions for new industries.
For the most part, this was brought about by the great spatial disparities in the economic development among the regions of the country,
but also by the multinational character of its people with their long
history of great and often violent ethnic cleavages. Already in its
First Five-Year Plan, Yugoslavia had attempted to lessen the economic
differences that existed among the various parts of the country by
specially designating "underdeveloped regions," areas with a per capita
national income much below the federal average.[19] These areas included the socialist republics of Bosnia and Herzegovina, Montenegro,
and Macedonia (see Figure 13). Their special designation from the
First Five-Year Plan on aimed at dramatizing the unequal relations
existing in the country. The drive for equality of opportunity among
all of its people was a political necessity for Yugoslavia; "in addition
to the economic dimensions, it covers equal conditions for education,
medical and social insurance, political influence and social mobility."
The plan also emphasized "evenness," meaning a "balanced economic
development of regions" through the location of new plants in the most
underdeveloped and backward regions of the country, instead in the
most advanced regions of Slovenia and Croatia only.[20] In the long
run, this caused economic as well as political problems inasmuch as
it meant that these two republics were to contribute a much larger
share of the new investments. Yugoslavia was the only country in
Southeast Europe that from the outset gave some attention to regional
development in the form of special aid and the planning of industrial
locations in its officially designated underdeveloped areas.

The economic blockade imposed by the Cominform in early 1949 was a major factor that contributed to the failure of the First Five-Year Plan. In part, this failure was also due to the nature of the plan itself, especially the overcentralization of all decision-making in Belgrade, the low priority of investments given to the most important part of the economy (agriculture), and certain overoptimistic goals of the plan itself. In addition, a severe drought had a devastating effect on agricultural production. The Yugoslavs now refer to the period 1946-50 as their "administrative period of bureaucratic centralism," a euphemism for a highly centralized, hard-boiled, and doctrinaire totalitarianism.[21] The Five-Year Plan was extended first for a year and by 1952 was abandoned, with the exception of the planned investments in "key" projects.

Assistance from the West in 1950-52 in the form of large shipments of agricultural products, some industrial equipment, and aid in modernizing and adjusting its armament industries avoided a complete economic and military breakdown in Yugoslavia and enabled the country to adjust to the complete loss of Soviet bloc trade. The ties with the West began a new chapter in Yugoslavia's economic growth, and 1950 was the beginning of a new road—their "own road"—of economic and political development. The aftereffects of the Cominform blockade and the "administrative period" were felt through the 1950s, but the failure of the First Five-Year Plan, the blockade by the Cominform countries, and the newly established ties with the West enabled the Yugoslav leaders to take a new look at the options available in their development strategy.

Greece

Greece emerged from World War II with a devastated economy and serious social and political problems.* A civil war shortly after the end of World War II further destroyed a great number of human and material resources. The period 1945-53 was characterized first by a struggle for survival (to 1950) and thereafter by a tremendous foreign and domestic recovery effort.[22] For this reason, long-term attention

---

*Devastation as a result of World War II and the German, Italian, and Bulgarian occupation included all major ports and 95 percent of the railroads, with industry at a virtual standstill and agricultural production, due to rural insecurity, at only 35 percent of the prewar level.

to economic development could not be expected until monetary and
political stability had again returned to the country. While American
aid was most impressive—it covered 68 percent of the Greek imports
and invisibles in 1949, exclusive of military aid, and amounted to over
$2 billion—it also created a real inflationary problem. Only after
thorough monetary and economic reforms, including a drastic currency
devaluation, was a more stable basis for future economic development
created. During the recovery period, Greece had already exhibited
some political instability, in part caused by the multiparty system for
which it was known from prewar times and from which it suffered
almost continuously during the postwar period. Its impact was felt
in every major economic decision and, unfortunately, much too often
in the lack of decisions needed for economic development.

SUMMARY

     The first postwar years had already established the pattern of
development strategy at least for the 1950s in all the socialist countries.
Greece, by the early 1950s, had just won the struggle for survival
against foreign intervention and with massive United States aid was
beginning a drive for recovery. While the various, though limited
options available for economic development at the end of the war were
quickly disregarded in favor of following the Soviet model, strategies
of economic development, discussed later in this Part, reestablished
to some degree the three-sector economy in Yugoslavia, and, during
the 1960s, showed signs of reducing the power of the central planners
in Bulgaria and Romania.

5

**THE DEVELOPMENT
STRATEGY
OF THE 1950s
AND 1960s**

The preceding discussions have shown that the first postwar years were devoted by all the socialist countries to a very rapid recovery and reconstruction of their war-torn economies, using a set of instruments nearly identical to those in use in the Soviet Union. Though some of these countries hesitated momentarily, Soviet-style institutions, including a centrally planned system of management of their economy under complete control of the Party and the state, were soon installed. This usually was referred to as the "command economy." Its long-term objectives obviously were of an economic, social, and political nature. Of the five countries of Southeast Europe, three followed this policy throughout the postwar period.

Yugoslavia's First Five-Year Plan (1947-51) in aims of structure was still a miniature Soviet plan. After Yugoslavia's break with the Soviet Union, its basic aims, as far as production priorities were concerned, remained unchanged for some time, at least on paper. With its increasingly independent economic system, however, including institutional changes in the management of socialist enterprises— from an administrative system to that of workers' management*—the economic and political makeup of the country, including its planning

---

*The basic law on workers' management was passed in June, 1950, as the first step in a series of reforms designed to transform Yugoslavia's basic economic, political, and social structure. Section 1 of the act described the principle of workers' management: "Manufacturing, mining, communications, transport, trading, agricultural, forestry, municipal and other public undertakings shall, as the property of the whole nation, be administered in the name of the community by

apparatus and its development strategy after 1952, underwent far-reaching changes.

Greece, on the other hand, pursued throughout the postwar years a policy of economic development based on market demand, with the private sector experiencing little state interference. Its whole economic policy was closely modeled after that of the Western European countries and thus differed radically from all other Southeast European countries. Still, restructuring its economic activities by greater emphasis on industrialization and modernizing its agricultural sector had top priority during the entire postwar period.

Centralized management of the economy[1] based on "social ownership of the means of production" as part of the theoretical basis of the socialist economic system, was modeled after the contemporary Soviet system, though its theoretical foundation was part of the classical Marxian economic laws of socialism.[2] It was argued that only by highly centralized planning under strict Party control could the proportional development of the economy be guaranteed and the disturbances in capitalistic economies, expressed in recurrent crises, be eliminated. An additional argument for the need of centralized bureaucratic management, one that still weighs heavily, was the example of the Soviet experience with the assumption that only centrally planned economies opposed to the market system could make such accelerated economic development possible. Based on the experience in economic development of all the socialist countries over the last twenty-five years, this argument, often repeated in Communist literature, could easily be refuted. Faulty planning with insufficient attention given to rational economic consideration and a management system that was unable to adapt to changing market needs has actually created large disproportions in the socialist economies, resulting, at times, in economic stagnation and even regression in several socialist countries. It was

---

their work collectives as part of the said economic plan and on the basis of the right and duties established by law . . . The collectives shall carry out their administration through the workers' councils and boards of management of the undertakings . . . (from International Labour Office: Legislative Series, 1950-Yu.2). The workers' council (radnicki savet) actually functions as the day-to-day decision-making body through a management board (upravi odbor), which it elects from its members. For one of the most comprehensive studies see International Labour Office, Workers' Management in Yugoslavia (Geneva: ILO, 1962).

largely this development by the late 1950s that forced one after another of the Eastern European countries into an overaccelerated economic reform, taking a new look at their Soviet-style institutions.

KEY ELEMENTS OF DEVELOPMENT STRATEGY

Much space has been devoted over the last 25 years to evaluating the working of the Soviet economic system, the stages of its development, and its impact on the postwar development strategy of the socialist countries of Southeast Europe.[3] All economic plans of the socialist countries of Southeast Europe closely followed the Soviet model, as was mentioned in earlier discussions. The key in the development strategy of the early postwar period—industrialization at a forced pace, with emphasis on heavy industry—was basic for all the socialist countries of the region and was designed to bring about a social revolution as well as to assist Soviet domestic and strategy aims.

The building of heavy industries received top priority, with coal and other energy sources and steel and metal production being rapidly expanded in order to meet Soviet bloc economic and military requirements. Light industries, investments in infrastructure (especially transportation and housing), and consumer-oriented industries received only secondary attention, largely depending on available resources. Hand in hand with the forced pace in industrialization went a modernization and enlargement of key raw-material exploitation. Foreign trade, which in the immediate postwar years already was reoriented to Soviet needs, was further closely tied to Soviet long-term industrial needs. In the postwar Stalin period (after 1956), direct Soviet economic intervention was reduced and replaced by Comecon, which was organized in 1945, but throughout most of the 1950s was little else than an arm of Soviet domestic planning.[4] Only during the 1960s did Comecon's expansionist activities have a more direct impact on its member states (the special case of Romania is discussed later in this chapter).

The economic policies pursued by the socialist countries of Southeast Europe are reflected in a greatly enlarged industrial base and thus are indicated in the rising industrial share of the national income (close to 50 percent). The increase in the GNP at factor cost (indicating GNP at real resource costs) in the period 1951-65 for all countries in Southeast Europe was mainly in industry, while agriculture's share rapidly declined.[5] The over-all growth for Romania, Bulgaria, and Yugoslavia, especially the industrial growth, was indeed impressive when it is realized that in 1938 more than three fourths of the people were still in agricultural pursuits. An important domestic base for the future expansion was established by the priorities set on metallurgy, machinery, and power, though the importance of consumer-oriented industries was only slightly raised after the events in Hungary and Poland in 1956. This type of industrial priority resulted in a major expansion in the over-all production output and contributed to a rapid structural change in all economic activities, including the distribution of manpower. In addition, this structural change, by concentrating on manufacturing industries, left its impact on the geographical distribution of the labor force by forcing them to seek their livelihood mostly in the existing urban concentrations either by moving from the many scattered rural settlements or, if feasible, by commuting to their places of work.[6]

Hand in hand with the industrial changes went a drastic reorganization in agriculture, including collectivization, much accelerated at the end of the 1950s, with the result that much agricultural output stagnated and remained low. In the beginning of the 1950s, the socialist countries were still largely agricultural economies, with two thirds or more of the total labor force in agriculture. Only Greece had little more than half of its manpower (57 percent) engaged in agriculture. This picture changed drastically during the 1950s, with substantial restructuring between agricultural and industrial employment occurring (see Appendix Table A.7 for details).

Closely connected with this emphasis on industrialization as the main vector for economic and social change was a massive effort to raise the output of vital domestic minerals. Ample supplies of minerals from newly opened and existing mines became essential to sustain the emphasis on heavy industries. Inasmuch as a large percentage of mining capacity before the war was geared to satisfy foreign demands (roughly estimated at 60 to 75 percent in Yugoslavia and Romania), the increased domestic demands could initially be satisfied without sinking new mines. This was especially true of the production of iron ore, bauxite, zinc, lead, copper, and chrome. A massive drive for fuel resources received high priority in all countries (see Figure 5).

The concentration on industrialization, especially on metalworking industries and later on general heavy industries, had a considerable impact on intra-Eastern European and Soviet trade, as well as on trade with the underdeveloped countries in the world. While trade with these areas was of little significance before the war, by the early 1960s manufactured products absorbed over 50 percent of the exports of Bulgaria and Yugoslavia and in turn accounted for 66 to 89 percent of the imports for Bulgaria, Romania, Yugoslavia, and Greece, with machinery and equipment accounting for 30 to 45 percent.

FIGURE 5

Trade within the Soviet bloc grew rapidly all during the 1950s, whereas trade with the West (specifically, the Western European countries) played only a minor role for Bulgaria and Romania (10 and 16 percent with all "developed countries," respectively), though it was substantial for Yugoslavia and Greece. Yugoslavia and Greece both decreased their share of foreign trade with the Western markets after the mid-1950s, when relations with the Eastern European socialist countries, including the Soviet Union, were again resumed (in Yugoslavia's case, when the Cominform blockade was discontinued). Beginning in the late 1950s, Yugoslavia also emphasized an adjustment of its cost price structure with the world market. Romanian trade with the West sharply increased between 1958 and 1967, from 16.2 percent to 38.1 percent. Bulgaria's economic links with Comecon, including the Soviet Union, were always extremely close, emphasizing industrial specialization and integration of its five-year plans with the bloc countries. Trade with the Western markets has increased, though at a much slower rate than, for example, Romania. Its foreign trade with the Soviet Union and the other Eastern European socialist countries was 81.3 percent of its total trade in 1958, though it decreased to 74.6 percent by 1968. Albania's trading pattern all through the 1950s and until its break with the Soviet Union in early 1960 was largely with the Soviet Union (nearly 50 percent) and the other socialist countries, with trade with the rest of the world minor. Changes in the trading pattern of the Southeast European countries are shown in Appendix Table A.1.

In summary, the basic objective of the development strategy of the 1950s for all the socialist countries of Southeast Europe was to bring about a rapid restructuring of economic activities, including a redistribution of the employment pattern, resulting in an ever-increasing demand for rural surplus labor. It was hoped that such a change would lead to increased production and demands for a variety of industrial products such as industrial goods, fuel and energy, and ultimately consumer goods and services. The effect of this on the whole economy in increased purchasing power, greater productivity, higher capital accumulation, and independence from foreign aid was obvious. It was the hope of all the Southeast European countries, including the free-market economy of Greece, that, once this was achieved and the mechanization of agriculture widespread, the surplus agrarian population would then find easy employment in the many new and dispersed industrial and tertiary activities. That such restructuring would bring about basic changes of a socioeconomic nature was to be expected.

Basic to this rapid economic expansion, with its emphasis on industrialization, was the need for sizable investments. To obtain them, the Soviet-type economic system established extremely high investment quotas regardless of consumer needs and the impact on the standard of living. This was achieved by relying on internal sources of accumulation obtained by forced savings, by the payment of low state-procurement prices for agricultural products, and by the physical allocation of resources in the industrial sector "so as to favor the producers' over the consumers' goods sector, and a relationship between income on the one hand and aggregate prices and taxes on the other could then be established to fit the plan."[7] The rising level of investment has been the major contributing factor to the entire postwar economic growth in all socialist countries of Southeast Europe, but their low productivity in spite of their larger share of the GNP than in the Western European countries is indicated in the slow growth of consumption. Maurice Ernst, in a study for the Joint Economic Committee of the U.S. Congress, feels that "a strong case can be made, therefore, for attributing the low productivity of investments to the economic policies and institutions that have characterized communism of the Soviet type."[8] Of special importance also is the distribution of investments, with roughly 45 percent of the total investments going into industry and construction (only 20 percent in Greece), with the bulk going into new plants.* Total labor intake into medium- and large-scale industries exceeded the total industrial employment in Bulgaria, Romania, and Yugoslavia in 1938. With the exception of Greece, the number of small enterprises rapidly declined.

Bulgaria and Romania received very little assistance in the form of credits from the Soviet Union for their postwar development programs. As a matter of fact, Romania through mixed cooperatives actually made important contributions to the Soviet Union. Yugoslavia and Greece received considerable U.S. aid, i.e., the former received up to 5 percent of its gross product in some years and the latter received up to 10 percent. Albania received considerable aid from the Soviet Union and, after 1961, from Communist China.

----

*According to Nicolas Spulber, "from 20 to 30 percent of the 'net material product (net material product, excluding services)' was methodically earmarked in each of the Communist controlled countries for gross fixed investments." It is obvious that such a rapid increase in the share of investments in income resulted in greatly increased capacity and output in industrial production of certain high priority industries. (Nicolas Spulber, The State and Economic Development in Eastern Europe [New York: Randon House, 1966], p. 76.)

From the general discussions thus far, it can be clearly seen
that, by reproducing the Soviet-type pattern of economic development
in miniature, a given pattern of investments was included—channeled
mostly to industry—with each one of the Eastern European socialist
countries putting great effort into the development of a whole set of
industrial activities nonexistent before the war.

The economic development in Southeast Europe, and specifically
in Romania, Bulgaria, and Albania during the period referred to as
the command economy, with its rapid over-all economic growth,
especially in certain types of industries, and the changes in the direction and structure of trade, were basically designed to follow the
course of Soviet economic and strategic priorities. Apart from Yugoslavia after its First Five-Year Plan (1947-51), the other socialist
countries of the area under discussion followed the Soviet model
throughout the postwar period, i.e., emphasis on rapid industrialization,
low priority to agriculture, and bilateral state trading monopolies.
Considerable growth was characteristic for most of the 1950s, and
the centrally directed planning of relatively few economic choices
was rather effective. This was especially true of the less-developed
countries of Eastern Europe—Romania, Bulgaria, and Albania. The
average annual growth rate for the countries amounted to 12.2 to 13.9
percent in the period 1950-55 and were only slightly less in the latter
part of the 1950s, 7 and 8.7 percent for Bulgaria and 9.7 and 6.5 percent for Romania for the early 1960s. Industrial output as a percent
of GNP was 47 percent in Romania and 45 percent in Bulgaria in 1963,
as against agriculture's 30 and 37 percent in the two countries, respectively. The latter over 50 percent in 1938.

Even though Romania, Bulgaria, and Albania had become economically dependent upon the Soviet Union in the early part of the
1950s, with their over-all economic development closely following
the Soviet pattern and Soviet bloc needs, over-all growth must be
judged a success. It must also be said, however, that the whole postwar economic development of the Eastern European socialist countries
in many ways was one of missed opportunities. Each of the socialist
countries developed its own economy along traditional autarchic lines,
avoiding specialization in production and large-scale economies. The
Soviet Union, for reasons of its own, encouraged bilateral relations
and did nothing to encourage a wider regional integration (as a matter
of fact, it opposed Yugoslav-Bulgarian integration in 1948). It was
felt that this was "an expression of their 'divide and conquer' approach
to Eastern Europe but from an economic point of view, the most significant missed opportunity of their dominance."[9] The absence of any
move for wider regional cooperation and integration during most of

the postwar period, except outright domination by the Soviet Union of
its weaker bloc partners, proved Spulber's statement of 1957 to be
prophetic as shown by developments since "Communism at the moment
of its expansion became more hypernationalistic than all the supra-
nationalists of the interwar period put together."[10]

THE DEVELOPMENT STRATEGY OF THE 1950s

The long-term development strategy in all socialist countries
of Southeast Europe was very similar. From the early 1950s on,
productive relationships differed between those following the Soviet-
type command economy—Albania, Bulgaria, and Romania—and Yugoslavia, the latter's now generally expressed as "market socialism."
Basically, all agencies and enterprises in countries following the
Soviet-type strategy were subordinated to a specialized branch ministry.
"Administrative and social agencies were budget-financed while productive enterprises operated on cost-accounting for current outlays
and budget grants for capital formation."[11] All financial transactions
were controlled by one of several specialized banks, e.g., agrarian,
investment, state, and so on, which were subordinate to the ministries
of finance. Payments made by socialist enterprises in the form of
turnover taxes and profit deductions were the main public revenue.
A State Planning Committee was responsible for coordinating all
planning proposals and had ministerial status. An advisory council,
with scientific and government consultants and a chairman and vice-
chairman comprised the working group. There existed, and with
minor modifications still exists, a complete interchange between the
state planning committees, the various enterprises, the ministries,
and a number of special agencies with both operational and consultative
functions, e.g., central statistical offices, state commissions on labor
and wages, and geological commissions. The heads of these are
usually members of the Economic Council, organized around 1957
and serving as a Committee on the Council of Ministers.[12] The pattern
of organization cited above is the one of Romania. It is broadly
representative of all the socialist countries, including Bulgaria and
Albania.

Management follows a form of horizontal integration, with
departments in each economic ministry for general policy (planning,
capital technology, finance, and sales) and operational direction of
the enterprises "grouped by the nature of the production processes."
In Romania, there was established also some vertical integration by
establishing so-called legal combines of enterprises run by the same
ministry.[13] Good examples of these are the Hunedoara Combine, for

joint supply of steel and coke-chemicals, and the Reşita Combine, for
joint demand of ore, silica, coal, and iron and steel, in Romania and
the Pernik & Kremikovtsi iron and steel works in Bulgaria. A similar
pattern exists also for foreign trade in the organization of product-
specialized monopolies. Adjustments of these organizations are common
and have been made since their establishment in the early 1950s.

Romania

    Romania's economic development in the 1950s was at best uneven,
in spite of a wide range of mineral, agricultural, and forestry resources
that were important contributions to the Soviet bloc partners and permitted it to benefit from economies of scale.[14] Romania's own production increases during the 1950s illustrate clearly its position as one
of the underdeveloped countries of the Soviet bloc. In 1960, it produced
only 8.7 percent of the bloc's steel (6.7 percent in 1950), 6.7 percent
of the electric output (4.4 percent in 1950), and 12.3 percent of the
bloc's cement (13.3 percent in 1950). The over-all rise in industrial
output was rather impressive, though limited in quantity. At 1955
prices, gross industrial output by 1960 was nearly 3.5 times the 1950
level, with chemicals, ferrous metallurgy, engineering, and building
materials ranking in that order. Basically, Romania's postwar industrial growth—and here development must include at least part of the
1958-65 take-off—as illustrated by data on per capita consumption in
1960 must be deemed a success. Per capita production in fuel, for
example, doubled between 1948 and 1960 (electricity increased 4.4
times) and production of steel and cement quintupled. Much as in
other socialist countries, agricultural output greatly fluctuated, and
the net output increased only slightly. Not until the accelerated drive
for the "socialist transformation of the countryside" in the form of
an accelerated collectivization (1959 to mid-1961) did agriculture
and forestry show an increase of roughly 30 percent in the national
income. Cereals, for example, increased by an estimated 10 to 15
percent in the 1959-61 period over the 1951-55 level.[15] Most of the
increases came from the recently reorganized state farms, which
received the bulk of the available fertilizers, machinery, and so on.
The gains in industrial production, according to John M. Montias,
were also matched by gains in productivity, especially between 1957
and 1961. The rise in net industrial output of 67 percent was accomplished with a rise in employment of only 22 percent.[16] Montias in
his studies draws the conclusion that the level of economic development
reached by 1960 was accomplished without sacrificing the standard of
living. Some Romanian statistics report that real wages had increased
20 percent in 1961 over 1937.

The turning point in Romania's economic development (proclaimed at a Party plenum in November, 1958) is closely related to the changes in its relations with the Soviet Union. The decision to concentrate on a more-independent economic policy, which could ultimately meet most domestic needs, set off Romania's dispute with the other Comecon members. Starting in 1958, emphasis in its economic planning was given to expanding its iron and steel capacities, its chemical and machine building potential, and its cellulose and paper industries. The Six-Year Plan (1960-65) promoted a policy of increased independence of external sources, emphasizing these new investment priorities.

There is no doubt that the rapid economic growth of the late 1950s and early 1960s, somewhat assisted by increases in productivity and agricultural exports, laid the basis for Romania's sustained growth of the 1960s. But at the same time, it also contributed to the need for economic reforms by creating a more sophisticated economy, thus exposing the need for a more-efficient management of the enterprises and the urgent need to improve trade with the West.[17] The efforts in the 1950s radically restructured and modernized the economic and social base of the country—not to mention the political changes—though it left serious imbalances and urgent tasks, especially in the development of a proper infrastructure and in the need for greater regional diversification in its economic development.

Bulgaria

Bulgaria's basic economic development strategy since World War II was a miniature of that of the Soviet Union.[18] On a per capita basis, Bulgaria is well endowed with natural resources, even more than Romania, but its small market was made up by specialization and close integration with the Comecon countries. Bulgaria is unique among the socialist countries in having recognized the need for continuous investments in the agricultural sector, though it can be argued that they have been insufficient considering the importance of this sector in the national picture. They averaged 18.8 percent (based on 1956 prices) between 1949 and 1957.[19] Bulgaria was the first Eastern European socialist country to achieve full collectivization (1958). As in other socialist countries, Bulgaria rapidly expanded state ownership of production and put a sharp limit on personal consumption. With the rapid expansion of production, the problem of allocation of capital investment, both with regard to branches and in terms of its spatial distribution, had come to the forefront in the discussions of the political leadership, as well as of the academic community.

Industrialization was again the main vector for restructuring the economic and social base of the country, and it depended on heavy imports, largely from the Soviet Union, besides making use of its own minerals. Metallurgy, chemicals, metal-using, and electric industries expanded most rapidly in the period 1948-58, as indicated by both the gross output and employment. These industries received 88 percent of the total investment outlays for the period 1950-58. The metallurgical industries alone received close to 17 percent of all centrally planned outlays, followed by the chemical industries. Before the war, integrated iron and steel works did not exist in the country. Pernik began operations in 1949, and a second plant was built at Kremikovtsi (both located in the Sofia basin) during the 1960s at great cost. Entirely new industrial branches were started, such as the engineering industries, which have been built since 1950 and accounted for close to 27 percent of the total industrial growth by 1960. The machine-building industry, which produced a variety of heavy capital goods, largely concentrated in Sofia, sold a large part of its products to the Soviet Union. As a result of the one-sided industrial building program, great structural disproportions arose and in future years undoubtedly will have a negative influence on the economic growth of the country. The important food-processing industries—in view of the importance of agricultural exports—were neglected during most of the 1950s.

Throughout the 1950s (and for that matter during the 1960s), the Soviet Union remained a model to be imitated in all important aspects of the economic and political life of the country. The need for the so-called great leap forward in 1958 was in part dictated to coordinate Bulgarian plans with those of the Soviet Union. The decision for an accelerated economic development was made by the Seventh Party Congress in June, 1958, and generally followed the aims of the Soviet Seven-Year Plan, which gave special emphasis to overtaking the West in per capita production. Bulgaria's role was closely coordinated with that defined by Comecon and was based on the division of labor according to "the natural resources of each country." It was Romania's objection to this division of labor that set its path apart from the other Comecon members, not Bulgaria, which, according to its first secretary of the Central Committee, Todor Zhivkov, made it clear that "independently of the historic traditions and particularities of our country, [Bulgaria] will develop exactly along the road followed by the Soviet Socialist State, according to the requirements of the basic laws for the development of the Soviet Socialist State."[20] As a result of the great leap forward, investments were increased, but certainly no decrease was made for the development of heavy industries. Still, considering the planned increase of 74 percent in two years, investments were totally inadequate (average investment increases in

agriculture during the 1950s were 2.4 percent). The anticipated progress in the standard of living did not materialize and left large parts
of the country backward and underdeveloped.

The results of this experimentation were devastating on Bulgaria's
economic progress. Few targets were met and a slowdown in the economy became obvious during the early part of the 1960s. According to
official statistics, over-all growth rates and agricultural production
had declined from 11.6 percent in the period 1956-60 to 9.6 in the
period 1961-65 in gross social product, and from 9.6 to 6.7 percent
in national income.* As a result of this slowdown, a far-reaching
reorganization of the whole economic system was contemplated by the
leadership and first discussed at the Eighth Party Congress in November, 1962, with guidelines presented at a Central Committee plenum
held in May, 1963. A new system of economic planning and management,
including the creation of a series of new mid-layer decision-making
bodies, associations, or trusts to coordinate the work of a number of
related enterprises was discussed.

Albania

Much less is known about the details of the development strategy
in Albania, though enough has been published that a general outline is
clear.[21] Basically, the country followed a policy not unlike that of the
other socialist countries, with emphasis on the development of an
industrial base to bring about basic structural changes and a general
neglect of agriculture. This was not an easy task, considering the low
per capita income of the population ($83 in 1950 and still only $151 in
1960 and $173 in 1965) and the general underdeveloped (or more

----

*The gross social product as well as the concept of national
income is based in all socialist societies on a less-comprehensive
definition than GNP, inasmuch as it excludes income from "non-produc-
tive activities" such as personal and social welfare activities, governmental services (education, administration, and cultural). The national
income (and product) includes only the material goods and productive
services (services connected with the production of material goods
and their distribution, such as trade and transport) valued at market
prices. Details for Yugoslavia are discussed in F. E. Ian Hamilton,
Yugoslavia: Patterns of Economic Acitivity (New York: Frederick A.
Praeger, 1968), pp. 327, 358-59 (footnotes 16-18). The above figures
are taken from Rabotnichesko Delo, October 31, 1967.

properly undeveloped) condition of the country at the end of World War II. Economic progress during the 1950s, based on available data, obviously was slow, and even in 1966 more than 65 percent of the working population was still occupied in agriculture. Only one third of the population had been urbanized.

Specific emphasis in the economic development of the postwar years was two-fold: the development of its rich raw-material resources (chrome, nickel, iron and copper ores, petroleum, sulphur, some low-grade coal, and natural gas, among others) and basic structural changes in the economy using industrialization as the main agent of change. In the first postwar years, Yugoslavia subsidized Albania's economic development, and during the 1950s and until 1961 the Soviet Union became the main source of aid. Since that time, Communist China has taken their place. Investment policies also followed the traditional pattern of Soviet-type development, and not until Soviet aid was discontinued, bringing a severe economic crisis to the country, were some of the priorities changed.[22]

Chinese technicians took the place of those from the Soviet bloc. Foreign trade could play an important role in Albania's development programs, but basically only two countries traded with Albania until very recently—the Soviet Union and China. During the 1950s, the Soviet Union accounted for more than 50 percent of Albania's foreign trade, while in the 1960s China accounted for approximately 70 percent. The Soviet Union saw in Albania's raw materials an important source for its own economic efforts, though much of these exports contributed little to Albania's economic development. In addition, while Soviet aid was important, it resulted in a very distorted development of Albania's industrial base. This, together with the political developments, precipitated the break between Albania and the Soviet Union. The developments of the 1950s—in essence, they continued throughout most of the 1960s—brought a slow transformation of Albania's essential agricultural base, but basic economic reforms, or even minor reforms, were put off until the late 1960s and the beginning of the 1970s.

THE ECONOMIC STRATEGY OF YUGOSLAVIA AND GREECE

While the basic developmental goals of Yugoslavia and Greece were not dissimilar, the accomplishment of structural changes and the institutional management and organization differed widely from the three socialist countries, Albania, Bulgaria, and Romania. The following brief discussion aims to point out the major differences

between the development strategy of Yugoslavia and Greece on the
one hand, and the three socialist countries of the area on the other,
without detailing developments or citing a mass of statistics, which
can be found in numerous publications in many languages.[23]

Yugoslavia

In spite of its expulsion from the Cominform, Yugoslavia followed
throughout most of the 1950s the same broad development strategy as
the other three socialist countries, though it differed in a number of
important institutional aspects.[24] Its agricultural policy condoned
private holdings after 1953; it relied on important Western and especially U.S. financial aid, as well as important military equipment; and
it introduced a system of workers' management, thus taking the first
step in decentralizing its huge centralized bureaucratic planning apparatus. The whole developmental strategy of Yugoslavia was greatly
influenced by the increasing development of an independent economic
system, tied neither to the economies of the Communist nor the
Western countries, though foreign trade with the Soviet bloc countries,
after having been completely discontinued between the late 1940s and
mid-1950s, slowly increased to approximately 38 percent of its foreign
trade turnover, while that with the Western countries, including the
United States, constituted over half of its total trade turnover by the
end of the 1950s. In comparison, in 1958 Bulgaria carried on 53 percent of its foreign trade turnover with the Soviet Union, 28 percent
with the other Eastern European countries, and 14.2 percent with the
West, whereas the figures for Romania were 51.5, 20, and 22.2 percent,
respectively.

Yugoslavia's 1947-51 plan, extended and finally discontinued in
1952, was its only centralized microplan; it was quite similar to those
of the other socialist countries. The main emphasis was on accelerating industrialization, specifically heavy industries, with large investments going into the development of power plants, mining, steel mills,
chemicals, and machinery and equipment production. The developments after 1952 were characterized by a slowly increasing degree
of decentralization in all aspects of economic and social development.
The Yugoslav doctrine emphasized decentralization and popular participation, using workers' management as the vehicle to counter the
excesses of the Stalinist-type bureaucratic planning and management
of the economy, but also to update the Marxist doctrine of "the withering away of the state." The new institutions launched what the
Yugoslavs call "socialist democracy" and what they believe constitutes
"a new and different type of socialism."[25] It also was hoped that by

closer involvement of the workers greater efficiency in production
could be achieved, contributing toward a lessening of the antagonisms
of the ethnically diverse society. Basically, this cautious development
continued until the drastic economic reform of 1965 greatly accelerated
the whole institutional framework of the country. This partial decentralization was achieved by the introduction of workers' management
in individual enterprises, by basic changes in the federal economic
plan (one of the main differences was that the state no longer issued
detailed output plans), and by the reorganization at all levels of the
administrative bureaucratic apparatus.

As the Yugoslav system evolved in the 1950s, administrative
instruments in planning were replaced with economic instruments,
the enterprises selling their products on a partially free market—
"market socialism," though with substantial government safeguards
remaining in the form of administrative instruments, e.g., foreign
trade, controls and currency regulations, tax policies, investments,
and prices. Yugoslavia used capital levies to which all enterprises
made contributions, while in Soviet-type planning a very inflexible turnover tax was the key planning instrument and a main source of investment funds.[26] Where Yugoslavia's development in the 1950s fundamentally differed from that of the other three socialist countries in
Southeast Europe was in regard to the institutional structure, specifically in her emphasis on the decentralization of state economic functions.

> The rigid, Soviet-type state plan was therefore replaced
> by a system in which the government became merely "the
> social regulator" of the nation's industry by direct controls
> drawn up by "the representative bodies of the country,"
> including workers' councils. Such a system maintains
> "the essence of socialism," prevents bureaucratic control
> and promotes production by "freeing the initiative of the
> producers to develop according to basic economic laws.[27]

The institutions that emerged during the 1950s reflected the
new theories introduced by the Yugoslav Communists, which set them
drastically apart from those modeled after the Soviet Union. According
to the Yugoslavs, these newly developed institutions launched "a new
and different type of socialism—socialist democracy." The institutional innovations are both governmental—a new constitutional law of
1953, modifying the 1946 Stalinist-type constitution—and even more
in the economic sphere. It is in the latter that the system has instituted the greatest innovations, especially in decentralized planning,
in the worker-management of enterprises, "and control of an economic

system that is relatively competitive and free (although not private) and socialist at the same time, and decollectivized, privately owned agriculture."[28] The period 1952-54 was a transitional one, with price and trade controls considerably relaxed. During the same period, local government received greatly increased autonomy, with an increasing role given to the citizen in public affairs, known as "social management." Most of the economic controls of the central plan were removed after 1954. Throughout the 1950s, the economy was broadly planned; the plan was not binding on the enterprises, only suggestive. It was decentralized in major parts of its decision-making processes, and economic enterprises were legally independent and, within limits, operated competitively.

The new powers of the workers' council had serious repercussions on the economy as a whole. Unaccustomed to these powers, workers' councils initiated huge wage raises that had to be covered by price hikes. The government was forced to reinstitute some price and wage controls, and enterprises were grouped into "chambers" for the purpose of better control of the actions through branch activities establishing broad policies and bringing "the self-interest of enterprises into line with national interests," including guaranteeing sufficient investment funds.[29]

On the whole, the relatively free and competitive market character of the Yugoslav economy during most of the 1950s oscillated; a greater amount of independence of the economy has been envisaged than turned out to be the actual case by the end of the 1950s. Important changes in the system of incentives and controls have reduced the freedom of action of individual enterprises in a number of spheres, though the reform of 1965 has restored these freedoms and even broadened them.[30] The Yugoslav economy was assisted throughout the 1950s by the International Monetary Fund (IMF) and a group of Western countries, in addition to considerable economic aid, mainly in foods and modern technology, from the United States.* This aid helped to free Yugoslav funds for important domestic projects and to adjust to a freer trading system and to protect the economy against inflationary pressures. In terms of foreign aid received from Western countries, Yugoslavia ranks close to Greece.[31] Yugoslavia also had been promised foreign aid from the Soviet Union, amounting to several

---

*Total U.S. assistance to Yugoslavia between 1950 and 1959 amounted to $1,157.6 million in economic aid and $724 million in military aid.

hundred million dollars. Several agreements were signed between 1953 and 1957 for nonmilitary aid amounting to $444 million. But actually, most was never made available because of Soviet-Yugoslav conflicts. Some writers actually feel that if the impact of the Soviet bloc's blockade against Yugoslavia is taken into account, the Soviet Union's aid may well have been negative.[32]

By 1960, Yugoslavia had achieved important economic gains. Industrial production grew at the remarkable average annual rate of 13.5 percent and produced a wide assortment of products, largely initiated since the war. Its industrial exports increased to three times the 1950 level. While the drive for industrialization obviously slowed down the production of consumer goods, a modest increase took place. The same can be said for an increase in real wages. Even agricultural production, in spite of serious interference by unfavorable weather conditions, reached a 1956-60 average output 35 percent above 1951-55. Certain developments of the late 1950s, such as price increases, too great a dependence on important raw materials and machinery, the huge repayment obligations of Western credits (over $900 million), too-rapid increases in investments (55 percent between 1959-61 alone) and personal income (37 percent during the same two-year period) brought about a 20 percent rise in the cost of living, as well as inflation close to 6 percent per annum and a high rate of unemployment. A rise of 32 percent in imports and only 19 percent in exports precipitated a huge trade deficit of $340 million that forced the government in 1961 to take measures to slow down the economy, especially its industrial growth.[33]

These developments culminated in a realization that something basic was called for to avoid the constant interference in the economic system, something that would seriously impair the development of market socialism. Also, trade with the Comecon countries, including the Soviet Union, had reached a level deemed dangerous to Yugoslavia's economic and political policies, including the modernization efforts for its industries with the help of Western technology. "The Resolution on the Basic Guidelines for Further Developments of the Economic System" in 1964 laid down the basis for important changes embodied in the important economic reform of 1965.[34]

Greece[35]

All domestic efforts and foreign aid to Greece focused on recovery rather than on development until about 1953. American aid and technical advice had a profound impact on economic recovery

(over 55 percent represented economic aid and loans), but an effort
to make really profound structural changes in the economy and to
"relieve some of the organizational weaknesses of the economy and
the society" was never really attempted.[36] Though economic, including
monetary, stability was successfully achieved in the 1950s, largely
with U.S. dollars and materials that assisted in expanding the economy
(this amounted to 10 percent of the GNP in some years), this dependence
on U.S. aid also had its disadvantages. First, it created a trade deficit
with the United States by financing imports above the needed standard
of living of the average Greek and thus contributed to an adverse
balance of payments. Perhaps even more serious were the large
imports that widened the traditionally existing trade gap, which made
it necessary after U.S. aid ceased in 1962 to find other sources of
foreign exchange in order to preserve the standard of living that had
been provided by U.S. economic protection.

Greece gave renewed attention to its long-term economic development once the immediate problem of recovery from the war, including
the civil war, had been accomplished, but a national development plan
was not initiated until the early 1960s, and even then it was expressed
in very general terms.[37] One of the main aims of this program was
the gradual elimination of disparities among the various regions of
the country, though "regional development was hardly considered in
the plan."[38] Throughout the postwar years, Greece had pursued a
policy of economic development based on market demand and supply
factors, with monetary policy as a major weapon of economic control.
It used government policy to provide assistance for economic growth,
especially industrial development, in most cases without controlling
it. Funds for a fairly large-size public investment program were
channeled through various semigovernment institutions, and government
plans until recently had little direct influence on economic development.
Generally, the private sector has met with little state interference,
and Greece's fiscal structure is based on providing incentives for
private and foreign investment. The only direct controls in use affect
agriculture, and the Agricultural Bank, organized in 1929, is the main
government vehicle.

In the 1950s, a number of steps were taken that in the long run
were to benefit the economy. Public works were initiated, a number
of new industries were established, and irrigation was extended; the
results of these measures were seen in the increase of the growth
rate of national income between 1950 and 1963 (the GNP in real terms
increased at an average rate of 6.3 percent, with agricultural and
industrial output more than doubling). But the real problem and
emphasis by all governments throughout the 1950s and continuing

right up to the present time has been that Greece's main export products were limited and often insufficiently competitive on the world
market (tobacco, raisins, and olive oil), and as a result exports were
insufficiently diversified and did not expand correspondingly to imports.
Income from the export of invisibles slowed down in the late 1950s
(and again between 1966 and 1968), but always played an important
role. Income from tourism and remittances from Greek workers in
foreign countries were on the increase since the late 1950s and played
a vital role in the economic progress of the country. Still, by the late
1950s they gave the economy a dangerous onesidedness. A study
published in 1961 came to the conclusion that "in spite of some improvements, the Greek economy displayed the same fundamental weaknesses
and symptoms as in the decade before World War II."[39]

THE CASE FOR ECONOMIC REFORM

The revolt in Hungary and near revolt in Poland in 1956 brought
home to all Eastern European countries, as well as to the Soviet Union,
an awareness of the need for greater flexibility and improvement in
their economic policies, including a greater attention to consumer
needs and the urgent need for more efficient planning and management
methods. For Bulgaria and Romania specifically, the need to placate
the peasantry took on special importance. The more-advanced and
sophisticated economies also had the greatest need for economic
reform, and this became especially apparent after the drastic slowdown
of economic growth in the German Democratic Republic in 1961 and
Czechoslovakia in 1962. Many reasons were advanced for this slowdown, but it was generally agreed that the real problem appeared "to
be largely symptoms of ailments which have affected all Communist
countries."[40] Institutional rigidity resulting in lack of flexibility in
adjusting to problems of economic performance affected both domestic
economic and foreign-trade conditions.

It is clear that economic reforms in the Southeast European
countries never could have been initiated without tacit agreement by
the Soviet Union. The destalinization program approved by Nikita
Khrushchev and the uprisings in Hungary and Poland in 1956 led to
a relaxation of police control and in institutions that enforced controls,
and this relaxation left its impact on certain Soviet institutions, e.g.,
drafting of labor, slowdown in collectivization in agriculture, though
of a temporary nature, the highly divergent wage system, and the
tightly controlled economic system of planning and management.
Poland after 1956, for example, decollectivized its agriculture, greatly
improved the position of its peasants, and instituted numerous measures implementing Polish reform. Montias argued that these

measures stopped short of basic changes. "The Polish planners will have to make up their mind at some point whether they wish to overhaul their economic institutions or whether they wish to keep the reins of power in Warsaw . . . Halfway measures toward efficient prices and decentralization are not necessarily an improvement over hidebound controls . . . "[41]

The Soviet Union somewhat reluctantly recognized "Yugoslavia's national road to Communism"; in 1959 it approved the lifting of previous trade on credit with Western countries and avoided countermeasures against Romania's opposition to Comecon's policies in 1961-62. A change in the Soviet Union's policies was also indicated by the 1962 publication of an article by the Soviet economist Liberman and others criticizing Soviet directive planning and management.[42] All these measures were an indirect go-ahead signal to the Eastern European countries to proceed with their own reforms. The retardation and stagnation of some of the economies gave a strong impetus to reform.

The economic reforms of the 1960s were initiated throughout Eastern Europe because of the deterioration of the economic performance of individual economies. In part, at least, this deterioration was the result of the economic level reached by the individual countries during the 1950s, demanding during the 1960s a more sophisticated approach in the planning and management of their economies. The domestic market was in need of greater flexibility in its decision-making processes as it underwent important changes "from the era of absolute scarcity and strictly controlled production and distribution into a stage of a limited buyers' market."[43] In part, this deterioration also was closely connected with the goal of each country to improve its economic competitiveness, especially in the Western markets. As Gregory Grossman pointed out, "the reform movement is thus in some measure a movement for at least a partial international re-orientation."[44] The latter was of special importance to Yugoslavia and Romania.[45]

The problem of economic slowdown was a less-serious one in the three underdeveloped socialist countries of Southeast Europe. This was in large part due to their less-sophisticated economies that carried their expansionist programs into the 1960s. Richard Burks, in a recent study, argues that "the need for economic reform in Romania and Bulgaria lay not wholly in the economic realm" but also in the political context.[46] H. G. Shaffer, on the other hand, feels that "there seems to be a somewhat better, though by no means perfect correlation between the timing of the introduction of reforms and the incident of economic slowdown."[47] Aside from Yugoslavia, Bulgaria was the first country in Southeast Europe to cite the need for economic reform, in December, 1962, after the devastating impact of its economic experimentation in the period 1959-61, the so-called great leap forward.

In Romania, the problem of economic reform did not really come to the surface until mid-1960 and was not formally initiated until 1967, a year after a noticeable decline in its economic growth.[48] Romania's over-all economic growth in the late 1950s and early 1960s, as described earlier, was impressive. Its policies of rapid industrialization and collectivization of the countryside, together with remarkable productivity gains, brought important economic gains from 1958 into the first part of the 1960s.[49] Because of these economic gains, the need for economic reform was not felt to be an urgent one, and Romania, together with Albania, was thus the last of the Eastern European socialist countries to continue its over-all economic development with instruments and policies originally adopted during the height of the postwar Stalinist-style growth policies. Albania did not initiate its first steps for a reform of its system of economic management until 1970. Yugoslavia, a special case, was also the trail-blazer in the movement for economic reform, which encompassed, during the 1960s, every aspect of the planning and management of the socialist countries.

Before discussing details of the reform movement of the 1960s, and specifically what it was to do and not to do, it is perhaps of importance to briefly summarize the major developments that led to these reforms. They have been well known to both Communist and Western economists and to a number of political leaders in the Soviet bloc countries. Much literature has been published on this topic, and the following discussions provide only the highlights.

In spite of the vigorous economic growth of the socialist countries, considerable imbalances and strains, which at times assumed an explosive character (the 1956 political upheavals and again the 1970 Polish upheaval), became obvious and often brought about stagnation in the production of individual products, which in turn affected the growth of the whole economy in various degrees. The Marxian emphasis in underdeveloped socialist countries on accelerated industrialization, with special emphasis on heavy industry and neglect of agriculture, creates repercussions on the whole socioeconomic structure, as well as on its worldwide trade relationships. With the Soviet-type economy prevailing in Albania, Bulgaria, and Romania throughout the 1950s, and for that matter during most of the 1960s, with its highly centralized, rigid, authoritarian, and generally primitive planning system, little leeway existed for changes in the decision-making process, including a transfer of certain decision-making powers to

lower echelons of the hierarchial structure. This rigid system with
its complicated administrative structure and constant political interference at various levels of the economy simply no longer met the
needs of the economy, once these countries reached a more-sophisti-
cated level of production and planning.

These negative phenomena in the economic growth of the socialist
countries, which Grossman divided into "static, dynamic and institutional phenomena"[50] came to the forefront after the mid-1950s, when
earlier high rates of growth declined and labor productivity in some
of the countries slowed down. They included, besides obvious imbalances in industrial production, stagnation and poor performance of
agriculture and the accumulation of unwanted goods, due either to their
poor quality or to changed market conditions that affected both domestic
and foreign sales. This was of special importance to Yugoslavia, where
a high percentage of its foreign trade was with the advanced Western
countries. Beginning in the early 1950s, this also affected Bulgaria
and Romania. Other causes included the wasteful use of resources
for production, insufficient attention given to the consumer and to
urgently needed improvements of the infrastructure of the less-developed regions of the Southeast European countries, the lack of understanding of demand and supply, and rising production costs, seriously
affecting the competitiveness even among the bloc countries. In addition, institutional causes also played an important role in the irregular
behavior of vital economic growth indices. Included in these are
overcentralization in decision-making processes, with cumbersome
lines of communication; a complicated administrative structure with
primitive methods of planning, including a rigid system of resource
allocations and investments; and the absence of initiative and a poor
system of incentives, the latter rewarding production increases at
any cost and thus penalizing innovations and production flexibility in
adjusting to consumer demands. Also, "dogmatic rooted impediments,
such as evidenced in pricing principles and in the opposition to virtually any private enterprise"[51] left its negative impact on the economy.

It is clear that these shortcomings of the system, expressed in
shortages of food and materials, a lagging technology, and unreliable
delivery schedules, of such importance in needed foreign trade, were
caused by the defects of the Soviet-type economic system described
earlier. As the economy grows and becomes increasingly sophisticated, these negative features have an increasingly important impact
on the economy.[52] The problems include the coordinating of an
increasing number of more and more sophisticated production units,
the proper allocating of skilled labor, satisfying the increasing
demands of the consumer, allocating vital imports with limited

available foreign currency, and the setting of priorities in the increased importance of foreign trade during the 1960s.

Another difficulty faced by all the socialist societies was the fact that centralized management of the economy did not prevent economic fluctuations, resulting in some years in a decline of the rates of total growth product. Sharp periodic fluctuations can be traced to fluctuations in investments, which in turn left their impact on rates of growth. Declines in growth rates of the net material product occurred in Bulgaria and Romania in 1954, 1956, in the early 1960s, and again in 1966. Spulber explained these strong cyclical fluctuations in all socialist countries by pointing out that the managers of the economies of these countries perceived

> only dimly the causes of the gyration of their economies and lacking adequate monetary and fiscal policies and instruments necessary for advanced industrial economies, the managers of the centralized planned economies of Eastern Europe were incapable of counteracting effectively the cyclical pushes. . . . Under these conditions the question of system redesigning (searching for new patterns of planning and management) gained momentum throughout Eastern Europe.[53]

It is clear that fluctuations in investments and investment priorities, both as to spatial distributions and branch of economic activity, left an important impact on the development processes of every country.

Nowhere was this more obvious than in the drastic transformation of agriculture, affecting the relationship between town and countryside and between industry and agriculture. Collectivization affected a large number of peasants and their families. It left its impact on employment, especially if mechanization and other modern technologies replaced the peasant. As long as industry was able to absorb the surplus population from the rural areas, the peasant could find work in the cities, and those remaining were able to put their energies into a more-intensive cultivation of their small plot of land, available for personal use. In spite of the importance of agriculture to the economies of the individual countries as a vital producer and consumer, as well as important foreign-currency earner, agriculture received little assistance and encouragement; in many cases it was seriously hurt by a discriminatory price policy, high taxation, and accelerated policy of forced collectivization of the remaining small, independent private holdings. The results of such a policy generally brought stagnation to agriculture, or even decline in the production of vital

food needs. The export surpluses declined or were completely eliminated. In Bulgaria and Romania, for example, changing growth roles
in the food industry have reflected year to year changes in aggregate
agricultural output. As a result of the structural changes, and this
largely holds true for the 1950s only, greatly increased industrial
output vs. declining agricultural production, changes in demands,
increased urbanization, changed food habits of the population, and so
on, considerable quantities of cereals had to be imported. For example,
an export surplus of cereals of approximately 3 million tons between
1934 and 1938 for Yugoslavia, Romania, and Bulgaria was turned into
a net import between 1955 and 1958 of close to 1.5 million tons.

The developments in the socialist countries throughout the 1950s
and most of the 1960s offer a classical case of misguided economic
development, with one-sided attention given to industrial development
and little if any attention given to agricultural developments. Benjamin
Higgins, in a recent study, discusses the interaction of industrial and
agricultural sectors and comes to the conclusion that "industrialization
and agricultural improvements are not alternative roads to economic
development, but are completely complementary."[54] The so-called
big push doctrine—efforts to push both industrial and agricultural
developments—was neglected by all the socialist countries, including
Yugoslavia, in part based on the previously mentioned "dogmatically
rooted impediments" so obvious in all Marxian societies.

It is then evident that pressures for economic reform, encouraged
by the economic managers of these socialist countries, in the first
place were derived from deficiencies and defects of the system as it
moved toward greater sophistication of their economies. The impact
of these defects, as R. V. Burks brought out in a recent study, became
especially obvious in their relations to "the exigencies of foreign
trade . . . if the ambitious development schemes of the planners in
Sofia and Bucharest are to be realized."[55] Pressures favoring
decentralization of the economic decision-making processes were
strongest in Yugoslavia, where reform of its Soviet-type economy
began in the early 1950s. Inasmuch as every economic reform also
has its political overtones, the ethnically diverse and often antagonistic
society of Yugoslavia also became the greatest and earliest proponent
for alternatives to the rigid Soviet-type political system. Closely
connected with these pressures was the need to earn Western currencies in order to enable these countries to obtain capital goods of the
most modern technologies which were only available from the advanced
capitalistic countries. This forced domestic producers to expose
themselves to foreign competition in technological quality. In turn,
this necessitated adaptability to change, a decentralization of

decision-making, and, most of all, a more rational pricing structure.
Montias pointed out that

> the lure of Western markets for primary commodities
> and the attractive prospects of obtaining "technologically
> progressive" capital goods from advanced capitalist coun-
> tries also presents a serious challenge to the cohesion of
> the bloc. These magnets tempt members to cater to their
> national advantage at the expense of proletarian inter-
> nationalism. The European Economic Community's
> pulling power is a case in point.[56]

Perhaps it is of importance to point out here that one of the
causes for seeking Western markets by the socialist countries of
Southeast Europe in early 1960 (with the exception of Albania) was
increased competition within the bloc markets, which was brought
about by the great duplication of productive facilities of the socialist
countries following basically the same development strategy. Yugoslavia, as explained earlier, for entirely different reasons was forced
to seek Western markets in the early 1950s. As production reached
greater sophistication in Bulgaria and Romania and they emerged
from scarcity into a limited buyer's market, it became obvious that
foreign markets in advanced countries, apart from those in underdeveloped countries, were essential for the successful pursuit of
economic goals. The need to earn foreign exchange by making their
manufacturing competitive on the Western markets, from the early
1960s on, became a major objective of their economic policy, and
this in turn necessitated a complete rethinking of many important
facets of Communist dogma and contributed greatly to the movements
toward economic reform that were the major characteristics of the
development strategy of the socialist countries of Southeast Europe
throughout the 1960s. The need to earn foreign exchange on the
Western markets, especially for Romania during its drive for greater
economic and political independence from the Soviet bloc, which was
most important throughout the 1960s, also had important political
implications. This need was of lesser importance to Bulgaria, with
its very close economic and political relations with the Soviet Union.

THE DEVELOPMENT STRATEGY OF THE 1960's

The development strategy of the 1960s was dominated by the
economic reform movement of the centrally planned economies. This
was first initiated, as was seen from earlier discussions, in Yugoslavia
in the early 1950s and continued with accelerated speed after the

reform of 1965. In a broad outline, it was presented by the Bulgarian leaders to its Eighth Party Congress in 1962 and published in some detail in 1963, but it was never fully implemented and was generally abandoned at the 1968 plenum. It was cautiously initiated by the Romanian leadership in 1967, with emphasis on the reorganization of its economic management system without basically disturbing the centralized decision-making of key economic policies. Albania was the last socialist country of the area to join the reform movement. Discussions have been going on since 1966,[57] but only after the Tenth Plenum (1970) was a campaign against "excessive centralism and bureaucratic management" instituted.[58]

The causes for this reform movement, which spread to all socialist countries including the Soviet Union, were discussed earlier in this chapter. Perhaps it is appropriate, therefore, not only to summarize what this reform is all about and its basic general and specific aims in individual countries, but also what it is not intended to do and finally to stress the major constraints as shown by the developments of this decade. In the process of these discussions, the major characteristics of the development strategy of the 1960s in the countries of Southeast Europe will emerge. The developments in Greece are presented in Chapter 8, which discusses regional development policies, inasmuch as the main emphasis of its development strategy in the 1960s was a continuation of its 1950 strategy, with some added attention to the regional aspects of its economic development.

Throughout the 1960s, and especially between 1965 and the Czechoslovakian crisis in 1968, all the countries of Eastern Europe frantically searched for new or improved ways to update their outmoded planning and management systems. While the economies of the Southeast European countries never went through the sharp deterioration and fall in performance as witnessed in some of the more-advanced socialist countries, such as East Germany, Czechoslovakia, and Hungary, their blueprints—with the exception of Yugoslavia—envisaged reforms of a more moderate and cautious character, with Party control maintained over key elements of economic decision-making.

The reforms of the 1960s assumed a variety of forms, but basic to all was the need for decentralization—the transfer of economic decision-making power—and for the delegation of important micro-decisions to lower echelons the enterprise or some enterprise association. The basic hypothesis of earlier years—that planning of every economic activity had to be carried out at the top only—was quietly dropped by the socialist countries of Eastern Europe, and a partial revision of the decision-making structure at least on the microlevel, as well as a reorganization of the incentive structure, became the guiding principles of all reforms of the 1960s. It must be understood that even these limited revisions did not come easy, and they suffered a number of setbacks (e.g., the developments in Bulgaria and Romania after the Czech crisis). On the other hand, decisions on the macrolevel, e.g., proportion of investments for various broad economic activities and aggregate consumption vs. aggregate investment, as expressed in the national plans, were left basically unchanged. More and more of the planning of consumer-oriented products was left to lower-level organizations of enterprises. Only in Yugoslavia did the national plan provide merely long-term goals for the economy at the marcolevel, with economic instruments (largely fiscal and monetary policies) used to influence developments on the microlevel.[59]

Basically, then, the major aim of the economic reform movements of the 1960s in Bulgaria, Romania, and lately in Albania was to improve the existing system of planning and management and <u>not</u> to replace it. Yugoslavia, ever since the introduction of workers' management and the reforms of the 1950s, has moved toward a new system, with the reform of 1965 initiating an ultimate complete withdrawal of all centralized (federal) economic decision-making functions and a great increase in the decision-making powers of the individual enterprises. Enterprises were permitted to retain a much-increased proportion of their net profits (71 percent as against 51 before the 1965 reform), and at the same time the share of enterprises and banks in total investment resources greatly increased, as can be seen in Table 2. This transfer of available investment sources to the local level and the autonomy of the producing enterprises has greatly reduced the role of the central planners. While the various reforms show certain basic similarities in all socialist countries— again, Yugoslavia is excepted—each country proceeded at its own speed, in large part dictated by local conditions and developments, such as its approach to underdeveloped areas and to the socialist division of labor. The reforms were closely related to foreign-trade policies with Western markets and dependence on the Soviet Union. Therefore, the scope as well as the speed of the reforms in Albania, Bulgaria, and Romania differ from those of the other socialist countries in certain basic details. Major differences were in the amount of decentralization, the freedom of distribution of investment funds available to the enterprises or associations, the number and type of the centrally fixed indicators transferred to the microlevel, and price and wage policies, though all countries proceeded in the latter with utmost care.

Inasmuch as the causes for the reform movements of the 1960s are much the same in all Soviet-type economies, the remedial

TABLE 2

Sources of Investment in Yugoslavia
(in percent)

Source	1960	1964	1966	1969
Business firms	31	26	39	34[a]
Banks (including investment in housing)	1	31	39	49
Government	63	37	15	16
Federal	37	7	-	9
Republic	7	8	-	3
Local	18	21	-	4
Other	5	6	7	1

[a]Data includes obligatory depreciation expenditures and contributions of "others" to gross investment.

Sources: Statistički Bilten SDK, 1961-69; and Statistički Godisnjak Jugoslavije, 1970.

measures proposed can be generalized within a broad framework. The research staff of the Economic Commission of Europe of the United Nations prepared a list of the types of action taken or proposed.[60] Harry G. Shaffer, in his study "Eastern Europe: Varieties of Economic Management," lists the major ingredients of the reform and indicates the gradient of acceptance by the East European socialist countries.[61] Grossman lists five main characteristics of various reform movements;[62] Burks stresses political factors in the reform movements and discusses four alternatives.[63] Using a modified form of these basic aspects of the reform as published and considering changes in the four countries of Southeast Europe since their publication, the present status of the acceptance of reform is noted in Table 3, though it must be realized that the major aspects of the reform constitute an integral part of its success. One thing is clear from Table 3. Yugoslavia is by far the leader in the economic-reform movement of the socialist countries of Southeast Europe. Romania's cautious attitude toward reform, mentioned earlier, becomes obvious from the acceptance of the various reforms: Bulgaria's planning and management apparatus has hardly changed during the last ten years; and Albania is just at the beginning of its reform movement.

TABLE 3

Status of Reform in Southeast Europe

Entry	Acceptance In			
	Albania	Bulgaria	Romania	Yugoslavia
Basic Reform				
Complete market reform and integration with free world markets				x
Integration of national economy with that of the Soviet Union by means of joint central planning on a bilateral basis		x		
Modified retention of a central planning system, together with pursuit of independence policy, hopefully with assistance of outside Western markets			x[a]	
Cautious domestic reforms, retention of all or some Comecon ties		x	x	
Cautious domestic reforms and some decentralization in the decision-making processes of the central planning apparatus; cautious establishment of Western trading ties	x			
Role of Central-Planning Authorities				
Role of central plan basically unchanged	x	x	x	
Central plan functions basically changed to long-term goals of the economy at the macrolevel; largely coordinating functions				x
Generally improve central planning techniques	x		x	
Change and reduction in centrally planned targets that are now mandatory for enterprises			x	
Delegation of Decision-Making Power				
General decentralization of administration apparatus responsible for the management of economy				x

	Acceptance In			
Entry	Albania	Bulgaria	Romania	Yugoslavia
Delegation of important decision-making powers in the economic field to enterprises (shift to microlevel)				x
Delegation of important decision-making powers in the economic field to intermediary bodies (associations), with only minor shifts to the enterprises			x	
Minor adjustments of administrative apparatus for the management of economy	x	x[b]		
Expansion of all investment funds available to enterprises and/or larger economic units (associations), with banks playing a major role				x
Increasing use of industrial investment funds by enterprises and/or larger economic units (associations and local political bodies) instead of central planning authorities (increased use of bank credits)			x	x
Concentration of industrial, as well as trading, enterprises into larger units with microeconomic responsibilities guided primarily by economic accountability (maximation of profits)			x	
Major changes in decentralization, extended to political reform				x
Role of Market in the Allocation of Resources				
Enterprises and/or associations have direct contractual relations with supplier and purchaser and thus greater flexibility based on market-consumer demands			x	x
Investment decisions based on enterprise and/or association initiative and on economic considerations (profitability length of repayment period), with bank loans available				x

(continued)

TABLE 3 (Continued)

Entry	Acceptance In			
	Albania	Bulgaria	Romania	Yugoslavia
Investment decisions basically unchanged	x	x		
Certain investment decision-initiative transferred to enterprise and/or association, but central planners' responsibilities basically unchanged -			x	
Economic Incentives				
Increased emphasis on remuneration of wage earners (workers and managers) depending on enterprises performance*c		x	x	x
Paid out of the enterprise earnings			x	x
Paid out of budgetary appropriations		x	x	
No changes from present system of established wage and salary scales, but enterprise profitability (or rate of production) increasingly important criteria		x	x	
Enterprises to retain a part of net earnings for a variety of responsibilities (e.g., investments, social welfare, profit-sharing)			x	
Price reforms, including changes in determination of prices and structure, to be more reflective of relative scarcity, or at least (average) costs, including greater flexibility of price changes (influence of market forces)			x	x

a Started out in 1967, but regressed in 1969.
b Until 1968 in Bulgaria.
c The real problem here is to what extent profits or gross income can be meaningfully used to establish enterprise performance.

In the long run, the crux of the reforms and the real issue has been the scope and speed with which this gradual transfer of the decision-making powers from the rigid bureaucratic central management apparatus to the new managerial class of the microlevel could be accomplished. The question was whether ultimately some form of market mechanism (market socialism) could be established. That this has succeeded thus far only in Yugoslavia is perhaps largely due to the willingness of its leaders to weaken the central administrative bureaucracy (and thus the Party oligarchy) in the interest of economic necessity and the greater political unity of its various ethnically diverse people.

The Yugoslav economic reform, therefore, at an early stage had two basic objectives (planned or not). It became both an economic and political necessity and in this process anticipated a "revision in the conception of society." According to Grossman's analysis, "this revision [of the conception of society] is perhaps the most fundamental ingredient in the philosophy of economic revisionism in present day Eastern Europe."[64] And while the ideological and doctrinal barriers are the most formidable obstacles to the appearance or progress of economic reform in Eastern Europe (including the USSR), the power-political and political-economic considerations may well be more decisive, although such considerations rarely make public appearance (on either side of an issue) without the benefit of proper ideological and theoretical garb."[65] Burks, in his recent analysis, is even more specific in his conclusion that "economic reform, then, is a political necessity" and "inevitably tends to spill over in political reform."[66] If this conclusion is correct, and there is no reason to doubt it, basic economic reforms in Communist countries have a momentum of their own and produce numerous political tendencies. Based on the Yugoslav and Czech examples, the cautious attitudes of the Bulgarian and Romanian leadership are clearly explained, as well as those of other socialist countries excluded from this study. This points up the seriousness with which the Bulgarian and to a lesser extent the Romanian leadership viewed developments in Czechoslovakia in 1968, in view of the Soviet Union's reactions and statements.

WHAT THE REFORM WAS NOT TO DO

Thus far in the discussion, what the reforms were to accomplish has been analyzed, and in this process their limitations and the types of constraints affecting the reform movement from their earliest inception have been indicated. In this section, it will be shown what the reform did not intend to accomplish. All the reforms (except

Yugoslavia) had certain limited objectives—decreasing the number of economic controls governing enterprises, creating a series of incentives for the system, but still maintaining strict over-all control, through modification—but <u>not</u> abrogation of the central plan. Furthermore, it must be made clear that an unrestricted market was never initially contemplated by any of the socialist countries, including Yugoslavia. The compilations in Table 3 indicated the trend. The following, therefore, is specific as to what the reform was <u>not</u> to do (except for Yugoslavia).

1. The reform was not to overturn the political monopoly of the Party, the basic socialist system, the trend toward rapid industrialization, and the basic organizational form of agriculture, even the future goal of "socialization of the countryside."

2. The reform did not affect the basic principles of central planning. This included comprehensive national planning with central decision-making of long-term fundamental aspects of the national economy, including its proportions and its speed.

3. Decentralization of economic decision-making does not mean abrogation of power. In effect, key decision-making powers remained with the central plan, though decision on the microlevel were to be transferred to associations and/or enterprises.

4. No significant amount of market mechanism has been introduced and only very cautious first steps were undertaken in shifting decisions concerning the use of certain resources to the enterprise level. The physical allocation of producer goods has not been changed, though in Romania, for example, enterprises and/or associations or local political bodies now have some additional decision-making powers in this area.

5. There has been no abrogation of price controls, and, while the principle of profits has been widely introduced as part of good management to be used as an incentive, with a certain amount to be retained by the enterprise, profitability has not become a guiding principle for the over-all economic development. Price revisions have been made only to achieve a satisfactory profit margin, and some profit has been permitted to remain with the enterprise as an incentive payment for its employees, as well as small internal investments (only in Hungary at the present time has price setting been partially freed from the central control).

It is clear, then, that the reforms of the 1960s—in Bulgaria, later in Romania, and most recently in Albania—simply aimed at a reorganization of the administrative apparatus—what the Albanians call, in their theoretical-ideological jargon, not unlike the Yugoslavs nearly twenty years earlier, "excessive centralism and bureaucratic management." This does not mean that some basic changes in all these countries cannot be expected in the future. Certainly, "economic liberalization is pregnant with political risk," as was shown so clearly in Czechoslovakia in 1968.[67]

THE DEVELOPMENT STRATEGY IN THE SOCIALIST COUNTRIES OF SOUTHEAST EUROPE

Having presented the reform movement in its broad outline, both what it was to accomplish and what it was not, it now is the objective in this section to be specific as to the developmental strategy in the individual socialist countries as well as to critically assess its impact, both immediate and long-term.

Yugoslavia

Of the socialist countries of Southeast Europe, only Yugoslavia has continued further on its road to decentralization. The specific goals of the Yugoslav reform movements of 1952, 1956, and 1962 were indicated earlier. They remain basically unchanged—introducting a market mechanism, with the "socially-owned" producing enterprises administered by their own workers' councils, now virtually autonomous. The search for institutions to carry out the marco-objectives of the state by micro-units continues and was one of the objectives of the 1965 reform. Because of the half-hearted measures of the 1962 reform, political interference by antireform forces, and the impact of decentralization, the continuous search for a proper framework for free-market socialism led to the 1965 reform.

The specific objectives of the 1965 reform can be expressed in five major changes:[68]

1. The economy was modernized by eliminating uneconomic investments and production, thus responding
   to forces of supply and demand, which meant a further
   expansion of the market mechanism
2. Economic efficiency was imposed in order to compete
   in the international market, which is of increasing
   importance to the Yugoslav economy due to surplus
   domestic capacities in a number of industries resulting
   in increased unemployment

3. Increased individual initiative was demanded, leading
   to greater flexibility in the production processes and
   technological innovations
4. By abolishing the General Investment Fund at the
   macrolevel and transferring investment objectives
   to the banking system, which was permitted to establish branches, thus allowing "depositors and borrowers
   to choose a bank in accordance with their judgment of
   the economic advantages present," Pejovich concludes
   that "the nature of the dependence of firms [enterprises]
   for outside funds should be expected to become increasingly more economic and less political"[69]
5. Finally, a far-reaching price reform was planned,
   with its major objective to abolish existing guidelines
   for the allocation of profit, thus giving the enterprises
   complete control.

Though anti-inflationary measures had to be reinstated shortly
after the promulgation of the 1965 reform by administrative controls
over most goods and services, some of which have been liberalized
since that time, fiscal and monetary controls are the ultimate objective,
thus ending direct government control.[70]

The economic reform, with its temporary controls on consumer
spending, produced a rapid decline in industrial production and a
serious increase in unemployment between 1965 and mid-1969, only
in part made up by those taking up work in Western Europe. The total
number of Yugoslav foreign workers at the end of 1971 amounted to
over 800,000 of which two thirds were employed in the Federal Republic
of Germany.[71] Numerous enterprises failed to adjust to the efficiency
drive and to the increased pressures of market forces and were also
seriously affected by the deflationary policies. Over 240 craft and
industrial firms were eliminated during the 1965-67 period, and many
more were in serious economic condition, including the so-called
political factories* established during the 1950s. Because of widespread criticism,[72] the government was forced to take a series of
administrative measures, such as relaxing credit terms, tariff raises,
freezing of certain wages, increased investments, especially in the

---

*"Political factories" in Yugoslavia are enterprises constructed
for political rather than economic reasons. They were subsidized for
their production losses, but this was ended by a law of July 25, 1965,
recognizing the need for a gradual normalization in its economy.

more-efficient enterprises, all of which left its impact, so much so
that by the middle of 1968 economic growth again started on its upward
movement. Inflationary pressure continued, however forcing the
government to intervene repeatedly in the economy.

A matter of real concern was the increased trade deficit, especially with hard-currency countries ($547 million in 1969 as against
$299 million in 1966). The balance-of-payments deficit, in spite of
increased tourist earnings (estimated at $360 million in 1970), was
highly unsatisfactory; it amounted to $375 million in 1970.[73] It is
obviously not the purpose of this broad review of the development
strategy of the 1960s to provide a mass of detailed statistical data;
only the broad developments during the decade can be summarized.
Those of the 1960s are obviously strongly influenced by the two
reforms—that of 1962, generally considered unsuccessful, and that of
1965, thus far mildly successful in providing an increased growth of
the economy, including an increased standard of living for the people
in spite of strong inflationary trends. (Data for all of Southeast Europe
are in Appendix Table A.1. A regional summary of Yugoslavia is in
Appendix Table A.2.) Improvements in the efficiency of production,
making competition on foreign markets easier, thus far has been only
moderately successful. The impact of the 1965 reform, after all, is
a long-term development and is greatly hindered by the small economies of scale that the Yugoslav domestic market provides. The reform
has been successful in providing a freer market (in spite of a retreat
in import liberalization and the full use of fiscal and monetary policies
and reducing political influence in economic decisions, although the
country's cumbersome political machinery is often slow moving, with
its proportional representation at all levels of economic and political
life from its ethnicly diverse population at varied levels of economic
advancement.

A law permitting direct foreign investments was passed in 1967
after much controversy,* but its immediate impact was small—$72
million in foreign investments were made by the end of 1971, as
compared with investments in Yugoslavia by the International Bank
for Reconstruction and Development (IBRD) of $415 million during the

---

*Yugoslav leaders were accused in parliament of "abandoning
the principle of class war, scrapping socialism, and hobnobbing with
capitalist companies." The advanced republics of Slovenia and Croatia
were especially interested in the passage of the law, hoping for sizable
foreign investments that would bring advanced technology to the country.

1960s ($98.5 million alone in 1970).[74] Yugoslavia had placed a number of serious restrictions on foreign investments, such as limitations on the amount of equity capital to be placed in any one joint venture (only 49 percent), taxation of profits at 35 percent, reinvestment of the first 20 percent of the net income in the country, with the transfer of profits outside generally depending on "the value of exports to hard-currency areas that the venture has generated." The total that may be withdrawn in any one year was limited to one third of the value of the exports. All these restrictions have limited foreign initiatives. After prolonged discussions in the Federal Assembly (the legislative body of the country) the existing legislation was amended in July, 1971, to make it more attractive to foreign investments. Also in 1970, a group of Yugoslav and Western banks and the IBRD organized the Internal Corporation for Investments in Yugoslavia (ICIY) to assist Western companies to invest in those Yugoslav enterprises where ownership was possible. The hope was expressed that close to $200 million additional capital could be placed at the disposal of Yugoslav enterprises.

Though steps have been taken to implement and liberalize the various reform measures, serious maladjustments remain and their solution is on the agenda for the 1970s. They include the great regional imbalances, the unsolved problem of the distribution of resources, the behavior of the enterprises where workers' management has often been more conscientious about increasing wages than in considering the needs of national economic priorities,[75] the nationalistic self-interest operating against capital mobility, and the future position and influence of banks, to mention only a few.*

Relatively little foreign investment entered the country thus far, and those republics now accuse the government of providing insufficient incentives, but internal developments balancing the various forces made the government steer a careful middle course, hoping to avoid criticism from the left. The government defends its policies as "being designed only to take account of the 'reality of economic forces.'" (Anthony Sylvester, "Yugoslavia's Consumers Call the Shots," East Europe, XX [January, 1971], 24.)

*The very basic question of the future role of the central government and parliament is by no means resolved. The long-term impact of the upheavals in Croatia and Kosovo in 1971 have left a shadow of uncertainties over many political as well as economic developments. One thing is again certain in early 1972, the forces operating against further decentralization and increasing the power of individual republics are still very powerful and the developments in Croatia in the

The impact of the numerous reforms experienced in Yugoslavia over the last twenty years has established a decentralized economic system allowing for individual initiative. Past experience has shown that in moving ahead in search for a satisfactory plan-market balance of its economic system, the future will bring further experimentations to improve the economy, both retreats and gains. The changes thus far have produced a uniquely Yugoslav system, rejecting the Soviet-type command economy as well as orthodox capitalism. It is the pattern of behavior of its new institutional framework, both enterprises and men in this unique Yugoslav experiment, that other socialist as well as nonsocialist countries are watching. It is impossible at the present time to forecast the extent, scope, and impact of the changes in planning and the market mechanism.

Bulgaria*

The development strategy of Bulgaria in the 1960s was generally a continuation of the 1950 policies, somewhat taken aback by the failure of the previously mentioned great leap forward. Ever since the leadership first mentioned its intention to undertake an economic reform in November, 1962, the topic has been uppermost in the minds of its economic and Party leaders.[76] The remarkable thing about the Bulgarian economic reform is that, while it was given much publicity, while its intentions were published in some detail (for example, the so-called Theses in December, 1965), and while certain features of the reform were actually experimented with, no complete document was ever published and implemented. The first time Party leaders spoke about an economic reform was in the disastrous aftermath of the great leap forward in 1962, when some details were discussed at the Central Committee plenum in May, 1963. Various information on the type of reform contemplated was published during 1964 and 1965, indicating ongoing experiments in the field of production committees elected by a general meeting of workers, for example, and other reform experiments.

The details for the broadly based economic reform expected to commence in 1965 never materialized. Instead, the Theses were published in December, 1965, containing some general and rather

---

fall of 1971 have given renewed ammunition to those opposing a further weakening of the remaining central power.

*See Appendix Tables A.1 and A.5 for a regional statistical summary.

advanced ideas on planning, price categories, the introduction of production committees, profitability, allocation of materials, and so on.[77]
These documents, which expressed some very advanced reform ideas,
were based on many centralistic assumptions, however. Lubomir
Dellin felt that "in its entirety it was considerably less advanced than
it appeared to be from reading some isolated verbal references and
their Western interpretation (especially the 'planning from below')."[78]
At the Central Committee meetings of April, 1966, the basic principles
of "The New Economic System of Planning and Management of the
National Economy" were approved, but many of its detailed reforms
were never implemented (price reforms were postponed). Dellin
comes to the conclusion that "the 1968 reversal toward centralization
tends to support those who questioned the extent and even the need of
economic reform in Bulgaria."[79]

The performance of the Bulgarian economy during the first part
of the 1960s was not unlike that of other Soviet-type economies, producing imbalances due to the high rate of industrialization and continuing a rapid reduction of those employed in agriculture. The basic
economic changes initiated during the period of the great leap forward
and again in the mid-1960s, which brought increased reliance on
imports from Western markets, forced Bulgaria to meet exports
under most difficult conditions. In part, the reform of April, 1966,
not unlike that of Romania in 1967 and even similar to that of Yugoslavia in its aim, though completely different in scope and approach,
was precipitated by the priorities brought about by increasing Western
trade, which it hoped would contribute to the availability of modern
machinery and other technological innovations. Bulgaria's trade with
the Western countries increased rapidly—a 19.8-percent average
annual growth rate during 1961-68 was achieved, as against a 12.8-
percent annual growth rate in its total foreign trade.[80] Imports,
however, were far greater than exports, and, in addition, Bulgaria's
exports consisted largely of agricultural products with a much lower
profitability than machinery; 18.2 percent of Bulgaria's total trade
was with the West. While tourism increased from 200,000 tourists
in 1961 to 2.5 million in 1969,* foreign exchange earnings in 1969
were estimated at $50 million or 3.6 percent of the total export
earnings.[81] The outstanding debt to the West in 1969 amounted to
$400 million, having a very depressing impact on the economic develop-
ment of the country.

---

*Of these, 180,000 came from the Federal Republic of Germany.

Many of the reforms planned in 1966 were never carried through, and the promised implementation of individual items never materialized. Dellin discusses and compares the promises under the Theses and the actual steps taken prior to 1968 and concludes that the economic reforms up to 1968 were a mass of suggested remedies, some of value, some questionable, and some contradictory, all aimed at some remolding and some basic changes of the existing system. It was his opinion that, in spite of obscurity and slow and piecemeal implementation, basically there was progress, though the promise of full implementation never came.[82] Among the most promising changes hoped for in the 1966 reform were proposed planning reforms—improving planning from below and reduction of obligatory indices—but it soon developed that neither existing institutions nor the role of the central plan was ever seriously in danger of change, nor was decentralization considered in any serious way. Instead, the stated goals were "to combine centralism with increased independence of the enterprise, and thus allowing for greater flexibility of the system."[83] The major change was the establishment of economic associations (trusts), a move generally interpreted as decentralization. In actual fact, it was little more than a reshuffling of management decision-making. The associations were authorized to act as their own agents in the field of foreign trade, but much of the obscurity made actual implementation nearly impossible. It was clear that internal disagreements among the leadership made the reform unworkable.

The July plenum of 1968, called unexpectedly during the height of the Czech crisis, followed by the November "Decree on the Gradual Application and Further Development of the New System of Management of the Economy," was officially called to perfect the 1966 reform and the earlier enunciated "Theses," but it is generally considered as having modified numerous key items that were considered essential for any real reform of the Bulgarian planning and management system, thus bringing a recentralization to the system.[84] The July plenum dropped every pretense of "planning from below," and "the need for increased planning as society develops" was then emphasized.[85] As a result of the July plenum, a series of new central controls over the economy were enacted, such as the Economic Coordination Committee, together with the organization of the newly created Ministry of Supplies and State Reserves, responsible for the central allocation of raw materials and supplies. During 1969, a number of other coordinating bodies were organized, such as the Central State Finance Control, a General Directorate of Quality, and State Inspectorates of Labor for every okrug (province), all with the objective to restrict further possible autonomous moves by enterprises.[86] Later, the power of the earlier established trusts was restricted and their number reduced, with their

main function outlined as serving as middle men between ministries
and enterprises. Raising labor productivity and introducing advanced
technology became their new responsibility. The decisions of the July,
1968, plenum were further elaborated in February, 1969. Any autonomy
remaining with the enterprises was abolished, and their position was
again typical of those in other Soviet-type centrally controlled economies. A minor change remained; the wage fund was made dependent
on profitability, labor productivity, the quality of the product, and the
conditions of the equipment. The position of the enterprise plans as
"draft plans" was abolished. The earlier established enterprise
production committee generally was downgraded.

Dellin summarized the developments of the 1960s, which were
characterized by two economic reforms—the reform blueprint as outlined in the Theses of 1965, few of which were ever implemented, and
the so-called reform of 1968, which in reality was a modification of
earlier reforms and really meant a step backward from the Theses of
1965.[87] The basic goals of the Bulgarian economy by early 1969 were
typical of the Soviet-type economies, including production priorities
and the primacy of the Party in all matters, including economics.
Confusion and ambiguity over actual implementation marked many
developments.

In addition to economic measures instituted, the July, 1968,
plenum also called for closer integration between the Soviet and
Bulgarian economies.[88] The impact of this decision was not immediately apparent. A series of far-reaching agreements were concluded
with the Soviet Union that in effect tied the Bulgarian economy even
more closely to Soviet needs (see also the discussion in Chapter 9).
Some argue that, in effect, Bulgarian production had become part of
the Soviet economic plans. By these agreements with the Soviet Union,
exports to Bulgaria, especially of vital raw materials such as crude
oil (2.7 million tons in 1967 and a projected 10 million tons in 1975),
were greatly increased. To support production and increased iron
and steel production, the Soviet Union agreed to increased steel shipments to the Metallurgical Combine Kremikovtsi. Joint developments
were agreed to for the timber production in Komi, Autonomous Soviet
Socialist Republic (ASSR) and for a cellulose combine in Archangelsk,
with Bulgaria supplying the needed labor for these and other projects;*
in return Bulgaria would receive products such as timber and cellulose.

_____

*It is estimated that over 12,000 Bulgarian workers are now in
the Soviet Union.

Bulgaria was to participate in the production of a variety of machinery parts for the Soviet Union and was to receive an atomic power station.[89] By June, 1970, Bulgaria and the Soviet Union had agreed to organize permanent working committees on specialization and cooperation in various industrial branches. Considerable credit for new Bulgarian industrial projects was made available by the Soviet Union, and, as a result of this close coordination of Bulgaria's production needs with that of the Soviet Union, a large proportion of its raw-material needs were supplied by the Soviet Union, e.g., 100 percent of its coal needs, 99 percent of its petroleum, and 87 percent of its iron ore. Bulgarian industrial production now is closely integrated with that of the Soviet Union. Vital Bulgarian production was financed by the Soviet Union, e.g., shipbuilding, with 100 percent of Soviet credits, and chemical and electrotechnical industries, with 50 to 75 percent. Altogether, 130 Bulgarian industries received substantial Soviet credits.[90] A near merger in vital industrial production obviously now exists. The two countries increased their trade, with Bulgaria's total trade with the Soviets to reach over 60 percent in the 1971-75 five-year plan.

Obviously, the July, 1968, plenum was the watershed for the Bulgarian Communist regime. It reversed the trend toward economic reform inaugurated in 1962, when it expanded trade with Western markets, and began a close division of labor with the Soviet Union, resulting in a near integration of the two 1971-75 five-year plans. Bulgaria's trade with the Comecon countries was to increase during the new five-year plan from 77.8 percent in 1970 to 83.7 percent in 1975, with the previously mentioned percentage to the Soviet Union of over 60 percent. With this assistance from the Soviet Union, Bulgaria's leaders felt safe in reverting in their economic policies to more orthodox-left procedures. A reorganization of the countryside in the tradition of Mao's communes and Khrushchev's agrograd was initiated,[91] though this reorganization obviously raised considerable internal opposition. Various other measures were taken, amounting to a general recentralization in the economy. This recentralization affected the earlier organized associations. The number of these associations was further reduced, from 120 to 65, of which only about 35 are predominantly industrial, but even they were to be abolished during 1971 and replaced with new ones covering a larger sector and an additional number of enterprises. In the process of this reorganization, the enterprises will be considered as branches or subdivisions of the newly organized associations.

The recently approved national economic plan for 1971-75, the Draft Directives for the new Sixth Five-Year Plan, published in February, 1971, makes few basic changes in Bulgaria's economic

policies as pursued during the 1960s.[92] Industrialization still has
first priority, though the production of consumer goods was slightly
raised. The only really new element in the plan was its greater
emphasis on scientific and technical research, with 1.85 percent of
the national income to be set aside for this purpose—approximately
200 million leva, as against 132 in 1967 (targets in the 1966-70 plan
were not achieved). Numerous reorganizations of the planning system
are contemplated, with only a few details available that deal mostly
with the procedure for the adoption of plans. Perhaps it is the experimentation and reorganization within the economy—e.g., agro-industrial
complex and new forms of management, including relations between
different economic institutions—that gives hope for a modest reform
movement.

Basically then, while the 1960s was a decade of experimentation,
the decade of the 1970s is to be a period of inward looking, with few
radical departures from the present planning and management system
of the economy. Burks, in his recently published analysis of events
in Bulgaria, draws the conclusion that the developments in Czechoslovakia in 1968 (and presumably those in Poland in December, 1970)
had a major impact on the reversal of Bulgaria's policy of economic
reform* and that Bulgaria simply "sought safety in the economic womb
of the Soviet motherland," suggesting that "Communist Bulgaria has
become in reality one of the weaker Socialist regimes, whereas it has
long been thought of as one of the stronger."[93]

Romania

Romania's whole development strategy in the 1960s must be
understood in the context of its political relations with the Soviet
Union, the need for maintaining independence, and its aim to hold
trade with the Soviet bloc to tolerable levels (not more than, say, 60

---

*Whether the recent Bulgarian developments are really the
result of the Czechoslovakian crisis of 1968 is naturally difficult to
assess, but the fact remains that the hopes for a real reform of the
cumbersome decision-making machinery were quietly abandoned after
1968 and Bulgarian-Soviet bilateral economic relations were greatly
increased in the last few years. Another point of view might be that
Bulgaria's close cooperation with the Soviet Union had nothing to do
with the Czechoslovakian developments and simply was one more
step toward long-term Bulgarian-Soviet cooperation.

percent of its total trade).[94] (See Appendix Tables A.1 and A.6.)
Romania has clung to its independence in economic matters and has
resisted a Soviet-sponsored policy of Comecon to "commit itself to
the import manufactures and the export of raw materials that the needs
of the more developed members seemed to imply."[95] Romania's policy
of rapid industrialization and the establishment of a broad economic
base ran counter to this Comecon policy. A more serious situation
developed with Khrushchev's proposal (originally proposed by the
Poles) for the establishment of "a unified planning organ, empowered
to compile common plans and to decide organizational matters. . . .
In order to select the investment projects there should be sectoral
plans, and projects once accepted could, if commonly financed, become
common property."[96] In view of Romania's strong opposition, the
acceptance of these proposals remained in suspense. In a declaration
made public in April, 1964, the Romanian Central Committee made its
opposition very clear:

> Our Party has very clearly expressed its point of view,
> declaring that since the essence of the suggested measures
> lies in shifting some functions of economic management
> from the competence of the respective state to the attribu-
> tion of super-state bodies or organs, these measures are
> not in keeping with the principles which underline the
> relations between socialist countries. The idea of a
> single planning body for CMEA has the most serious
> economic and political implications . . .[97]

The basic argument put forth by the Romanian leaders kept
creeping up repeatedly—the question of economic relations on the
"principle of complete sovereignty . . . that forms of cooperation
different from those unanimously agreed upon with CMEA . . . can be
decided by them alone is a sovereign way."[98] Romania again successfully stopped Russia's initiative in moving Comecon toward a supranational approach in the development of economic relations. Bilateral-
ism was strengthened during the next few years, in part due to the
necessity to coordinate the forthcoming five-year plan (1966-70)
among the members of Comecon. Romania continued to resist the
strengthening of Comecon and stressed sovereignty, in large part
due to Romania's suspicion of Soviet motives. (See also the discussion
in Chapter 9.)

In view of Romania's generally satisfactory over-all economic
growth prior to 1966, the urge of economic reform and democratization
of the system was less urgent than in some of the other socialist countries of Eastern Europe. Still, after 1965 pressures for reform

emanated from various sources, including the Party, and this finally resulted in a Party directive in late 1967 initiating a cautious restructuring of Romania's economic management system.[99] This directive was not fully implemented until 1969-70, and numerous adjustments were made during these years.

The major aim of the development strategy in the early 1960s (Sixth Five-Year Plan, 1960-65) was "to promote increased self-reliance and independence from external sources" based on the Party decisions in November, 1958.[100] These decisions of 1958 were those that set the stage for Romania's new industrialization policies, working toward greater independence from Soviet-bloc economies. The policies enacted for the Sixth Five-Year Plan were, on the whole, successful. They greatly increased factor productivity and industrial development, with actual production coming close to the plan's goal. A growth rate of 14.5 percent per annum in the gross output of industries was achieved in the 1959-65 period. Collectivization accelerated after 1958 (only 17.5 percent of the arable land was completed by April, 1962) without serious interruptions of agricultural production, in part by its liberal reimbursement provisions in the nationalization of private land.

Exports were to grow faster than imports, but emphasis in imports was on machinery and equipment to meet industrial expansion and thus to establish greater independence from Comecon deliveries. It was estimated that a cumulative trade deficit of $417 million for the period 1960-65 could easily be carried.[101] Romania hoped to increase its trade with the West and to continue imports of a variety of complex equipment for its industrial-modernization drive. This meant a radical change in the distribution of its foreign trade, with Comecon's share falling to 50 to 60 percent of its total trade. Great efforts were put into this drive and foreign-trade operations were slightly decentralized; it is generally agreed that "it was these efforts which produced the economic reform" and resulted in the new directives mentioned earlier.[102]

Basically, the reform initiated in 1967 is being continued to this date with varying intensity. The main objective aims at improving planning and management methods by decentralizing certain economic operations, with "multiple responsibilities" set up at all levels of the management system. Basic central-planning policies remained unchanged, but by instituting a multilevel system of authority it was hoped that innovations could be encouraged and that there might be greater flexibility in the decision-making processes and greater efficiency and responsibility at lower echelons in the decision-making hierarchy.[103] Most important in this newly established multilevel system—State Planning, branch ministry, industrial association, enterprise,—are the functions of the associations or trusts (called "industrial centrals").* These centrals assumed important duties of the branch ministries, which were reduced in number, and later were charged with the management of either the vertically or horizontally organized group of enterprises acting as relatively independent economic entities.[104] By late 1969, most industrial enterprises were under the direction of the centrals, and a number of responsibilities held by other central authorities were transferred to these associations. The centrals assumed considerable authority over the enterprises, e.g., they were responsible for capital for current operations, modernization, new investments (by 1970, these centrals had available from their own funds slightly over 50 percent of all investments), ensuring supplies of basic materials (based on quotas established by the appropriate ministries); they had charge of all employees, administered the wage fund of the enterprises, and were responsible for many research and development activities. A new National Commission for Scientific Research was responsible for the coordination of research and development activities, and research institutes had considerable financial autonomy.[105]

Generally, only centrally planned functions were transferred to the Centrals. Ministries were now responsible for the national plan, centrals were responsible for the management of the enterprises, including the setting of an increasing number of production indicators, and enterprises were responsible for the actual production, including certain market research. The reorganization also affected the system of prices (based on costs), with wages and salaries tied to profits and the introduction of a system of bonus payments. Banks also assumed an increasingly important role and became important sources of capital for the Centrals. Other reforms affected profits, a percentage of which was to remain with individual economic units. The percentage was raised in 1970 from 10 to 35 percent.[106]

---

*The Industrial Centrals might be compared in concept with a large multiplant U.S. corporation in which the central management controls the broad outline of targets but leaves the details of the production process itself in the hands of the individual plant manager, who is told what he will produce, the number and breakdown of the work force, wage structure, material allocation, profit level, credit limits, and so on, but not necessarily exactly how to do it. The centrals apparently will have much more leeway than in the past to recommend new investment, within limits, and have authority to carry out certain types of projects without reference to higher authority.

A reform initiated at the time that had great possibilities is the organization of "workers assemblies" at the enterprise level and a new system of collective responsibility at all levels of the industrial hierarchy from the minister councils to the centrals and the enterprise, with a board of directors consisting of members appointed by the centrals and members elected by the "workers assembly" of the enterprise. The director of the enterprise became the chief executive officer. The centrals' responsibilities in foreign trade were somewhat limited, with the Ministry of Foreign Trade in over-all charge of allocations and basic directives. This represented somewhat of a retreat from earlier published directives. A great many details went into the reorganization.

All these measures, according to Nicolae Ceausescu, were taken with the hope of achieving greater decentralization in operation, of establishing "greater initiative and direct participation, as well as unified leadership in all the levels of management of the socialist activities," and of rapidly introducing technological innovations. Two tendencies are very clear here—centralization and additional controls "go hand in hand with expansion of local autonomy."[107] Some local industries, such as food industries, became the responsibility of People's Councils (local governing bodies) at the judeţe (province) level. The economic reform gave these People's Councils limited responsibilities, including their own sources of revenue, thus becoming less dependent on the central budget. On the other hand, a newly estab-lished General Directorate for People's Councils, as well as a State Committee on Local Economy Administration, were the officially appointed watchdog committees, something typical for the socialist countries.[108] The Romanian reform did not go beyond a restructuring of the planning and management apparatus.* The introduction of market reforms was not attempted, mainly due to the Party's fear of a runaway political situation—not in the domestic sense as in Bulgaria, but in its foreign relations specifically in its relations with Moscow, which might provoke military intervention.

That the introduction of all these measures of decentralization did not always go smoothly was obvious from various talks by Party leaders and a variety of publications. But, unlike the reforms in Bulgaria and even in Yugoslavia, opposition came less from the Party

---

*Officially, it was not even called "reform." Instead, Romanians spoke of "perfecting the planning system." Rather than using the term "profit," the term "sound benefits" was used.

leadership than from the specialists—the managers who tried to slow down or who were openly opposed to this decentralization, which forced many of them to move away from the capital in Bucharest or even other from regional capitals. Other difficulties arose with the delegation of power to the newly decentralized organizations. Both the ministries and enterprises were reluctant to give up responsibilities. The years 1969 and 1970 were marked by problems brought about by these reforms by retreats as well as advances. The position of the Party often remained ambiguous, and at the December, 1969, Central Committee meeting the economic role of important Party organs was increased, contrary to the 1967 directives, but this increase, contrary to the developments in Bulgaria, was not necessarily brought about by outside events. It gave the Party a stronger control over the implementation of economic policies. One of the new organs was the Central Economic Council and its counterpart in every judeţe, whose task it was to accelerate the implementation of the reform.

It is obvious then that Romania's foreign relations, and specifically its relations with the Soviet Union and to Comecon's drive for greater integration among its members, was the decisive impulse for its development strategy. Statistical data shows that in the late 1950s Romania's share of trade with the Communist countries was 67 percent of its total foreign trade. By 1969, it had reoriented an important part of its trade toward the West: 46 percent was with the non-Communist world, of which 36.3 percent were with the developed capitalistic countries, as against 55 percent with the socialist countries, of which 48.9 percent was with the Comecon countries. It also had successfully resisted Comecon's pressure for closer economic integration. Russia's invasion of Czechoslovakia, which Romania's leader publicly condemned, put it on the defense. Romania's concern over Russian criticism (as well as that of neighboring Bulgaria) about its economic policies, its unfavorable trade balance with the West due to ever-increasing imports that accumulated huge deficits (about $800 million in 1968), and a general economic slowdown forced Romania, in 1969, into a modification of its policies toward multilateral cooperation with Comecon. Romania's growth economic dilemma, which could be solved only by increasing Western trade (80 percent of its iron-ore shipments were from Russia for example) in spite of increased tourist income (93.5 percent of the total foreign currency earnings in 1969) and perhaps long overdue increasing agricultural exports gave it little choice.[109]

Certain of Comecon's integration programs were and still are opposed by Romania, such as joint enterprises, "the majority's right to dispense the Comecon's bank capital, including minority contributions," the problem of transferable rubles, the exact obligations of bank members, the role of the bank staff, and an old problem under the new name of "rationalizing Comecon's production by eliminating inefficient operations."[110] But because of its economic dilemma, it had little choice other than establishing closer cooperation with Comecon. After some hesitation, Romania joined Comecon's Investment Bank in December, 1970, and several other Eastern European multilateral organizations, such as Intermetall (a separate branch organized by Comecon). With the finalizing of the new five-year plan (1971-75), numerous economic bilateral agreements with individual Comecon members were concluded, indicating Romania's new position with regard to the other socialist countries. One of the earliest indications of Romania's new position in regard to integration was the signing of an agreement with the Soviet Union to help in the construction of a nuclear power plant.

The years since 1969 have not been easy ones for Romania. A natural catastrophe (the flood of 1970),[111] an economic slowdown, and huge Western trading debts, all have forced Romania's policy-makers to move increasingly closer to Comecon and the Soviet Union economically. Romania has not given up economic cooperation elsewhere, especially in the expansion of its trade with the Western markets. This has become clear with the recently signed agreement to establish a Franco-Romanian bank, mixed Colombian-Romanian oil explorations, the trade delegation to the United States, and the fast-rising Sino-Romanian trade. According to a recent statement by Romania's Party Secretary, Comecon's share in the 1971-75 period will amount to more than half of Romania's trade. Inasmuch as imports from the West will be held down, with exports increasing for the payment of Romania's trade debts of the 1960s, these Western imports may very well not be able to provide a growing stimulus to investments and modernizing industrial production, as was the case before 1969. Romania's inability to achieve success in exporting more to the Western markets and its own inability to meet Western demands (in part due to the underdevelopment of its key resources, such as agriculture, light industries, consumer-goods industries, and foodproducts), in addition to its huge Western debt, produces a serious economic dilemma for the country.

These are all factors in forcing Romania into closer relations with the socialist countries. Romania's 1971-75 five-year plan, with the stress on raising the standard of living, repaying its debts to the West, and a continuation of its drive for industrialization, will give it little leeway in continuing its policy of the early 1960s of defending its economic sovereignty by taking an independent stand against Comecon's pressures. The economic and political developments of

the last few years clearly indicate the restrictive parameters available
for Romania's development strategy in the 1970s.[112]

Albania

Albania's development strategy in the 1960s was a continuation
of those of the 1950s, with the exception that China took the place of
the Soviet Union as a major contributor to its economic development.[113]
Albania's basic agrarian character still dominates, though a variety
of industries have been established during the last twenty years and
a better balance between industrial and agricultural production exists
(for statistical summaries, see Appendix Tables A.1 and A.7). Only
one third of Albania's population can be considered urbanized. Roughly
22 percent of its population is now occupied in the industrial sector,
which contributed 46 percent to the national income in the late 1960s.
Economic cooperation with China has continued and even expanded
during the 1960s, and the latest agreement signed by the countries
gives every indication of continued collaboration with and increased
assistance by China during Albania's 1971-75 plan.[114]

The need for economic reform was not felt in Albania until the
economy had developed greater sophistication, not unlike the developments in other socialist countries. The Seventh Plenum of the Party,
in December, 1968, discussed for the first time modifications in
economic planning, improvements in the administrative apparatus,
needed changes in wage policies, and so on.[115] Albania took initial
steps in reforming its economy, though it was a long way from either
an actual restructuring or even modification of the planning and
administrative apparatus. Articles that appeared in the Albanian
press during 1969 and 1970 discuss in greater detail new directives
of the Central Committee dealing with extensive decentralization of
power within the state and economic agencies.[116] Few details are
available, but that Albania's drive for decentralization also had internal
enemies is clear by Haki Toska's statement that "of course no one
opposes these great principles [extension of power]. However, when
the time comes to implement them, there is reluctance and they tend
to become ineffective . . ."[117]

The drive now underway basically is designed to improve economic management and to decentralize decision-making, not unlike
the other socialist countries in Southeast Europe. It is also obvious
that in Albania a highly centralized "controlled productive-resource
distribution system no longer fits current conditions."[118] The decentralization drive in Albania started from the center, with the major

stress on decentralization of power from the district level down to the lowest echelon, the People's Councils. These now have the power to draft their own economic and budgetary plans and to administer their sociocultural institutions and artisan enterprises. Local units now hire specialists for a variety of needed services. Ultimately, the People's Councils will become involved in the administration of health centers, schools, postal and communication services, and so on. Decentralization is proceeding with great speed, as can be seen from numerous newspaper articles, and includes People's Councils in villages, localities, state farm enterprises, city boroughs, and cities. Part of the decentralization drive will be turnover of elected officials "by replacing old and inefficient elements with new cadres." Obviously, some of these policies aim at replacing old Party members with new blood, again not unlike the Yugoslav situation, something that broke the back of the Bulgarian economic reform by the refusal of the established, old Party members to approve basic reforms.

From the available reports, Albania's decentralization drive is especially marked on the local level. This became obvious as a result of the national elections of September, 1970. Less was said about decentralizing important decision-making powers of national bodies though the assuming of important new functions by these lower administrative bodies would presuppose these shifts. It is much too early to forecast a trend for the 1970s. It is obvious, though, that this drive for decentralization at this stage is simply a restructuring of the administration apparatus to bring greater efficiency into its various decision-making organs. It certainly is not a basic change in the planning or central decision-making apparatus concerned with the running of the economic and political life of the country. The Albanian reform has a number of innovations, such as extending new powers to local units without establishing a middle man, which was the case both in the Bulgarian and Romanian reforms (associations and centrals, respectively). Presumably, the size of the country plays some role.

Hand in hand with these reforms are increased efforts by the Albanian leadership to expand and diversify its foreign trade by signing trade agreements with a larger number of countries. Trade and political discussions with neighboring Greece were initiated in 1970, and diplomatic relations were established in 1971 for the first time since the founding of the Albanian state. Relations with Yugoslavia have improved, and cultural relations have been increased with the large Albanian minorities in Yugoslavia and especially in the autonomous province of Kosovo, sponsored by both governments. Obviously, changes have taken place, and for the first time in many years Albania is again establishing foreign economic relations and easing restrictions

to foreign visitors. Albania thus has joined other socialist countries
in up-dating its economy and undertaking essential economic and
administrative reforms.

SUMMARY

It is clear from the preceeding discussions that the decade of
the 1960s will be known in the socialist countries as the "decade of
economic reform." All four of the Southeast European countries spent
much time and energy in preparing and implementing economic reforms.
Many of the hopes that the reform movement encouraged did not materialize; many of the reforms were stopped before they could have any
impact; and constraints of both an internal and external nature blocked
many of the reform goals, or never permitted a genuine attempt at
reform. The same basic ideas appear in Bulgaria and Romania—a
desire to modernize the planning and management apparatus, in part
to improve their competitive position, especially in the Western
markets, and to facilitate participation in technological innovations,
in part to encourage initiative and efficiency among their enterprises.
To accomplish these goals, certain controls to which the enterprise
was subjected were cut and additional incentives were provided, while
at the same time the tight over-all control remained unchanged and
often was increased (see the earlier discussion of Romanian policies).

Only Yugoslavia has been consistent in its policy of reform,
and it is here where economic reform spread to political reform and
to a true market socialism, forming a unique Yugoslav system. But
it is also in this ethnically diverse country where the reform from its
inception was to serve both economic and political ends, where it is
forced to undergo constant compromises precisely because of the
differences and rivalries between the peoples who in the first place
encouraged this reform. Romania and Bulgaria moved with extreme
caution in attemption reforms of their planning mechanism. It was
never contemplated to be more than a restructuring of some of the
most obvious abuses of its planning and management apparatus.

Both internal and external pressures constrained the reform
movement. Romania continues, at the present time, a cautious move
toward decentralization that is, as far as can be seen at the present
time, unhampered by internal factional disagreements, though Romania
is eminently aware of the physical proximity of the Soviet Union.
Bulgaria's reform generated much internal opposition, especially from
old-line Party members. The events in Czechoslovakia in 1968 and
those in Poland in 1970 proved decisive for Bulgaria, and to a lesser

degree for Romania. Reform in Bulgaria became too risky and was mostly abandoned, and therefore further economic developments were worked out in close collaboration with the Soviet Union, bringing about a near merger of the Bulgarian and Soviet economies by the beginning of 1971. Albania only recently took the road to limited economic reform.

It is precisely because of the many divergent internal and external forces that influenced the reform movement during the 1960s that the development strategy of the 1960s has been analyzed both for the area impact as a whole and for each individual country. Many of the basic ingredients of the reforms, their scope and aim, were much the same in every socialist country of the area. The constraints also left a remarkably similar impact. The reform movement, which at the beginning of the 1960s was about to sweep the region, slowed down markedly by the end of the decade. It certainly has run its course for the present in Bulgaria, will continue on its cautious and slow road in Romania, has just begun in Albania, and presumably will continue its road toward a true market socialism in Yugoslavia, if internal centrifugal forces and certain outside pressures closely connected with the future of the whole state will permit its expansion. The road of economic reform is fraught with dangers, but also with hope, if the socialist countries of Southeast Europe can ultimately build a technically sophisticated and viable set of economies and compete on the world markets. The new technological age demands the most modern machinery, the latest scientific methods, and the most efficient use of the administrative apparatus of every state.

The preceding discussions presented an analysis of the development strategy and changes in the postwar period of the five countries of Southeast Europe. From these discussions it is obvious that a very vital part of the development strategy of these countries is influenced by political constraints operating because of pressures exerted by the Soviet Union, which often greatly reduce the economic and political leeway available to the socialist governments of the area. In part these constraints also depend on the wider world political scene. In addition, the role assigned to the various regions of the country in the over-all developmental planning has a very important impact on the development strategy. This role and the relationship between national and regional forces will now be discussed in some detail in the following chapters.

The three chapters in Part III are therefore devoted to an analysis and assessment of regional development policies as part of the national strategies of the five countries of Southeast Europe—specifically, the concepts of regional development, the implementation of policies, and the processes and application of special regional policies in the countries of Southeast Europe. It has been found necessary at various stages of past discussions to clarify the concepts used in the field of national and regional development and, specifically, to analyze the interaction between national and regional development policies. Because there was a need for clarification earlier in this work and taking into account recent developments and their practicality within the field of regional development, Chapter 6 is devoted to a brief review of the most-important terminology in the field of economic development, including regional development, in order to clarify these concepts and to avoid misunderstandings in the discussions to follow. Included in the discussions in Chapter 6 is an analysis of the concepts of growth poles and growth centers and a brief discussion of the relationship between these concepts and a regional economic policy.

Chapter 7 discusses the various models of institutional measures taken to increase greater regional participation in decision-making processes. Basic to an understanding of regional-development processes is the role the various interest groups played and their impact on the development strategy of the countries of Southeast Europe. In the second part of Chapter 7, the institutional changes are briefly analyzed under the headings of administrative changes, the scope and the relationship of the central plan to regional planning measures, the financing (investments) as they relate to regional development in general, and, finally, the problem of locational decisions and, specifically, spatial development of industry.

Chapter 8 is devoted to a comparative analysis of specific regional locational and planning policies in the countries of Southeast Europe, including the spatial complexity creating regional imbalances. Following Rosenstein-Rodan's dictum, based on his study on the south of Italy, the study is based on the premise that "accelerating the development of a region should be considered primarily as part of an optimization policy for the whole country of which the region forms a part."* The discussions in Part III aim to show that a viable national planning policy must be concerned with both the over-all socioeconomic development (sectoral and branch policy), as well as with a maximization of the region's contribution to the national well-being, which, as part of the over-all strategy, includes the full integration of the underdeveloped and depressed parts of a country.

---

*Paul N. Rosenstein-Rodan, Reflections on Regional Development, Massachusetts Institute of Technology, Center for International Studies, C/63-25, July 31, 1963.

Economic-development policies, and specifically regional policies, demand a comprehensive approach, that is, a problem-oriented, integrated approach to various types of human activity: economic, social, cultural, as well as institutional, with special attention given to the problems of the interrelation between agriculture and industry, the various types of investment, education, in- and out-migration, and so on. It must be emphasized, however, that a comprehensive approach does not mean development in every area, but rather the establishment of a clear set of priorities with regard to a specific set of propulsive forces affecting different types of human activity. It is also of importance to make clear that the term "development" is a very general one, but in the context of the discussions here it is understood as contributing to both quantitative growth and qualitative change of numerous economic and social variables.[1] Quantitative growth basically consists of an increase in the productivity of a country or a part of the national territory (regional development) producing, as Antoni Kuklinski noted, "the welfare effect of economic growth and the productivity effect of social factors."[2] According to Benjamin Higgins, "economic development" is viewed as "development in terms of those objectives which can only be achieved through the efficient and organized use of scarce resources of an area."[3] Expanding on this, Andrezj Wróbel views economic growth "as an outcome of this complex process, which embraces generation and adoption of innovations not only in the technique of production, but also in the broad field of culture and social organization."[4]

Organizing the best possible distribution of available resources (including human resources) for the accomplishment of a set of goals

145

is referred to as "planning." Let it be first acknowledged that planning is a method of guiding development toward a specific goal[5] and that it requires social and economic action, movement, and change and thus produces a complicated system interaction that includes economic and social processes. Planners include everyone actively engaged in the planning process, and, as the late Yugoslav economist Rudolf Bićanić wrote, "in the repetitive cycle of preparation, decision, implementation and control of plans several groups of actors take part."[6] Their interaction raises problems of decision-making at various administrative levels, with regional pressures often playing a decisive role, thus establishing a variety of targets. Whether planning can take place at any sequential level or only at certain levels of economic and social development is a much-discussed question among Soviet theoreticians as well as Western economists, but is of little relevance for the specific problem here.[7] It is also clear, based on ample evidence, that planning for different economic sectors varies and especially that the advanced technological processes demand a variety of the most-sophisticated planning procedures. Thus, "planibility" depends on certain economic factors.[8]

Planning is easier for manufacturing industries than for agriculture. For example, basic industries that by nature are slow-changing (e.g., electricity) require comparatively fewer decisions than light industries, which usually have a more-rapid change in the volume and type of products. The developments in the Soviet Union are a good example, since they began with electricity (GOELRO plan), continued with natural resources, and finally gave attention to agriculture. The latter caused the greatest problems, though planning was restricted to compulsory or commercial deliveries of products and ignored the problem of production planning. Consumer-goods planning also cause some serious problems.[9] Nonsocialist countries such as Greece first planned their financial policy, including the allocation of credits for developmental processes. In the Soviet planning model, the main emphasis is on institutional change, and planning is considered possible only by completely abolishing private economy and introducing socialist collective economy.

One other term is in need of clarification. This is "development planning," which includes all of the procedures required, carefully structured and pursued for the purpose of coordinating various human activities, thus exploiting the existing potential of the physical and human resources, e.g., an appealing climate, a favorable location in relation to communications and transport, and a nucleus of rapidly growing industries. Numerous studies have concluded that to be successful development planning must give special attention to the process of interaction as it relates to both national and regional planning. This encompasses

> "a gradual shift of emphasis from the problems of the individual region to the problems of growth and change within a system of regions that are tied together by a number of inter-exchange and competitive relations, . . . the integration of an increasing number of factors of development which has enlarged the scope of regional planning schemes . . . to include all relevant aspects of development; that is social, cultural and institutional as well."[10]

The literature is abundant with discussions on finding a generally acceptable definition of the concept of "region," consideration of which is beyond the scope of this study.[11] For the purpose of the discussions here, the term will be used to denote simply geographical and administrative subdivisions and their activities, for which development plans can be promulgated on a subnational (regional) level. For analytical purposes, two basic functional factors of regions are usually recognized: (a) those related to the problems of the region themselves, e.g., promulgation of special policies to assist underdeveloped regions, such as social assistance, establishment of an infrastructure, or improvements of outmoded structures; and (b) the national objectives related directly or indirectly to all regions of a country. In its broadest sense, there are two main reasons for a regional policy: social concern for the less-advantaged regions of a state and the administrative-economic necessities expressed in the decentralization of important economic, social, and institutional bodies.

Regional policies must be comprehensive and are formulated according to conditions found on the subnational level, i.e., developed, underdeveloped, and lagging.* Sometimes only the terms "developed"

---

*Relating the term "underdeveloped" to countries, Gunnar Myrdal characterized such as having "large and increasing gaps in productivity and income among major regions, advanced countries by small and diminishing ones." Benjamin Higgins defined an underdeveloped country as "one with large and increasing differences in per capita income among major regions, and with a large proportion of the population living in the poor and lagging regions; an advanced country has small and diminishing gaps among regions, and only a

and "backward" are used. Sometimes areas are referred to as
"stagnate" or "depressed." The terms "congested" and "depopulated"
also are used. Niles Hansen, for example, uses three types of analytical regions—congested, intermediate, and lagging—and explains
this division as coming "to grips directly with the problem of overconcentration of population and economic activity in some areas."[12]
Eastern European scholars often used the term "depressed," whose
meaning is related to the intermediate or stagnate region. This refers
to regions that have reached a certain level of development, usually
with sufficient infrastructure, but that, because of changing economic
activity and political-historical developments, have been left behind.
Largely because of the absence of modernization and/or changed
strategic aspects, such regions are considered depressed and very
often lagging in development. The character of Hansen's "intermediate region" is closely related to the above-cited depressed or
stagnate areas. These regions are in need of structural transformation—the previously cited agrarian region of Slavonia, in northeastern Yugoslavia, is an example of this type of region. For the
purpose of this study, the terms "developed," "underdeveloped," and
"depressed" or "lagging" will be used in regional descriptions.

It is obvious that in the process of converting underdeveloped
and lagging regions, changes and adjustments of a sociocultural
nature play an important role. The developments in the various
underdeveloped and lagging regions of the countries of Southeast
Europe during the last twenty-five years and cited in this book are
proof that the socioeconomic changes in these regions are accompanied
by major cultural changes among its people. This is easily verified in
the case of Yugoslavia, with not only mass internal migration but even
more important external emigration.* Expectations and motivations

---

small proportion of the labour force is employed in the poorer and
relatively lagging regions." As far as "lagging regions" are concerned,
Higgins' statement will find general acceptance, that before too much
time they must be converted into leading ones, "otherwise the agglomer-
ative pull of the leading regions may become so strong that lagging
regions become chronically poor ones." Benjamin Higgins, "Regional
Interaction, the Frontier and Economic Growth," UNRISD/71/C.49,
GE.71-11332 (Geneva: United Nations Research Institute for Social
Development [Programme IV-Regional Development], May, 1971)
(Mimeographed). p.29.

*Of the total Yugoslav population 3.6 percent, or 15 percent of
the total registered nonagricultural labor force (excluding private

are strongest among the people of the more-advanced sectors (foreign emigration is strongest from Croatia) and among the better-educated in the underdeveloped and lagging regions of the country.

Another term used is "congested" (or even "overcongested") areas, defined as "areas in which the economic growth has reached a scale in a given time that is bigger than the optimal from the point of view of internal environmental conditions of the over-congested region and the development of other regions of the country."[13] In the countries of Southeast Europe, congested areas are still few, e.g., the primate cities of Athens and perhaps Belgrade and Bucharest.

It must also be stressed that the emphasis on and implementation of regional policies and plans goes far beyond the attention given to individual problem areas. It encompasses basic concepts of economic development, the implementation of such policies, including the vital problem of disaggregation of national plans, and various institutional policies. Whereas regional policies can solve one specific problem, generally they are more comprehensive in nature. Policies are of short-term or long-term character, and it is possible to "distinguish various types of instruments: comprehensive planning or programming; financial inducement and restrictions; and administrative measures."[14] The main function of regional planning is one of coordinating over-all economic social growth, though a distinction must clearly be made between federal and unitary states. The term regional development and regional policy as used in the context of the discussions here, therefore, is a broad one involving both social and economic activities administered by the national and/or local governments. The recent emphasis on decentralization of certain planning and management activities of the economies of the socialist countries, as discussed in Chapter 5, has enhanced regional participation.

Most of the countries of Southeast Europe lack comprehensive regional-planning policies and some scholars question whether they have any regional policies at all. Yugoslavia experimented more in this respect. All of its republics have their own short-term and long-term macroplans, but the country as a whole lacks a comprehensive over-all microplan, not to speak of an integrated regional plan. Other Southeast European countries have over-all national planning, but they are sectoral and branch plans that do not take into account regional differentiation, and their plans are without regional

---

peasants, including self-employed, jobless, and the socialist sector), was working in foreign countries in 1970.

disaggregation. Greece only recently, in the late 1960s, organized seven planning regions and recently added seven administrative districts (for details, see Chapters 7 and 8). Yugoslavia has gone furthest in urban planning: a Federal Planning Institute, Republic Planning Institutes, and many metropolitan planning bureaus exist.

Much theoretical writing dealing with regional development and concepts of regional planning is available.[15] The United Nations Research Institute for Social Development (UNRISD) in the last few years has published a series of relevant theoretical studies. Numerous other publications in the United States and Europe have appeared. Hansen, J. Hillborst, Antoni Kuklinski, and others recently critically examined the existing theories and models of regional development.[16] The aim of the following discussions, therefore, is simply to synthesize existing theoretical thinking for the purpose of clarifying the later discussions, and concentrate on two aspects—how growth is transmitted between regions and the concept of growth poles.

NATIONAL GROWTH
AND REGIONAL POLICIES

Over-all national growth can be accomplished by using two types of regional policies. One stresses the attainment of over-all sustained growth by maximizing the growth of the few existing centers with the greatest growth potential. This, according to Albert Hirschman, brings benefits to the less-developed regions through "trickling-down" effects. Such effects as transfer of capital, interregional trade, and labor transfer will very likely occur, according to this theory, if a certain degree of complementarity exists between the two regions—the growth center and the hinterland.[17] Hirschman discusses the interaction between two regions of a model of a national economy in terms of a "polarization effect"—or, according to Francois Perroux, the "effets de stoppage."[18] These effects take place when activities in an underdeveloped region are slowed down due to the competition of a richer region. Also, when employment opportunities are not adequate, the labor force in the poorer regions tends to migrate to the richer regions or, as has frequently been shown, seeks employment in foreign countries.

It is clear that, in the short-run, the benefit of national economic growth will be accomplished by allocating considerable investment to the advanced region, with economic growth in the less-developed regions a long-term goal. Kuklinski speaks of the time horizon as the crucial factor here.[19] Gunnar Myrdal uses concepts similar to

Hirschman. His terms "spread" and "backwash" effects coincide with Hirschman's "trickling down" and "polarization" effects, but he is less optimistic about the ultimate accomplishments of reducing regional imbalances, believing that the polarization forces are stronger than the trickling-down forces.[20] In essence, the question of this relationship between the richer and poorer regions is closely related to the over-all long-term competitive position of the poorer region, but it must be recognized that the various regions of a country neither develop at the same speed nor are all aspects of growth established at the same time. As Hillhorst plainly stressed, "the most obvious reason for the transmission of growth in space seems to be interregional trade."[21] Only as the effect of trading becomes more obvious in the degree of specialization of the underdeveloped regions, facilitated by the growth of a sufficient infrastructure of communication and transport and an increasing per capita income bringing higher savings, can economies of scale with its increased productivity take effect.

While Myrdal is less optimistic than Hirschman about the success of his spread effects, even he considers the possibility that polarization effects are predominant in the earlier stages of development and that they may be slowed down or even reversed in the later stages, further increasing regional inequalities. It very much depends on the over-all competitive position of the underdeveloped regions, including the availability of commodities at competitive prices, to the more-developed regions (the alternatives are foreign imports and less interregional trading).[22] Hirschman also considers that in the early stage of industrial development regional imbalances are not reduced and may even grow.

The economic-development theory of "unbalanced growth" developed by Hirschman is explained by a concentration of economic activity in selected growth centers, therefore making for special concentration of economic activities. It is based on the fact that economic development is essentially an "unbalanced process" that is transmitted "through chains of disequilibrium."[23] Perroux' growth theories based on growth poles are essentially similar to Hirschman's theory. Both of these theories are in considerable part the result of a reaction to the "balanced growth" theories developed earlier by G. Cassel and expanded by Ragnar Nurkse and Rosenstein-Rodan.[24] Balanced regional growth as opposed to unbalanced growth refers to similar growth rates for all regions or induced growth in the slower-growing regions to enable them to advance more rapidly and thus ultimately catch up with the more-developed ones. This is also referred to as "evenness" in growth, or "equalization," a term explained later in this chapter.

A second type of hypothesis in the pursuit of national growth aims at the priority development of the underdeveloped regions, giving special attention to industries based on local resources and going hand in hand with an expansion of its infrastructure, thus gradually increasing interregional trade. The ultimate criteria is closely related to the long-term comparative advantage of the under-developed region. Neither hypothesis has undergone sufficient empirical tests to draw conclusions as to their ultimate success.* But from the available evidence, it is clear that regional growth to be successful must depend not only on possibilities of economic diversification but also on social equality in interregional policies to reduce interregional differences in the standard of living.[25] It is also clear that institutional developments and the model used in the over-all development are key factors influencing regional differentiation. These goals are met in Yugoslavia, for example, by giving special assistance to its underdeveloped regions as part of a sacrificial contribution by the richer regions for social equality. According to Kuklinski, "in such a situation, economic growth and social equality are conflicting goals in regional policies, but this conflict exists only if the short-run perspective is accepted. In the long run, the situation might be quite different."[26] The question arises as to what will happen to the poorer regions if the trickling-down or spread effects do not work or if in time the comparative advantage of the poorer region to the more-advanced region starts to decline or even disappears None of the existing theoretical generalizations on regional economic growth has conclusive proof, and only by extensive empirical tests will it be possible to foresee the future development of the poorer regions.

GROWTH POLES AND CENTERS

The second important aspect of the theoretical discussions of economic growth and regional development has been centered on the concept of development poles, pôles de croissance (focal points of growth), together with related concepts such as growth centers, growth areas, core regions, development nuclei, and so on. These concepts provide a useful tool for theoretical discussions of national

---

*Niles Hansen expressed it succinctly when he emphasized that future progress in the theoretical details and classification no doubt will be determined by the extent to which they are associated with hypothetical studies of growth at the regional level.

and regional planning.[27] The basic contribution to the concept of
growth poles was made by Francois Perroux.[28] Perroux defines
"growth poles" only in relation to abstract economic space and not
in relation to geographic space. He distinguishes between three
types of abstract economic space: space as defined as a plan, space
as a field of forces, and space as a homogenous aggregate. His
growth poles are thought of in the realm of their relationship to the
second type of abstract space. He defines growth poles as "centers
[poles or focii] from which centrifugal forces emanate and to which
centripetal forces are attracted. Each center being a center of
attraction and repulsion has its proper field which is set in the field
of all other centers."[29] To Perroux a growth pole must consist of
one or more enterprises that contribute to economic development in
a region. He also stresses that economic development does not come
about at a uniform rate, but rather concentrates on a few nodes, which
results in spread effects to the whole economy. He refers to the
"domination" of one national, regional, or local economy over others.
According to Higgins, this domination can also be brought about by a
particular industrial city generating "growth in the region as a whole
through the spread effects of its own growth."[30] Such an interaction,
with forward and backward linkages (according to Hirschman), can
result when several important industries (propulsive industries) are
located at the pôle de croissance. But the fact remains, as many
have pointed out, that "a 'propulsive industry' must be large, it must
be fast-growing, and it must generate substantial spread effects."[31]

In part, the rapid acceptance of the growth-pole theory in
France was a reaction to the central-place location theory. French
regional economic analysis thus differed from the traditional, rather
static location theories promulgated by August Lösch and Walter
Christaller.[32] It was Jacques Boudeville who elaborated on Perroux's
general theory and included geographical dimensions in "economic
space."[33] Wróbel, in a recent paper, made it clear that "this transition from abstract economic space to geographical space has been
always the weak spot of the spatial 'growth pole' theory (and a source
of considerable confusion), since the rules of transformation of one
space into the other have never been satisfactorily formulated."[34]

Since the first writings by Perroux, the contents of this theory
and his concepts have been much broadened and generalized, with
the result that they lost a considerable part of their original content
and meaning.* Originally, the concept of pôle de croissance was

----

*Partly due to Perroux's ambiguous original statement, in part

thought of as an "explanation of development and underdevelopment in the past," but, as Higgins made clear, "since growth proceeds through the appearance of pôles de croissance, in regions where no growth is occurring it is necessary to create pôles de croissance by active intervention."[35]

Thus, poles have become an instrument of policy with development poles clearly influencing the system of structural relationships. To avoid misunderstanding this broadly used term—it often has become a slogan in the discussion of regional problems—a clarification of the term "poles of growth" as well as "polarization" must be made, since they have been used differently by English writers and by the French school of regional economics. Perroux's definition of "pole" or a pôle de croissance was explained earlier. He understood "polarization" as a process by which poles are created and enlarged by "a succession of different fields of forces which generate a changing sequence of different vectors over functional and geographical space." To English writers, the image of the term conveyed "is that of a continuum being gradually stretched towards its opposite extremes; that of two opposing poles generating forces which gradually alter the ordering of the elements in the space between them, attracting them."[36] Thus, there must always be two poles, while in the French interpretation more than two poles can exist at the same time. Today, the development-pole theory is largely applied to a regional context— that is, geographical space. Even Perroux himself was

> primarily concerned with economic growth as manifested in organizational and industrial space, i.e., the appearance, growth and stagnation of firms and industries, the mutual interrelations between poles prevailing in these spaces, and the move forces and mechanism behind the changes taking place . . .[37]

In Boundeville's definition, a "polarized region" is "a heterogeneous continuous area localized in geographical space, whose different parts are independent through mutual complementary and interplay relations centered around a regional centre of gravity."[38]

---

due to poor translation from the original French into English, and partly due to the confusion of many authors, the term "growth pole" has had a wide but also very diverse interpretation.

In summary, it is generally agreed that the functional character of a growth pole is obvious, though its locational and geographical aspects must also be considered. Inasmuch as the growth pole is also used as one measure of dispersion leading toward polarization, geographically it must be accepted, otherwise growth poles cannot be useful in discussions of regional policy.* Still, Hermansen made it clear in his detailed analysis that growth-pole theories are basically nongeographic.[39] Others conclude that it has only a limited theoretical value in a locational context. Though Darwent stresses that, "despite the flimsy theoretical background and the lack of empirical verification, there is nonetheless a great deal of intuitive appeal in the notion of growth center in which economic and social development is initiated and transmitted to an area around it."[40] Alan Gilbert commented "that the growth pole concept has created more darkness than light for the regional planning processes,"[41] while Meus en Ruimte probably expressed the consensus about the relationship between growth-pole theory and regional economic policy by stating, "while concepts and terminology of the development poles must be made more precise and consistent," nevertheless, "through the principles of regional concentration, the growth pole theory furnished a contribution to regional economic policy."[42]

Perhaps one other important point should be made. This is the fact that most of the theoretical framework for the discussions of the regional problem originated as a response to the problems in

---

*Kuklinski clearly distinguished between growth poles of "national significance" (their effect on the structure of the regions in which they are located, on interregional reciprocity, and the whole country) and growth centers, which are intraregional in character only. Antoni R. Kuklinski, "Growth Poles and Growth Centres in Regional Policies and Planning: An Institutional Perspective (discussions)," (Geneva: United Nations Institute for Social Development, 1969) (mimeographed).

Kosta Mihailović argues strongly for the use of the term "development pole" instead of "growth pole," indicating a broader concept of poles and at the same time stressing that it can only be understood in the context of regional conditions. See Kosta Mihailović, "The Dynamics of Structural Changes as a Context for the Growth Pole Theory, with special reference to Yugoslavia." Mimeographed draft paper, Belgrade, February, 1971, pp. 18-19. The author of this book uses the terms growth pole and development pole interchangeably, but follows Kuklinski in the use of the term growth centers.

industrially advanced economies, with a corresponding lack of regional-development theory related to the problems of underdeveloped countries. (The J. Friedman and R. Misra studies are probably notable exceptions.[43]) On the other hand, M. Penouil pointed out that many of the theories and conceptual frameworks of economic development (formulated largely at the abstract level) can be transferred to the problems prevalent in underdeveloped regions.[44] In addition, some of the theories have been determined independently in underdeveloped countries.

The problem in the-less developed countries is not as much one of leveling out differences between regions or of development per se, but rather one of economic growth by the development of new growth impulses, thus creating spread effects. That is not to say that the concepts of growth poles and centers do not relate to the problems of the less-developed or underdeveloped countries. These concepts must be adjusted to their peculiar situations and needs. Essential questions that must be answered, and the countries of Southeast Europe serve as a useful case study for less-industrialized countries, are directly related to the spatial allocation of resources, to the development of new resources, and to the organization of an administrative hierarchy aware of regional and interregional relations, with a carefully disaggregated regional plan. These questions include the location of propulsive industries (including their proper size, which will exert strong growth impulses in the surrounding hinterland, as well as in a larger area); the role (including possible expansion and/or transfers) of existing industries; the integration of labor supply in the production processes, especially of new industries; the delineation of administrative regions and centers; the contribution of the service, including the relations of the public-service sector to the whole developmental processes; the problem of in- and out-migration of rural and urban settlements; and the designing of a proper infrastructure, including both expansion of existing insufficient facilities and the erection of new ones.

Developmental spatial planning, based on growth-pole and growth-center policy theory certainly can offer a valuable framework and tool for integrating these theories into the over-all policies of economic growth and the regional-development policies of the less-developed regions. Its success will greatly depend on efficiently coordinated functionally and spatially integrated administrative decisions. Later, discussions will show that none of the countries of Southeast Europe at the present time meets this criteria, though various experiments have been underway in nearly all of the countries.

IMPLEMENTATION
OF REGIONAL
DEVELOPMENT
POLICIES

The previous discussions analyzed the various concepts of economic development and their relationship to regional policies. The discussions in this chapter relate these concepts to the problems of implementing regional development policies. Before analyzing the ways in which national and regional policies are implemented, it must be recognized that such implementation largely depends on the national goals (parameters) set by the society and the values and expectations created by national-development policies. Basic to a successful implementation of regional development policies is not only the type of relationship existing between the national policy emphasizing sectors and branches and its coordination with regional goals, but also the type of model of development used for both the economy as a whole and the regions of a country. Kuklinsky summarizes the design of regional policies and developments and recognizes four problems: (a) an analysis of resources and means; (b) an analysis and identification of barriers for economic, social and, cultural progress; (c) the proper selection of regional development strategies (with particular attention given to the proper choice of growth poles and centers) and; (d) the proper choice of methods and models that should be used in the design of the regional plan.[1]

Most of these problems have been mentioned in earlier discussions in the context of the analysis of development strategies. The types of development strategies vary among the five countries of Southeast Europe, as does their implementation. The choice of growth poles (see above) leaves its imprint on both the economic activity and demographic structure on a national scale, while the proper selection of growth centers and their role in the economic and social transformation leaves its impact on the regional level, on the surrounding region, on a system of regions, and, ultimately, on all socioeconomic activities of a country. The choice of growth poles and centers is greatly influenced by the goals expected to be reached and is of special importance for the underdeveloped and lagging regions of a country.* Marxian theory applies concepts generally identical to the writings of Western scholars for the creation of propulsive power for territorial structures. The work by N. E. Kolosovski and his followers on industrial territorial complexes expresses similar theories of economic development.[2]

In implementing regional policies, it is of importance to distinguish first of all between the two models of regional planning, known under different names as adaptive and developmental, passive and active, or allocative and innovative. The basic characteristics of these models have been presented by John Friedman and are summarized by Kuklinski and Tormod Hermansen.[3] Basically, "developmental," "active," and "innovative" distinguishes itself from "adaptive," "passive," and "allocative" in that it recognizes the interrelationship between economic development and spatial change and identifies and promotes processes of swift economic development, including economic, social, and cultural objectives. This type of planning "is concerned as a response to the pressures and requirements of national economic development."[4] The distinction between the two models of planning is not always clear and often depends on the planning objectives in a given country.

Implementation of regional policy depends on the interaction between the decision-makers and the economic system, with considerable differences in the type of economy existing: the Soviet-type, centrally planned (command) economy, generally prevalent in Albania,

---

*It must be made clear, however, that the impact of growth poles in underdeveloped regions as, Gokhman and Karpov emphasized, may "serve as an incentive to the economic development of the region as a whole or of a significant part of it . . . it may barely affect the region at all since the basic interests of the pole will fall outside the regional limits . . . it may cause part of the population to shift from outlying areas into the zone of the growth pole and thus adversely affect conditions in the main part of the regional territory (momentarily or for a longer period)." See V. M. Gokhman and L. N. Karpov, "Growth Poles and Growth Centres," in A Review of the Concepts and Theories of Growth Poles and Growth Centres, UNRISD 70/C.6, GE. 70-24266 (Geneva: United Nations Research Institute for Social Development, November, 1970), p. 199.

Bulgaria, and, with some modifications, in Romania; and the mixed type (federal type) of economy prevalent in Yugoslavia, with decisions initiated and implemented by different levels of administrative organs, or by individual enterprises, or a different type of mixed economy with a strong private sector and a strong central governmental influence, such as in Greece. Measures implementing regional policies leave their impact on a large group of activities: stimulating and expanding industrial growth; development and expansion of an infrastructure, especially with the view toward benefiting underdeveloped and lagging regions; labor mobility, especially from rural to urban centers; education, including vocational training; and aid to social welfare. All these measures are dependent on a coordinated policy between national and regional planning (regional and sectoral agencies) affecting investment decisions, something at the present very inefficient and arbitrarily handled in all socialist countries of Southeast Europe.

To bring greater efficiency into planned economies, especially affecting locational and production decisions, special attention must be given to achieving more-efficient organizational structures, with the view toward improved data collections. Ian Hamilton cites recent efforts and approaches discussed in the socialist countries.[5] They include

> Liberman's decentralized market-mechanistic system, . . .
> the approach by Lange, Birman and Sik, in which decen-
> tralization reduces the volume of information to be proces-
> sed at the center . . . and raises the economic efficiency
> of decentralized decisions by market pricing, . . . the
> cybernetic approaches . . . in which progress is achieved
> by the design of a highly efficient information processing
> system yielding efficient decisions.[6]

Most of these approaches thus far are found in theoretical discussions only. Both existing political constraints and insufficient data make these changes only a long-term objective. Still, experiments with different types of organizational structure with a view toward obtaining increasing efficiency in planning and production processes, including a greater integration of regional contributions, has been going on at various degrees, as is obvious from the discussion in Chapter 5.

DECENTRALIZATION IN DECISION-MAKING PROCESSES

The various economic reforms of the 1960s had a common goal—to bring about greater efficiency by introducing in various degrees some method of decentralization in the system, thus transferring responsibility to different levels of decision-making.[7] The organizational structures facilitating decision-making in the five countries of Southeast Europe were mentioned earlier. But with varied regional emphasis and policies becoming increasingly common in the over-all economic-development policies of the countries of Southeast Europe, a need arose for new regional machinery and specific guidelines for decision-making on different levels. Yugoslavia has gone farthest in this institutional reorganization, transferring important parts of its planning apparatus to regional bodies and greatly increasing the decision-making power of local bodies. Countries with a centralized administrative system experimented with several solutions, largely by transferring vital economic decision-making processes from the center to micro-units. The Communist leadership (with the exception of Yugoslavia), as well as the leadership of Greece (both before and after the military takeover), have been reluctant to permit a great degree of decentralization in the various economic decision-making processes. In the highly centralized bureaucracy of the socialist countries, however, the inability to quickly attain institutional reaction, thus providing for some earlier recognition of problem areas, is a most serious situation. The changes made during the 1960s increased regional participation in decision-making processes, and this was accomplished by several institutional measures, the alternative models of which are briefly summarized below.

In essence, the reforms retained the basic central-planning mechanism but attempted to improve the economic decision-making processes by decentralizing key decisions and their machinery of implementation by the establishment of new institutions—industrial aggregates called trusts, referred to in Romania as industrial centrals. They were assigned many of the functions formerly held by central-planning bodies, but also some from individual enterprises. At the same time, the latter, subordinated to a trust, received greater autonomy (this was especially true in Romania), assuming responsibility for planning and investment decisions based on the success of marketing their products.[8] The trusts also were expected to assist weak enterprises, which themselves maximized their profits when sales were judged by value.

The second alternative envisioned no new institutions. The emphasis was on the use of existing institutions, and the main concern was with a decentralization of the excessive state apparatus by encouraging enterprise initiatives and the granting of additional power to lower-level government agencies (district and local units). Beginning in 1968, this approach was also initiated in Albania, with increasing emphasis.[9]

A third alternative provided a radical shift in authority from the center to republican or even communal bodies. This basically is the Yugoslav model, which aimed not only at decentralizing many aspects of the decision-making apparatus (e.g., investments, micro-planning decisions, and marketing arrangements), but also meant the abandonment of rigid central planning. This shift from the centralized, Soviet-type model in the decision-making structure to a participatory model called direct democracy can be explained by the Yugoslav belief that key decisions should be made by the workers and the enterprises themselves. It fits the peculiar Yugoslav situation, where increased emphasis was placed on workers' self-management and on the problems inherited in a multinational society. With increased information available to local units (communes and enterprises), it was the enterprise and its management that were the initiators and were the groups interested in diffusion of the decision-making apparatus. The central-planning apparatus, with its micro-decisions, has been abolished, and the key decision-making authority now has been vested in the enterprise itself, assisted by communes and the republic. Yugoslavia's planning now concentrates on macroplans when forecasting broad economic activities. They are microplans when they are concerned with a specific project, such as the key projects still financed by the federation through the annual budget, the Iron Gate hydroelectric project, land reclamation in the Vojvodina, and the Bar to Belgrade railroad. Generally speaking, with the exception of the above-cited specific projects, the main central-government influence is confined to fiscal policy and taxation.

It is obvious that the changes in Yugoslavia were radical ones that affected the transfer not only of economic decision-making processes, but, as expected, those of self-management of the enterprises, leaving their impact on a wide area of economic and political developments. The shift in Yugoslavia produced a pluralization of the polity and menaced the leading role of the Party by shifting authority from the state to the local level and from the Party in general to the various state offices and parliamentary bodies. The danger here was the effect on a continuing process of pluralization both in the economic and political structure of the country and the political risks involved in this type of radical reform.[10] The Czechoslovak development prior to August, 1968, is a good example of this type of pluralization of the economy and of the danger of the spillover to the polity that threatened the leading role of the Party. It certainly left its impact on the Hungarian reform, which moved much more cautiously since the fateful August days in Czechoslovakia.

Greece is sometimes mentioned as another example of the implementation of regional policies, though the reader must be

reminded that the Greek national plan is simply "an indicative plan
on the macro level for the private sector of the economy," strongly
defending the principle that the "effective operation of the free market
is the best means of promoting the country's economic development."[11]
The plan specifically stresses that "the State will initiate business
ventures, through organizations operating on a strictly entrepreneurial
basis, only when the projects are of fundamental importance for the
industrial development of the country, and provided that private
initiative takes no interest in the matter."[12]

   The very broad planning directives in Greece emphasize decentralization of the decision-making processes to a very limited extent
only. Most of all, it is not in the tradition of Greece's economic and
political development to operate on various decision-making levels.
At the same time, the present conservative government also is
cautious about intervening too actively in the economic and social
structure, although Greek governments at various times have intervened
to various degrees, especially in agriculture, by channeling investment
funds into projects or even regions when it was felt that such measures
were in the national interest. But the over-all attitudes and policies
of Greek governments have, in themselves, acted as a constraint on
the decision-making structure. The highly centralized government
apparatus, with the Ministry of Coordination supervising the broad
aspects of economic development, has shown concern for the great
spatial imbalances of the country as indicated by figures for the
national product and per capita gross regional product in its regional
distribution.[13] Therefore, the government's concern was more with
the actual control of regional inequities and the establishment of a
broad regional development strategy than with the actual decentralization of decision-making processes.

   The 1968-72 plan, the first enacted by the new government, expressed the hope that, by establishing and naming specific planning
regions, an appropriate organization of regional administration and
hierarchy, an expansion of the role and jurisdiction of the newly
organized Regional Development Councils (in part brought about by
the reorganization of the former Regional Development Services),
and the preparation of feasibility studies, ultimately the structural
problem can be successfully attacked and ameliorated. The whole
regional plan is still based on largely voluntary cooperation, but for
the first time a detailed implementation of the needed steps has been
provided, and the weight of the government is often decisively felt.
It is hoped that the proposed association of Greece with the countries
of the Common Market could offer the needed incentives for accomplishing these goals. Thus, the Greek model for implementing its

regional policies depends on strengthening existing institutions, and the organization of new ones that will provide an opportunity for greater regional consideration in the light of the background, needs, and potentials of the country. Regional authorities under this model offer advice and prepare detailed technical studies, but the final decision-making authority lies with the national government. To obtain fuller cooperation in its policies and at the same time decentralize the cumbersome central machinery, seven administrative districts were recently proposed, with regional governors "vested with decisive executive power."*

In tampering with central planning, the Southeast European socialist countries are faced with a real dilemma of either completely abolishing it, as in Yugoslavia, or improving its operation by increasing decentralization of the decision-making structure. Two basic problems exist. Either little is gained in efficiency by decentralization, and

---

*The recently proposed administrative regions (regional districts) are similar to the earlier (1965-67) established planning regions, with the exception of northern Greece, which was broken down into central and western Macedonia, with a base in Thessaloniki, and eastern Macedonia and Thrace, with Kavala as the administrative capital. It should be pointed out also that as of this writing the newly established administrative regions are inoperative. They were recently declared void by the State Appelate Court in its decision of November 11, (Symvoulion Epikrateias).
The seven Planning regions are:

1. Athens, Attica, and the Aegean Islands; headquarters in Athens
2. Northern Greece, including Macedonia and Thrace; headquarters in Thessaloniki
3. Epirus and the western islands; headquarters at Ioánnina
4. Thessaly; headquarters at Lárisa
5. Peloponnesos, the western islands, the western part of central Greece; headquarters at Patras
6. Crete; headquarters at Iraklion
7. Central Greece; headquarters at Lámia.

See Economic News (Ministry of National Economy), XXXI (Athens, September, 1971), p. 3.

the regimes seeing no alternative are simply falling back to a centralized, authoritarian, repressive command economy, thus taking a short-
term, easy way out; or countries ultimately are being forced to abandon
central planning altogether, replacing it with market socialism, but
in this process risking political pluralization, thus ultimately weakening
the leading role of the Party, which might well put an end to the
totalitarian system. The Yugoslav model of market-type reform,
initiated in 1952, has served as a danger signal for many of the more-
orthodox Eastern European socialist leaders.

Changes in the method of planning and management in all five
countries are continuous, without a real and theoretically integrated
design, and are closely related to changes in social relations and
production potential, both on the macro- and micro-economic levels.
They include a wide range of developmental and behavioral problems
affecting every aspect of the societal spectrum, e.g., the organizational
structure of the economy, the use of economic instruments to influence
decisions at various levels of policy, the status of the enterprise, the
growing importance of external economic relations, and the whole
problem of regional differentiation. The choice and type of these
decisions for Romania and Bulgaria, as pointed out earlier, lies not
solely with these countries, but greatly depends on developments in
Moscow. Only small, independent Albania is to a certain extent in
its own house. Yugoslavia has made its decision, at least during the
lifetime of Marshal Tito, though external economics and internal
pressures may ultimately have a major influence.

Finally, the question is raised whether there exists perhaps
a middle ground for implementing meaningful regional policies. Inasmuch as it has been shown that no one type of policy can achieve a
satisfactory solution (complete market reform and regional priority
in decision-making certainly are no guarantee for competitive efficiency
and continuous economic growth), the slowly evolving decentralization
policies of Romania focused on a triple approach could very well be
the answer for a viable model for a number of socialist countries in
the immediate future and ultimately could serve as a new model for
taking account of regional pressures.* These policies now evolving
in Romania are based on the following: (a) sectoral and branch policies
on the macrolevel and, for key projects, on the microlevel set by the

---

*Hungary, too, is slowly evolving its own model, but the absence
of an ethnically diverse population puts the regional problem in an
entirely different perspective than in Romania or Yugoslavia.

central plan; (b) encouragement of greater regional and local initiatives by delegating increased authority to the newly organized territorial-administrative units of the country (People's Councils); and (e) at the same time transferring important microdecisions in the economic sphere to the newly organized "trusts," while also enlarging the role of individual enterprises, including their competitive positions. It is too early to judge the results of the slowly evolving initiative taken by the Romanian government, but these developments bear careful watching.*

Interest Groups

When it is considered that all operations of a modern national economy result from a constantly increasing multitude and complexity of decisions, it can readily be seen that the highly centralized system of decision-making used until recently by three of the four socialist countries of Southeast Europe has come under increasing attack from its own interest groups, the managerial elite, the industrial interests, the Party, and a variety of those with regional interests. To this must be added, in Yugoslavia, an increasingly effective parliamentary structure, trade-unions syndicate, the press, and the pronounced and often diverse multinational interests, with their dislike for a strong central government.[14] While the Yugoslav Party is no longer a monolithic hierarchy and while it has been badly split by multinational divisions and conservative-liberal battles over basic differences in economic policy, it still wields considerable power, and, according to a recent study by M. George Zaninovich, "fills the role of an integrating and modernizing elite in Yugoslav society."[15]

---

*In more than one way, Romania is perhaps an ideal country to serve as a model for the medium-size and perhaps even small countries. With its population of 21 million, with limited to good endowment of natural resources, with certain regional loyalties both among the Roman-speaking people and the two large minorities, the Hungarians and Germans, and with a rapidly changing economic structure, Romania does not have the great spatial imbalances of either Yugoslavia or Czechoslovakia, nor does not have the great ethnic-cleavages prevailing in Yugoslavia. It therefore avoids some of the strong and diverse pressures on the central government in following certain necessary sectoral and branch long-term priorities.

In addition, as Kosta Mihailović in a recent study has pointed out, regional leaders serve two masters, and this is even true in Yugoslavia.[16] They must promote regional interests, but they also must take into account national interests, inasmuch as their behavior will make advancement in the Party hierarchy possible. The danger in such a position is a real one. If Party leaders become known—and this holds true for all others in a position of leadership (directors of enterprises and the various specialized bank officials of the Investment Bank and Agricultural Bank, for example)—as localists and particularists, their advancement in the national hierarchy and their dream of moving to the national capital can be seriously affected. It also should be pointed out that the behavior of the leadership in Yugoslavia greatly differs from that in the other socialist countries. Their regional interests very often have priority over national interests. Their behavior also differs in developed and underdeveloped regions. It depends on more personal relationships and impact on national decision-makers in underdeveloped regions; in the developed regions it is less personal, more indirect, and institutionalized. The individual Party members in the Yugoslav society, with its many centrifugal forces and pronounced and often contradictory regional interests, are thought of as a stabilizing force with an inherent feeling of obligation to the Yugoslav system,[17] though the developments in Croatia and Kosovo during the constitutional debates in 1971 even question this.

Yugoslavia is not only an excellent example of a country with an articulated regional consciousness permeating all levels of the society, but it is the only country in Southeast Europe facing up to these problems. In Yugoslavia especially, awareness of this regional consciousness and concern with regional interests and reactions influence every economic and political decision of the national leadership and its institutions. In a society with deep regional-ethnic cleavages and their resulting strong regional interests, often contrary to national interests, it is of major importance to remove obvious contradictions in these relationships. Yugoslavia is a long way from its desired goal, though its ultimate success may very well decide the stability and viability, perhaps even the very existence, of the Yugoslav state. The problems faced by the behavior of different and often-clashing regional forces are unique, inasmuch as only a few countries in the world have such deep regional-ethnic cleavages as in Yugoslavia.*

---

*One of the most perceptive analyses about Yugoslavia's problems has recently been published by the well-known Yugoslav

The similarity of the interest groups, their behavior, and often the perception of their leaders, especially as they refer to the regional problems in all socialist countries, can be explained by the type of economic problems faced and the advances in economic development made since the war. Differences in Greece are largely due to its polity and to some extent to the differences in its economic system. In countries with a highly centralized decision-making structure, regional interests are either handled by the central authorities, of which Albania and Bulgaria are good examples, or by carefully selected regional institutions taking the brunt of regional pressures (Romania), or by instituting regional advisory bodies, mostly problem-oriented study groups (Greece). Thus, countries with a centralized decision-making structure determine interregional relations at the highest decision-making body and thereby control and reduce active participation of regional forces. At the same time, a unilateral expression of regional problems is generally considered "anti-Party and anti-State." The behavior of regional leaders in these societies is judged by their performance and their loyalty to the national Party and leadership. Non-party individuals, again, have only a very minor role to play in the various decision-making processes. The result is usually a minor or secondary role for regions in the decision-making processes. And while these remarks relate largely to their role in the polity, in the field of economic development the transfer of a variety of decisions from central to local-regional authorities has proceeded with increasing speed, though, as the example of Romania shows, key decisions are not made by the enterprises themselves, but rather by the coordinating bodies, the previously mentioned Industrial Centrals.

At the present time, and with the scientific data available for analyzing behavioral processes and values, a thorough analysis of the behavior patterns of political leaders in socialist societies, especially with regard to their emphasis on interregional relations, is not possible. This is especially true for a spatial analysis of political behavior, inasmuch as insufficiently tested variables of individual social behavior either are not at all or only insufficiently available; this also holds true for Greece. It must be stressed, however, that an analysis of the role of the League of Communists and, to a lesser extent, of other Communist parties in influencing

---

economist Branko Horvat. His paper appeared first in Gledišta (Nos. 5-6, 1971) and was translated "Nationalismus und Nation," Wissenschaftlicher Dienst Südosteuropa, 8/9 (August-September, 1971), pp. 136-146.

changes in the political and social system is possible, in part due to the large amount of documentary material available, though on a more traditional basis. The behavior and attitudes of the various interest groups discussed provided the governments of the area with a difficult dilemma regarding the efficiency and proprieties of decision-making, the degree of decentralization conducive to efficient operation of the economy, the influence of regional forces, and the way in which decisions are conceived and implemented.[18]

Regional Consciousness

Before analyzing the decision-making structure and organs within their institutional context, a word must be said about the broad problem of regional differentiation and the impact of regional consciousness on the development strategy of the countries of Southeast Europe. Here, one is really considering two not necessarily similar regional problems. Most countries in the area have a serious problem of regional disparities, in part brought about by historical and political circumstances, in part by physical deficiencies in natural endowment. Perhaps with the exception of small Albania and, to a lesser extent, Bulgaria, these perennial problems, which divide countries into developed and underdeveloped regions, are here to stay for some time. The second type of regional problem is closely connected with linguistic and ethnic factors that create regional ethnic cleavages expressed in regional consciousness and loyalties. This is one of the most difficult problems to solve and is closely related to the ultimate viability and survival of the state. (Figure 6 and Table 4 show the ethnic breakdown in Yugoslavia).

Perhaps another type of problem exists, though it may very well be only a stage in the larger picture. At the present time, it is most strongly developed in Bulgaria, but it is also found in Greece. It is not specifically focused on the problems of national vs. regional development. This problem recognizes the general backwardness of most parts of the Bulgarian space economy, in its initial stage of economic development. Perhaps certain regions are less endowed by nature and therefore receive less attention, even encouraging

----

*Even among western scholars, the large-scale decentralization in Yugoslavia is viewed with concern when taking into account the most efficient way of decision-making for the economic and political viability of the Yugoslav state.

TABLE 4

Yugoslavia: Size and Growth of Ethnic Groups, 1953-71[a]
(in thousands)

Ethnic Group	1953	1961	1971	1961-71 Increase	Average Increase (percent) 1953-61	Average Increase (percent) 1961-71	Distribution (percent) 1961	Distribution (percent) 1971
Serbian	7,066	7,806	8,432	626	10.7	7.7	42.09	40.52
Croatian	3,976	4,294	4,803	509	11.7	10.9	23.15	23.09
Slovenian	1,487	1,589	1,718	129	9.2	7.7	8.57	8.26
Macedonian	893	1,046	1,203	157	18.7	13.9	5.64	5.79
Montenegrin	466	514	608	94	21.3	16.9	2.78	2.93
Moslem		973	1,219	246	26.9	22.4	5.25	5.86
Yugoslav		317	409	92	-	25.1	1.70	1.96
Albanian[b]	754	915	1,243	328	26.2	30.5	4.93	5.98
Hungarian	202	504	515	11	2.8	2.0	2.72	2.47
Turk	260	183	222	39	22.3	19.2	0.99	1.06
Slovak	85	86	90	4	7.1	4.0	0.47	0.43
Romanian	60	61	60	- 1	- 1.4	- 1.1	0.32	0.29
Bulgarian	62	63	63	0	1.5	0	0.33	0.30
Ruthenian	37	39	41	2	8.3	6.3	0.20	0.19
Italian	36	26	—	—	-30.0	—	—	—
Gypsy	85	32	48	16	18.8	40.2	0.17	0.22
Other			132	4	1.9	1.6	0.69	0.63
Total	16,937	18,549	20,806	2,257	16.1	11.4	100	100

[a]Attention should be directed to two specific developments: the rapid rise of the Albanian population—26.2 in 1953-61 and 30.5 in 1961-71—in comparison to the major population groups, the Serbians and Croatians; and the 25-percent increase in the population indicating "Yugoslav" as a nationality.
[b]The name "Albanian" appears first in the 1971 census. Earlier censuses listed the people as "Šiptari (Shiptars)."

Sources: Popis stanovnštva 1953, 1961 and preliminary figures for 1971; Statstički bilten, Godine i Demograsfka statistika za godine 1953-1971, as printed in Sociologija, II (1971), pp. 278, 282.

FIGURE 6

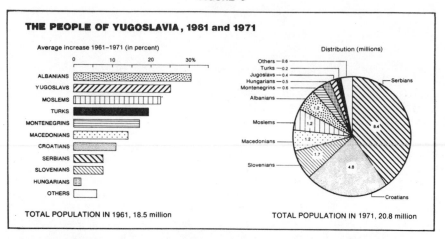

THE PEOPLE OF YUGOSLAVIA, 1961 and 1971

Average increase 1961–1971 (in percent)

Distribution (millions)

TOTAL POPULATION IN 1961, 18.5 million

TOTAL POPULATION IN 1971, 20.8 million

large-scale migration (for example, in many of the mountainous parts of Bulgaria and Greece) from areas without a real economic potential. In a relatively small country such as Bulgaria, with its highly centralized planning apparatus, the absence of a strong regional consciousness and a rapidly increasing dispersion of a variety of economic activities create regional problems of a different character. Regional pressures are presented by a variety of largely economic interest groups pressuring for greater decentralization and local initiatives in the decision-making processes. This type of development is obviously present in all countries, socialist and nonsocialist. On the other hand, it is very possible that, as time goes by, local interest groups may very well develop regional loyalties and demand ever-increasing participation in the various economic and ultimately political decision-making processes. At least for the time being, the transfer of decision-making to regional and local authorities is a minor issue, though much has been written and said about encouraging local initiatives. Central planners thus far have been reluctant, more so than in any other country of Southeast Europe, to transfer any meaningful authority to lower-level administrative bodies or enterprises.

It is, after all, a fact of life so well brought out in a study by Janusz Ziólowski for the United Nations, that regional consciousness or regional sentiments, sometimes referred to as "regionalism," exist in most parts of the world and do not diminish in developed countries.[19] It can be expressed, as Ziólowski rightly noted, in a social and political protest against the extreme dominance of some privileged regions of the country or even against certain decisions by centralized government bodies. Such an expression can be a state

of mind, a regional chauvinism, and, in extreme cases, separatism
and secession.[20] The problems of regional differentiations in the
Southeast European countries have most frequently been associated
with extreme centralization, but at times criticism also has been
leveled at the parochialism of local communities and the value system
of a specific society. There really is no simple answer to this complicated and usually highly emotional problem. The important thing
is awareness of the problem by political leaders and a constant compromise or reconciliation (of particular importance when there exists
a strong regional consciousness) between centralized initiative and
control and local autonomy. But let it be made clear, the author
here refers to the destructive aspects of regionalism, not to those
absolutely needed in modern societies (multinational or not), such
as the fostering of indigenous regional cultures, regional initiatives
in economic and polity developments, and so on.

The problem of these regional differentiations in the individual
countries of the area—for a time following World War II they were
simply ignored—has even become more pronounced and serious due
to the greater transmission of ideas, better and faster communications,
travel and education, and the general spatial mobility within and
between countries. As has been pointed out by a number of writers
during the last few years, and as can easily be observed by the
searching traveler, in spite of the greatly increased spatial mobility
of the people of the area, or because of it, people still wish to "belong."
The home environment is all-inclusive. The movement into anything
new cannot fully replace the "home system." Even when living in
the impersonal environment of a large city or at far-distant places,
people like to preserve their ties with their place of birth, with the
remaining members of their family, or simply retain with a certain
memory, and this, in turn, encourages a feeling of regional consciousness and regional sentiment. Every government in Southeast Europe
must face the problem of increased regional awareness for a variety
of reasons (political, economic, or simply a certain vague perception).
It is precisely for this reason that movements toward decentralization
of important governmental functions and emphasis on regional participation and initiatives have a stronger foundation than may generally
be assumed.

INSTITUTIONAL CONTEXT

The interrelationship between regional and national interests,
the area in which a variety of interest groups—regionally and structurally based—are most clearly visible, is in the institutional context.

From the discussions thus far, it has become clear that increasing regional and local pressures by a variety of interest groups has succeeded in decentralizing numerous functions of the central-planning apparatus, though this was accomplished, with the exception of Yugoslavia, without or with only slight basic changes in the prevailing system. In part, these pressures are the result of a more-complex and technologically progressing economy in its "intensive stage of development," demanding flexibility in the adaptation to rapidly changing conditions. In part, they are the result of the forces of nationalism prevailing in every one of the countries of Southeast Europe.[21] These changes have increased somewhat the authority of local bodies, People's Councils, and communes, and certain decision-making powers have been delegated to them. While actual policies differ greatly among the socialist countries of Southeast Europe, the broad aims of decentralizing important decision-making functions to permit greater participation by regional and local bodies are generally accepted. It is also generally agreed that regions cannot have independent goals contrary to those of the national interest, but at the same time it is acknowledged that every type of economic and social policy of a state has both national and regional implications. The more advanced and refined an economy becomes, the more crucial become the links between various levels of central authority and the initiative of local groups.

The emphasis on more fully integrated regional policies has increased in every one of the five countries, regardless of their ideology, though economic and political developments to a great extent have determined the basic policies applied and have influenced the type of conceptual approach. In the case of Yugoslavia, officially at least, it is stated that its policy "is an attempt to implement the old Marxian concept of the withering away of the state and its replacement by the self-governing local community."[22] The absence of a model assisting in the establishment of regional policies in decision-making is one of the reasons that changes in the decision-making machinery present such a painful and difficult experiment for some of the more orthodox socialist leaders in the area, specifically in Bulgaria. On the other hand, the type of institutional instruments available and the measures used to implement regional policies may very well determine for some time to come the relationship established between the various regions and interest groups in the countries of Southeast Europe. Moreover, it is extremely difficult and at times nearly impossible to isolate measures specifically affecting regional policies. This is especially the case in sectoral activities, which nearly always have both a national and regional impact, e.g., heavy industry and shipbuilding. Massive, centrally planned programs also give priority to the development of underdeveloped regions; to the development of new areas (e.g., the industrial zone of Thessaloniki in northern Greece and Galati in Romania or those that influence development of the infrastructure, such as the Bar to Belgrade railroad); to education, especially vocational training; to manpower mobility; and to social welfare, which has both a national and regional impact.

In Yugoslavia, as stated earlier, central-planning decisions in effect do not exist, and the only remaining centralized activities are certain key projects (which are being phased out) and the Fund for the Development of Underdeveloped Regions, which, due to its size and long-term aim, influences a variety of regional policies (see the discussions p. 218. The federal government allocates 1.85 percent of the national income in the socialized sector to the underdeveloped regions. These funds are channelled through banks to the regions, mostly in the form of soft loans. While the republican governments act as channels for the transfer of money from the federal government, they have the major say in how these funds are used, even though most of the money is simply transferred to the communes. The Fund has several functions: it compensates underdeveloped regions for their unfavorable trade position, assists in financing investments proposed by the underdeveloped regions, and grants subsidies out of the federal budget for social expenditures, called in Yugoslavia "expenditures on collective consumption." These grants from the federal treasury amounted to 9.2 percent of the total federal budget in 1971, with Bosnia and Herzegovina receiving 40 percent of these funds, Kosovo 30 percent, Macedonia 19 percent, and Montenegro 11 percent.

Emphasis on regional development policies is relatively new for the countries of Southeast Europe, and the measures applied for their implementation vary greatly, though the locus for making decisions and implementing such policies in its broad sense is remarkably similar, inasmuch as all five countries have some type of central-planning organs, though with greatly differing functions. A fully coordinated sectoral and regional policy, with the close coordination of a variety of policies initiated at various levels, really does not exist, though recent developments in Yugoslavia come close.[23] If planning is done on several levels, the central-planning body has the task of coordinating the work of the many organizations involved and preparing a cohesive draft plan in terms of regional and/or sectoral and national objectives. The locus of decision-making in countries where there is a centralized planning apparatus has in general sharply focused decision points, but the decisions themselves, contrary to many reports, are the result of numerous individual and group interests representing various activities in the decision-making scale. The final decision rests with the central political authorities.[24]

The general scope of regional development policies indicates certain related processes tied to a variety of production characteristics, e.g., increased complexity and diversification of the distribution and consumption of the type of production. This also depends on the way government functions and services organized and related to the economy. The number of departments, agencies, and ministries engaged in some planning functions in the countries of Southeast Europe is large, and it is for this reason that the central-planning machinery, with its coordinating functions, comprises a huge bureaucratic apparatus. In addition, all countries have several specialized financial institutions funding sectoral and/or regional programs. The precise point of decision and the machinery for transmitting strategically important planning decisions to various local activities is an important question inasmuch as other decisions on various levels usually depend on these decisions, even though the number of decisions not planned is far greater than those that are. In part, it is for this reason that the trend in socialist planning has been toward reducing the number of plan indicators of the central plan, while at the same time increasing the decision-making power of the lower planning levels and enterprises. Yugoslavia originally initiated some of these changes and has become in some aspects a model for similar experiments among both socialist and nonsocialist countries.

Territorial-Administrative Changes

By restructuring various territorial-administrative units and by shifting certain decision-making functions to different levels, the foundation was laid for transfer of important decision-making functions from central to regional authorities. This restructuring facilitated measures of decentralization and thus contributed to greater regional participation, though, with the exception of Yugoslavia, no real regional machinery was available. Local participation and government was largely advisory in nature.

The type of administration prevailing has always played a significant role in determining spatial patterns. The spacial administrative patterns that prevailed in the countries of Southeast Europe at the end of World War II generally were inherited from the past. Those in the socialist countries were quickly reorganized and "modeled on the forms of the highly centralized public administration and economic management prevailing in the U.S.S.R."[25] It soon became apparent

that the multitude of administrative units created in the early postwar
years in these relatively small countries, largely to ensure centralized
Party control, soon showed their obvious disadvantages by being too
limited and numerous for efficient planning and for seriously effecting
obvious economic linkages between long-established as well as new
industrial plants. As the economies assumed greater sophistication,
industrialization spread, a greatly improved modern network of
communications was established, unnecessary duplications became
obvious, and thus a number of territorial-administrative adjustments
became necessary. The numerous postwar changes in administrative
regions are detailed in an article by Thomas Poulsen, who aptly
observed that they do not fit into as common a pattern as was the case
in the early postwar years."26 Figures 7-11 show the present major
administrative boundaries for the countries of Southeast Europe.

In Yugoslavia, the territorial-administrative changes affected
a number of districts (srezovi or kotari) and communes (opshtinas
or opcine), which were drastically reduced or, in the case of the districts, completely abolished by 1968. Only the traditional republican
boundaries remained unchanged (they included the autonomous provinces of Vojvodina and Kosovo). In the case of Romania, the 28 provinces
(regiunes) established in 1950 were reduced to 18 in 1952 and 16 in
1956 and were replaced by 39 provinces (judetete) in 1968. The 177
districts and more than 4,000 communes (communas) established in
1950 were reorganized in 1968 and the districts were completely
eliminated.27 With the territorial-administrative reorganization
into 39 provinces, People's Councils received specific decision-making
authority of "all local activity of the state in the economic, sociological and administrative fields, as well as in construction and the defense
of socialist property."28 Bulgaria organized 14 provinces (okrugi)
in 1949, which were reduced to 12 in 1951. In 1959, 27 provinces
subdivided into 867 districts (obschinas) replaced the earlier system.
Since that time, the number of districts has declined. Albania retained
its territorial-administrative organization throughout the postwar
period, with its 26 districts (rhethi).

It is obvious from the many territorial-administrative changes
in the socialist societies of Southeast Europe that they made difficult
meaningful comparative assessments of both economic and demographic
changes, inasmuch as these units formed the basis for statistical
units. Only in Greece and in Yugoslavia is such a comparison possible,
on the nomos and republican level. The impact of these territorial-
administrative changes is far-reaching. Many governmental services
were located in these administrative centers and in turn have exerted
a considerable "pull" on other activities. As a result, they became

FIGURE 7

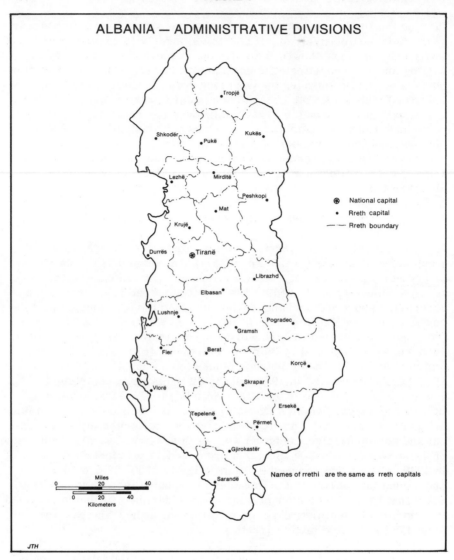

ALBANIA — ADMINISTRATIVE DIVISIONS

Tropjë

Shkodër
Pukë
Kukës

Lezhë
Mirditë

Peshkopi

Mat

Krujë

Durrës
⊗ Tiranë

Librazhd

Elbasan

Lushnje

Pogradec

Gramsh

Fier
Berat

Korçë

Vlorë
Skrapar

Ersekë

Tepelenë
Përmet

Gjirokastër

Sarandë

⊗ National capital
• Rreth capital
—·— Rreth boundary

Names of rrethi are the same as rreth capitals

Miles
0   20   40

0   20   40
Kilometers

JTH

176

FIGURE 8

BULGARIA — ADMINISTRATIVE DIVISIONS

headquarters of new industrial establishments and thus influenced the distribution pattern of economic growth. All the province and district capitals showed a rapid increase in the rate of annual population growth. Poulsen and others have pointed out that "the nodality was further strengthened by the selective improvement or establishment of completely new transportation facilities focused upon the newly named centers."[29] Therefore, changes in provincial and district boundaries very often meant a corresponding change in and often loss of administrative and economic activities and services.

Arguments, especially in Bulgaria, for unity of the functions of administrative and economic regions were in many ways a continuation of the discussions on regionalization that filled so many pages of Soviet and certain Eastern European journals. The economic region so derived "is a result of historical processes, born and changing in time, extending from past into future, and its development similarly to the whole socio-economic progress is due to quantitative and qualitative growth of productive forces."[30] But in spite of being neglected, the economic regions have an important administrative-economic purpose.[31] Planners in Bulgaria, for example, have been concerned

**FIGURE 9**

GREECE — ADMINISTRATIVE DIVISIONS

1. Evros	14. Kozani	27. Kefallinia	40. Arkadhia
2. Rodhopi	15. Kastoria	28. Zakinthos	41. Argolis
3. Xanthi	16. Grevena	29. Aitolia kai	42. Messinia
4. Drama	17. Ioannina	Akarnania	43. Lakonia
5. Kavala	18. Thesprotia	30. Evritania	44. Khania
6. Serrai	19. Preveza	31. Fthiotis	45. Rethimni
7. Kilkis	20. Arta	32. Fokis	46. Iraklion
8. Thessaloniki	21. Trikala	33. Voiotia	47. Lasithi
9. Khalkidhiki	22. Larisa	34. Evvoia	48. Lesvos
10. Pella	23. Kardhitsa	35. Attiki	49. Khios
11. Imathia	24. Magnisia	36. Piraievs (Piraeus)	50. Samos
12. Pieria	25. Kerkira	37. Akhaia	51. Kikladhes
13. Florina	26. Levkas	38. Korinthia	52. Dhodhekanisos
		39. Ilia	(Dodecanese)

FIGURE 10

ROMANIA — ADMINISTRATIVE DIVISIONS

for some time with the establishment of proper economic territorial units, the so-called administrative economic regions, as functional, economic regions, to serve as regional groupings for functionally and spatially integrated economic activities following the Soviet example (territorial-production complexes), which reflect the economic and political aims of the system. Ideally, as Tormond Hermansen brought out, administrative areas should be so organized to make possible their most efficient use, both as a framework for spatial planning and for the efficient coordination of decisions.* But with

_____

*Tormond Hermansen proposed two types of changes in the system of political-administrative decision-making that will improve developmental spatial planning. "First, administrative areas should be rearranged so as to coincide with the functional areas of the spatial organization. Secondly, the decision-making system within the administrative areas should be reorganized so that functionally and spatially interrelated decisions are efficiently coordinated." United Nations Research Institute for Social Development, Spatial Organization and Economic Development - The Scope and Task of Spatial Planning, UNRISD/69/C.68, GE 6923863 (Geneva: [Program IV: Regional Development], July, 1969), p. 83.

FIGURE 11

few exceptions, the administrative regions of the socialist countries were not thought of as planning regions, though some became involved in "centrally coordinated areal programmes of economic and social investment developed in conjunction with financial planning, but also operational plans for agriculture, retailing, local industry, education, health and welfare elaborated by local people's councils."[32]

This rigidity in the purposes of the territorial-administrative structure is more surprising inasmuch as they form a decided handicap to an effective system of spatial interaction and development. With the future clearly emphasizing increased transfer of important deci-sion-making functions to many different levels on the hierarchial ladder—for example, regions, districts, communes, or individual enterprises—the present regional uniformity often adversely affects the creation of economics of scale. Ultimately, this is bound to be replaced by administrative units offering greater flexibility and closer integration with the economic and social requirements of the country. Yugoslavia already offers a good example, with opčine councils faced with new and difficult decisions having to rely largely on their own funds rather than on federal allocations for investments of productive and nonproductive nature. Increased emphasis on cooperation, special-ization, and sharing of facilities with each other, often accompanied by the reestablishment of traditional patterns of spatial organization, are the results of the political and economic decentralization of the 1950s and 1960s. This reestablishment of traditional patterns now has a more-adequate economic base, with the addition of numerous industrial plants, new transportation facilities, skilled labor pools, and so on. These changes will have a lasting effect on the geography of these countries, including the effectiveness of administration.[33]

The Central Plan and Regional Planning

Much recent literature discussing the problems of regional planning has been devoted to the relationship of national to regional planning, the evolving function of the central plan in Soviet-type economic systems related to the changing spatial behavior in planned economies. The real problem here is that central plans generally are concerned with the development of sectors and branches, and their disaggregation into regional components is usually disregarded. On the other hand, effective spatial planning must take into account regional objectives and conditions. Also, the aggregation of regional plans, based on prior investigation of regional needs, with special attention given to regional conditions such as developed, underdeveloped, or lagging, is completely lacking in the spatial planning of the countries of Southeast Europe. The designation of regions as developed and underdeveloped, as is the case, for example, in Yugoslavia and to a lesser degree in Romania and Bulgaria, and the special attention shown them by the state has had little impact on a globally integrated regional planning policy.

The countries of Southeast Europe show significant differences in their approach to regional planning, and this is reflected in the role of the central plan, of institutional measures, and of the performance of the market mechanism. Two approaches or concepts are here dominate.[34] In one concept, the central plan still retains its leading role as a directive instrument in the development of the economy, which obligates all economic organizations, but which, due to the growing intricacy of the economy, pared down the number of plan indicators that are transferred to the economic units. Either at the same time or in addition thereto, use is made of economic instruments for the purpose of inducing the successful completion of the planned targets. In another concept, the central plan serves as a guideline for the central authorities, and, when implemented, it regulates the market mechanism that develops when the economic units operate independently in accordance with fundamental economic rationality. In this case, the central-planning organ's main task is to regulate the instruments of the economic policy that will encourage economic units to direct their activity toward central-plan objectives. Obviously, here central planning must take into account the market environment, but it does have a responsibility and an opportunity to influence its workings by introducing structural changes in economic and social development.

The rapidly changing economy, especially of Romania and, to a lesser degree, Bulgaria, necessitated not only adjustments in planning objectives, but certain experimentation, including retrenchments (in Bulgaria), which are reflected in the type and emphasis of directives and economic instruments used and in the changing relations between the various units of operation and the central plan. Both the cause and effect (increased efficiency and rationality in economic management) of the economic reforms of the late 1960s are similar in the socialist countries of Romania, Bulgaria, and even Albania. New planning and management methods, by increasing the flexibility of planning methods and instruments, should contribute to improving the workings of the socialist economies.

Governments use a combination of regional policy measures, such as financing infrastructure and development projects, for improving occupational mobility by increasing opportunities for vocational training, welfare, housing, and education, by a variety of stimuli for industrial expansion, by direct budgetary assistance to underdeveloped regions, by special key projects, and by a number of tertiary activities (e.g., tourism). The types of measures used for the implementation of regional policies and their techniques are much influenced by the planning model in use, details of which were cited in earlier discussions.

Planning instruments are generally divided into two main groups— administrative and economic[35]—with administrative instruments based on the use of power by the authorities (pressures by the Party) and economic instruments largely those stimulating or restricting activities of enterprises and material interests of the individual. In Soviet-type planning, various administrative instruments are used, such as tax policies, fixing of prices and wages, budgets, subsidies and aid, various credit policies, public recognition in the form of awards, bonuses, and punishment if plans are not fulfilled. Yugoslavia replaced administrative with economic instruments in the early part of the 1950s. Greece has generally used economic instruments only. To encourage greater individual initiative and productivity, Romania, Bulgaria, and lately Albania have also made use, to varying degrees, of economic instruments, especially those associated with creating both personal and market stimulation. In Yugoslavia, the enterprises assumed increased responsibilities, selling their products on the free market, with workers' management acting autonomously, taking the place of bureaucratic decisions. Romania has taken initial steps in increasing the autonomy of its enterprises by increasing their decision-making authority, especially in the field of production and marketing. Generally, it can be said that in the more centrally planned economies the market mechanism plays a secondary role, though certain elements of the market are now appearing in the planning apparatus. The major features of this evolution are decentralization, increased independence of enterprises, and initiative in areas of the producers' self-interest, all pointing toward a shift of major functions, or at least a decrease in the influence of central planning, and the transfer of certain decision-making functions to local bodies. But this does not imply a policy of integrated regional development—far from it.

Financing Regional Development

The major institutional measures implementing regional and local development are in the field of finance and location planning, including the previously mentioned organizational structure

(associations and enterprises) and locational (especially industrial)
policies. The analysis will of necessity be brief and will serve simply
as background for later discussions of the regional development
strategy.

The essential conditions for financing economic and social
developments lie in the "mobility of the accumulated resources," of
considerable importance in investment allocations. The final decisions
determining territorial allocation of investments, with the exception
of Yugoslavia and Greece, are in the hands of the central authorities,
though they are based on a series of compromises, which are reflected
in the distribution of available resources.

The problem of sectoral vs. regional investment decisions will
be unresolved as long as central budgetary resources are committed
without integrated planning policies, thus effecting the unbalanced
growth of regions. In Yugoslavia, the problem is a completely different
one, for accumulated resources are decentralized, and enterprises
are generally independent in matters of investment decision.[36] The
investment resources, therefore, are for the most part attached to
branches and regions, with banks playing a vital role in their distribution through the control of credits. With investment funds from government sources much reduced during the last few years (see Table 2).
Because of the general decentralization and the emphasis on market
forces, the mobility of accumulated resources for a time had become
a very serious question. This left a special impact on the underdeveloped region. To imporve the territorial mobility of capital accumu-
lations a solution was found, with the establishment of the previously
mentioned Fund, with income contributed by all the republics, the
purpose of which was to finance economic development of underdeveloped republics and regions and thus to provide capital on a more
competitive basis. Prices of raw materials were also permitted to
increase, but inasmuch as prices of manufactured goods remained
uncontrolled and rose more quickly, the situation for the underdeveloped
regions on balance did not improve.

Also the expected transfer of capital from developed to underdeveloped regions unfortunately did not materialize; in part because
of the lack of surplus capital in the developed parts of Yugoslavia,
the absence of economic motivation, and the domination of the capital
market by enterprises that acquired the financial means to control
investment decisions, though banks and local communes still played
an important role. Also, republics in order to assist their own underdeveloped communes, were forced to change priority in the distribution
of budgetary resources. Decisions for financial allocations to regions

were made by central authorities. Often, they were marred by regional
and interregional conflicts. This was partially due to the lack of
coordination of republican and national plans. In Yugoslavia, certain
key investments are made directly by the central authorities, using
central budgetary allocations, thus by-passing the regions, but they
have been much reduced and are generally older commitments.

In Romania, investments also are slowly being decentralized,
though the central plan still has a major responsibility for establishing
both the volume and the structure of distribution. Related experiments
in Bulgaria were soon thereafter reversed. But a trend had begun to
restrict this responsibility to key investment projects, setting financial
limits for less-important investments are transferring responsibility
to lower planning levels (enterprises, trusts, or associations) or to
banks. By establishing planning authorities on lower and intermediate
levels (often an organizational unit), these authorities also had to
assume full financial responsibility for planning results on the local
level and for the weaker associated enterprises. In addition, alterations
in planning methods, usually during the last few years, have resulted
in the increased financial responsibility of lower-level economic
branches. This resulted first in a shift of authority—in the case of
Romania, to industrial ministries and later to administrative bodies
under the ministries—and finally these bodies were transformed
into associations, directorates, or trusts with full financial responsibility for the associated enterprises, including their profits. This
was closely related to giving the enterprises greater rights and responsibilities in production and marketing. In both Romania and to a
lesser extent Bulgaria, enterprises now obtain small development
funds from their own resources, which gives management a somewhat
freer hand in extending their services. Financing from enterprise
development funds also extends to social and cultural activity.

Increased authority in decision-making at the regional and
enterprise level naturally has raised questions concerning the authority
of state-appointed directors, a question closely connected with the
position of the director between the central authority, the associations,
and the enterprise and its work force. Questions at the present time
are settled individually as they arise, but the problem is a serious
one. Closely connected with enterprise initiative is the slow removal
of administrative decision instruments and their replacement with
economic instruments.[37] In Romania, as a result of shifts in the
decision-making authority, the method of disbursing financial assets
for investment from the central budget to regional territorial authorities (both political and economic) is now under review, including the
entire tax system.

The problem is different in Greece. Budgetary allocations assume responsibility for the financing of key projects such as irrigation, improvements in the infrastructure, and projects not handled by private initiative but deemed of importance for the country's over-all economic objectives. A series of specialized banks, e.g., the Agricultural Bank and the Industrial Development Bank, are the agencies through which financing is accomplished. Certain projects are jointly financed by governmental allocations and private interests.

Locational Decisions

It has often been stated that "the decision of where to locate a new project is as important as the decision to invest in it."[38] The locational factor becomes even more important because of an articulated regional policy. This is not only because of the existence of various regional forces, often contradictory and fighting for influence in the central decision-making organs (of particular importance in a multinational society in which some projects have important local or regional impact), but also because of certain locational factors. Even the lack of a specific regional policy will give certain places an advantage in terms of preferential conditions for the location of projects by making investment cheaper due to its advantages in terms of infrastructure, availability of labor, education, and other factors. If, in addition, an active regional policy exists, the careful study of those factors contributing to a maximization in locational policies, ultimately expressed in the planned allocation of investment funds, will be essential for a successful regional policy, especially in countries with scarce capital and in their early or transitional stage of economic development. It has been pointed out, therefore, that a combination of sectoral allocations and regional priorities, with a close coordination of both policies, would ideally contribute to a policy of balanced regional growth. (See Figure 4.)

Every country in Southeast Europe recognized the importance of industrial-location policies, though these policies vary greatly from country to country. The importance of industrial-location decisions is of more basic significance to individual regions than any other issue, in part because of the greater strategic significance of heavy industry and its impact on a variety of key developmental factors.[39] Locational policies can be simple encouragement to move to certain areas, based on locational factors or on factors of local preferential conditions in terms of local, regional, or government inducements in the form of subsidies or other fiscal concessions (this is very common in Greece). In this way, manufacturing industries

or other projects receive inducements to move to areas of unemployment or to regions of potential and actual migration. Greece has both
a policy of government inducements and outright laws and, in taking
advantage of such policies, industry must then follow established
policies.

Socialist countries consider industrial-location decisions as an
integral part of Party and state policy. They follow either a policy
of dispersal, by which every region should receive its fair share (see
the discussions on Bulgaria in Chapter 8) or a policy, followed in the
1950s in Yugoslavia and to a lesser extent in Romania, of concentrating
on existing growth centers at or near advantageous locations of natural
resources or at development poles and axes that for various reasons
have a potential of ultimately expanding.[40] Criteria for locational
decisions changed following the introduction of the principal of "profit
or rentability"[41] and the decentralization of important decision-making
functions in Yugoslavia in 1954 and in the other socialist countries
during the late 1950s. Rentability now is the key criteria and serves
as an important success indicator for the allocation of investments.
The distortion of the pricing system in countries Romania, Bulgaria,
and Albania makes it difficult to calculate rentability objectively,
but changes here are also under consideration. The distorted pricing
policies also have an impact on location decision-makers, inasmuch
as it is difficult for this reason to calculate precise average costs
and profits.[42]

Locational decisions, in reality, emerge from a complex series
of decisions brought about by both conflicting and complementary
economic, social, and political pressures and behavior. Industrial-
location decisions in the countries of Eastern Europe "respond to
the system as it is, without entering into its rationale or logistics."[43]
Hamilton, citing the example of Yugoslavia, comes to the conclusion, however, that "the market factor explains the locale of industry in or near major metropolitan and industrial centres and in
transport nodes throughout the region" in Yugoslavia.[44] Conflicts
between vested regional interests exist in every country, but information is more plentiful and easier to obtain in Yugoslavia. The professional planning commissions in the various countries serve as important links between local pressure groups and the top decision-makers.
This includes all types of location decisions, for individual projects
and for branches, agriculture, industry, and tertiary activities.
Ideally, a spatial approach that takes into account the rate and type
of contribution that each region can make toward national progress
should be followed, but regional interests, even individual ones, very
often are subordinated to national needs. In Yugoslavia, the results

of these conflicts very often are resolved by moving into and expanding earlier industrial areas and bringing about lower short-term production costs, as opposed to expanding into underdeveloped areas where long-term production and social costs would be lower.[45]

No socialist country has made really optimal location decisions. The reasons are many; Hamilton's analysis of them is summarized here.[46] First, there exists basically an information gap, in part based on insufficient awareness of problems. Information relating to the coordination of important linked activities at local and regional levels usually is unavailable. The arbitrary setting of prices and hence costs and profits remains. Second, basic information is of poor quality, and the innovation of efficient processing of data by computers and linear programs in determining optimal planning solutions often is considered a threat to the authority and creditability of Party officials. Third, planning agencies lack the ability to study objectively competing projects or simply are insufficiently trained or even unwilling to figure project costs, profitability, or tenability. Fourth, planners often are rational only in some social and political issues,[47] and their ideological conviction influences the sequential attention given to the principles of location and to other important planning objectives (e.g., defense and assistance given to specific regions). In deciding on alternatives, the planner's rationality depends upon his awareness of the relevant spatial activity sphere: i.e., certain specific locations that should be studied for the purpose of evaluating the availability of relevant information in order to compare their advantages and disadvantages to actual plant-location choices. The planner's knowledge and personal preference for the environment plays a vital role, as evidence indicates, especially in Yugoslavia (see discussions earlier in this chapter). Last, adaptive location decisions that are made in response to a careful analysis of environmental opportunities and economic efficiency have become more important for decision-making in the socialist countries. This is contrary to the earlier adoptive approach practiced during the command economy, which encouraged poor and distorted perception of the environment (the Nikžić steel plant and the Lukavac plant for manufacturing high-grade coal products from poor brown coal). These were the so-called political factories of the 1950s, which were largely motivated by powerful local interest groups[48] or by a desire by the Party to demonstrate its concern for the underdeveloped regions of the country by changing the regional economic structure.

The basis for industrial-location decisions changed radically, as the changes in the whole decision-making process from a command economy with the Party as the sole decision-maker to decisions based on economic principles became established policy. Such a policy brought an increased interaction between individuals, groups, and area interests and took into account both regional and national needs based on important criteria for evaluating economic efficiency.[49] Again, there exists a great difference between Yugoslavia, Greece, and the three other socialist countries of the area because of the prevalence of more-rational economic prices and more-objective decision-making processes. Even though regional pressures often cause serious problems in the division of available investment funds, their rejection or absence in other socialist countries is no guarantee of a more serious and objective attempt in location decisions. The lack of meaningful spatial economic data in relation to production, transportation, investment, and social costs hinders a more-meaningful locational analysis in various branches of the economy.

SUMMARY

The whole area of institutional relations clearly illustrates the interrelationship between various regional forces and institutional measures. The various forces in financing, planning, organizational structures, and location decisions have their regional consequences. Regional forces generally were disregarded, until recently, in the centrally planned economies of Romania, Bulgaria, and Albania, as well as in Greece. Therefore, the Yugoslav practice, though heavily influenced by its multi-ethnic nature and experience, serves in numerous cases as a model. In the past, it was often stated that the harmonious social development of a country demanded a disregard of regional forces, including foregoing the initiatives of their people. Now it is slowly being realized that harmony can also be achieved by full integration of regional-territorial forces and local initiative with national development planning, as well as greater efficiency in the planned spatial activity sphere. Emphasis on sectoral priority in the past, together with the absence of disaggregation of national plans, has not always accomplished the most desirable results in national economic development, often aimed at "evenness" or "balance" in socioeconomic development. The greater realization of the need for regional and local participation expressed in the decentralization of an ever-increasing number of planning indicators is obvious proof of the increased fluidity and flexibility of the existing planning system.

8

THE SPATIAL ORGANIZATION OF ECONOMIC ACTIVITIES IN SOUTHEAST EUROPE

THE SIGNIFICANCE OF REGIONAL PLANNING

Discussions in the preceding two chapters presented a theoretical framework for the analysis of regional policies as practiced by the countries of Southeast Europe. These discussions already made it clear that a viable national development policy must be concerned with the over-all socioeconomic development of a country, as well as with a maximation of the region's contribution to the national well-being. Because of the existing spatial complexity, which created considerable regional imbalance, choosing the right type of regional developmental policies and, specifically, the interrelationship between national and regional objectives are closely tied to the over-all level of the economic development of individual countries, their long-term developmental aims, and the type of society, its values and goals.[1]

If national development planning is to stimulate economic development in a country, it certainly should be regionally oriented and thus contribute to the full integration of all regions of a national territory. Unfortunately, Soviet-type central plans have resulted from decisions by central-planning authorities and administrative-professional bodies without executive power, usually without realistically prepared and closely integrated regional plans. Numerous examples exist in Romania and especially Bulgaria, where even existing intersectoral relations and important structural units often have been disregarded. Kosta Mihailović pointed out this problem when he emphasized that the "centralized economies stressed the sectorial structure to such an extent that the position of regions became a passive one."[2] In the past, national planning gave top priority to sectoral and branch policies. Its disaggregation into regional plans simply did not exist.

The establishment of comprehensive and consistent policies for regional development, closely integrated with national sectoral priorities, including detailed locational studies, assumes a greater and greater role in the rapidly advancing and technological economies of the countries of Southeast Europe. Broad regional objectives, in order to be successful, must be set within and closely coordinated with the national priorities and goals. Increased emphasis on regional development policies will not only contribute to better integration of underdeveloped regions, but also to a better integration of the more-developed, yet depressed regions, those in need of converting an outmoded structure to accommodate the demands of a modern economy. Well-integrated sectoral and regional development policies contribute to the modernization of the industrial agricultural structure (called the Agro-Industrial complex [APX] in Bulgaria[3],) redirect and bring about a better integration of the infrastructure, encourage increased interregional trade, and thus contribute to the changing over-all socioeconomic structure of the individual countries by increased diversification in all economic activities.

Basically, a policy of regional economic development must have two goals, both of which have two distinct components: an emphasis within the region on the most advantageous allocation of material and human resources and a wider national emphasis. One is concerned with the best possible distribution of resources, considering outside conditions, and the other is concerned with the effect of interregional relations, how they will influence economic performance, the make-up and growth of the economy as a whole, and what the consequences might be with regard to individual regions. The problem of relating the role of individual regions to the goals and the implementation of national policies is a relatively easy one, wherever there is an absence of strong regional loyalties and initiative on the local level. On the other hand, strongly expressed regional interests in the form of localism and particularism will complicate the execution of regional policies—Yugoslavia is a good example.

The Underdeveloped and Lagging Areas

The full integration of the underdeveloped and lagging areas of the country into a national policy in which they can contribute their share to the national progress must be a part of any long-term

development policy. This is of special importance for the countries
of Southeast Europe, inasmuch as their underdeveloped and "lagging
regions are [often] dominant elements, partly because of their magnitude and partly because some of these regions may have extraordinary
growth potentials."[4] It goes without saying, therefore, that problems
of such magnitude complicate claims for the distribution of limited
capital and available skills desperately needed for the development
of diversified economic activities.

So-called regional development* policies in most Southeast
European countries were expressed in specific policies affecting the
underdeveloped areas of a country and the prevention of supercon-
centrations of excess economic activities and population in urban concentrations (Figure 12). The specific policies affecting underdeveloped
regions were related to investments, including the activation or enlargement of national resources, the contribution of social costs
(welfare and education), and the building of manufacturing industries
in the early postwar years, which were able to absorb rapidly large
numbers of untrained people. With the expansion of educational
facilities and additional investment funds becoming available, developmental policies were directed toward an increased emphasis on dispersion of economic activities, the building of small- and medium-
size industries, preferably based on local resources. While increased
attention was given to the problems of the underdeveloped regions
per se, in most countries of Southeast Europe—Yugoslavia has specifically designated its underdeveloped territories since the First
Five-Year Plan—attention to lagging or depressed regions has been
minimal, beyond the sectoral emphasis of the national plan (Figure
13). It will be shown later in this chapter, however, that a slowly
increasing emphasis on dispersal policies, with emphasis on growth
poles (development poles) and growth centers and axes development,
is clearly emerging in all countries (see Figure 14).

---

*Kosta Mihailović distinguishes between "regional development"
and "regional aspects of economic development." The first refers
to the concept of region as an independent economic entity. The
second denotes an approach to regional problems from the aspect of
the development of an economy as a whole. Kosta Mihailović, "The
Regional Aspects of Economic Development," in Yugoslav Economists
on Problems of a Socialist Economy (series of articles by Yugoslav
economists), Eastern Europe Economics (New York: International
Arts and Sciences Press, 1964), pp. 29-45.

FIGURE 12

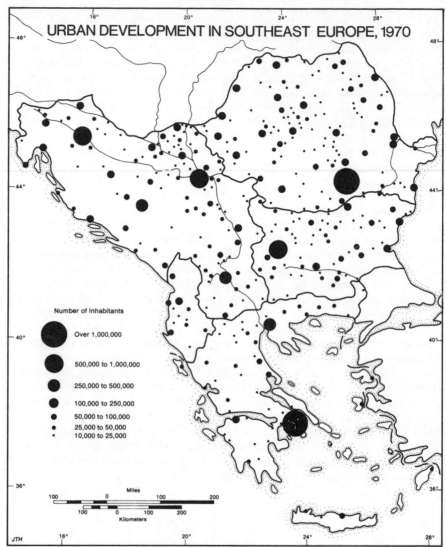

URBAN DEVELOPMENT IN SOUTHEAST EUROPE, 1970

Number of Inhabitants

Over 1,000,000

500,000 to 1,000,000

250,000 to 500,000

100,000 to 250,000

50,000 to 100,000

25,000 to 50,000

10,000 to 25,000

Miles

Kilometers

JTH

Data based on Norman J. G. Pounds, Eastern Europe (Chicago: Aldine Publishing Co., 1969); Bernard Kayser, Géographie Humaine de la Grèce, Centre des Sciences Sociales d'Athènes (Paris: Presses Universitaires de France, 1964); and various official statistics.

194

FIGURE 13

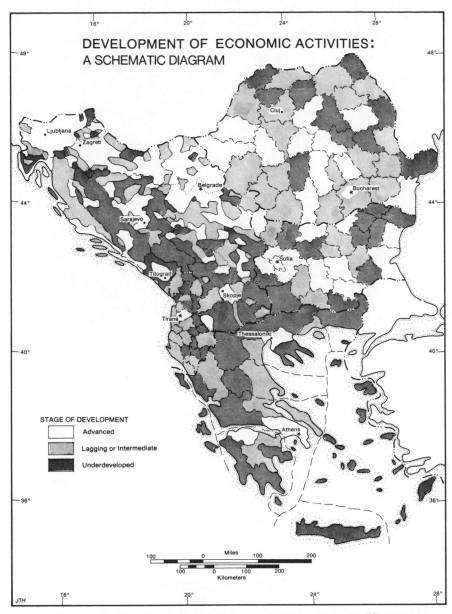

DEVELOPMENT OF ECONOMIC ACTIVITIES:
A SCHEMATIC DIAGRAM

STAGE OF DEVELOPMENT

Advanced

Lagging or Intermediate

Underdeveloped

Note: The stage of development for Albania, Bulgaria, Greece, and Romania is based on late 1960s regional data for industrial output, percent of GNP, and percent of total investments over a five-year period. For Yugoslavia the stage of development is based on 1970 data for per capita income in the socialist sector only and on regional percent of GNP and industrial output. Such bases result in some distortion, especially with regard to the classification of lagging and underdeveloped regions. The reader is reminded that comparable statistical data obtainable for the socialist countries often omit the private sector of the economy. Also, economic development for a given area may reflect only a single industry, such as tourism, or one factory in a single place. Conversely, highly developed agricultur e in some places may result in considerably high per capita income in spite of the fact that little or no industrial development is present. Comparability of the different stages of development between the five countries is difficult to assess. The over-all picture represented by the schematic diagram is based on both the latest available statistical data and extensive first-hand field observations.

195

FIGURE 14

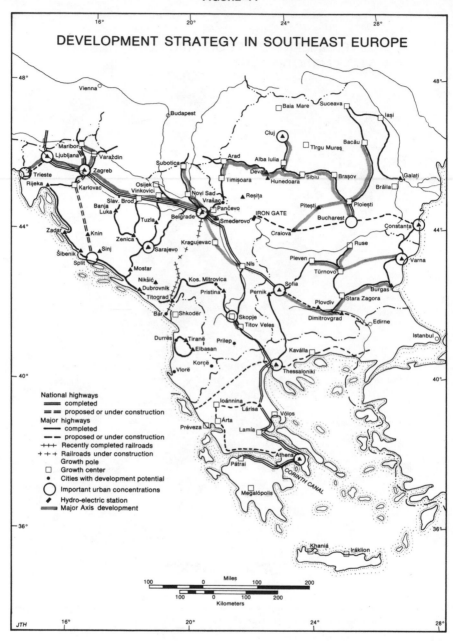

DEVELOPMENT STRATEGY IN SOUTHEAST EUROPE

National highways
━━━ completed
══ proposed or under construction
Major highways
━━ completed
--- proposed or under construction
+++ Recently completed railroads
+ + + Railroads under construction
Growth pole
☐ Growth center
• Cities with development potential
◯ Important urban concentrations
◆ Hydro-electric station
▬ Major Axis development

Obviously, integration of underdeveloped regions into the national economy is of utmost long-term importance, in part at least because many of the "poor regions are poor because they are imperfectly integrated."[5] A national social and economic transformation must give special attention to the structural changes and full integration of its less-developed regions. This is essential in order to gradually reduce the interregional disparities. The establishment of inter-regional connections certainly can make important contributions here and must receive high priority. Also, the problem of population mobility—the migration from certain regions with limited potential—has received some attention.[6] Stabilizing population in regions with a low development potential may very well prolong conditions or even worsen the problem. The examples of Yugoslavia with its so-called political factories and similar ones in Romania and Bulgaria in establishing certain industrial facilities in less desirable regions are ample proof. The large-scale migration from underdeveloped regions to cities and towns was generally accomplished without a preconceived plan, though in later years in the planning of economic activities an effort was made in some of the countries to lead this migration into directed channels favoring small- and medium-size towns.

In some regions and countries, the establishment of new indus-trial activities in smaller towns brought about a fairly wide dispersion of economic and noneconomic activities; Slovenia, Bulgaria, and to a lesser extent Romania are good examples. After some criticism about the early growth pattern in Bulgaria resulting in concentrations in a few large cities—in Sofia, Plovdiv, Varna, and Pleven—the location of new industrial activities followed the principle of full dispersion, though polarization in a few centers had not been completely avoided. In some regions of Southeast Europe, industrial activities are con-centrated in a few medium-size towns, often the regional centers, that have a high potential as development poles. Such a policy of emphasizing development poles and growth centers comprising both economic and noneconomic activities is of special importance in Yugoslavia, where investment policies are highly decentralized. Such an emphasis is also noticeable in the other socialist countries and is also being considered as the basic development policy by the government of Greece.

Finally, the effects on regional development of the mass emi-gration to foreign countries from Greece and Yugoslavia must also be emphasized. These large-scale emigrations already have resulted in labor shortages in certain agricultural regions of Greece (Northern Greece) and industrial centers in Slovenia, but at the same time they eased the problem of the underdeveloped regions by supplying the needed manpower and in addition aided over-all development by the influx of considerable foreign earnings from its workers abroad. Total receipts by Greece in 1970 amounted to $345 million from a working force of roughly 200,000. Yugoslav foreign emigrations—the total number of workers abroad reached over 800,000 in 1970—generally have been from the most-advanced regions of the country— Croatia, Vojvodina, and Slovenia—but an increasing number of mainly younger people from underdeveloped areas in the country take up work in foreign countries.

During a recent visit to the steel works in Nikžić, information was received that as many as 20 percent of their engineering supervisory force seeks work in foreign countries, chiefly in the Federal Republic of Germany. Inasmuch as the most highly motivated and best-trained people find job opportunities easiest, this type of emigration has a most serious impact on the whole economic development of the country. It is estimated that approximately one fourth of the labor force of Croatia is now abroad. While the short-term aspects of seeking better earning opportunities abroad can be beneficial to the country, long-term aspects, with the danger of permanent emigration of the most productive groups of the population (75 percent of the emigrants are in the age group between 20 and 40), are indeed a serious danger signal for the long-term economic development of the country.[7] But for the moment, at least, it relieves the pressure on the domestic labor market and brings certain consumer goods, such as automobiles, television sets, refrigerators, and washing machines, and also agricultural implements, such as small tractors, to a rather widespread group of inhabitants without costing the state valuable foreign currency. In addition, the transfer of foreign income has increased constantly, so much so that it contributed $350 million to the Yugoslav balance of payments in 1970.*

It must be made clear, however, that in the author's opinion the solution to the problems of the underdeveloped regions and the widespread unemployment do not lie with temporary or permanent emigration. The long-term dangers certainly outweigh the short-term

-----

*Politika, in a report on November 4, 1971, speaks of 1971 earnings as high as $600 million from those "temporarily employed outside the country." It also mentions that a marked slowdown in workers leaving the country for the Federal Republic of Germany was noticed during 1971, with unskilled workers (68 percent of those departing in the first nine months of 1971) being in the majority.

advantages (permanent emigration, impact on demographic structure of the population, and so on). The solution must be sought through the creation of basic conditions for increased geographic mobility, especially from the underdeveloped regions. Brief mention has already been made of the workers from Bulgaria in the Soviet Union. The motivation behind this move is connected with labor shortages in the Soviet Union and the import needs of the Bulgarian economy.

Balanced vs. Unbalanced Regional Growth

Soviet-type planning has perpetually had difficulty reconciling the twin goals of rapid economic development with the decrease and ultimate elimination of regional inequalities. The Soviet model stresses "evenness" in economic growth, implying a balanced regional development, thus achieving social equality as the ultimate goal in the socioeconomic development of its society. Actually, within this model two often contradictory policies were followed: one with emphasis on balanced regional growth, with all regions growing at similar rates and with the least-developed region receiving special assistance in the form of specifically allocated aid to catch up with the rest of the country, thus conforming to the stated principle of evenness of socioeconomic development (see the example of the underdeveloped regions in Yugoslavia); and the other, again within the over-all goal of evenness, a policy of balanced sectoral growth oriented toward a rapid growth rate, with the optimistic assumption that ultimately the existing regional differences can be successfully overcome. This latter policy, with emphasis on heavy industrialization, received top priority in all socialist countries of Southeast Europe during most of the 1950s. Such a policy of forced and rapid industrialization was instrumental in the early period of the Soviet-type planned economies in changing the economic as well as the social structure of the whole society, but it certainly neither brought evenness in economic growth, nor did it eliminate regional inequalities.

The term "evenness" was much debated in the early postwar planning period of the socialist countries. It gave the people, especially of such a regionally diverse country as Yugoslavia, the hope that inherited regional imbalances might well be overcome should an "even" territorial allocation of investments by a proper (even) allocation of productive forces be made. Sometimes the term "evenness" is used synonymously with the term "equality." This latter term expresses social equality as a value and implies balanced regional development as distinguished from polarized development.

Mihailović explains that not only a social goal is involved, "but also the initial assumption that there is or at least should be no conflict between economic and social goals."[8]

Planners in the socialist countries were continuously confronted with a dilemma when choosing the correct policy for regional development. Should priority in planning be assigned to achieve evenness, which in the short and even medium run would presumably slow down economic growth in the more-developed regions of a country? Or should priority be given to spontaneous growth, offering more-rapid national growth, especially in the short and medium run, but creating polarized developments and leaving or even increasing regional disparities in this process?

Other contradictions in the development of the socialist countries of Southeast Europe that affected regional policies were related to the copying of the Soviet experience, including the emphasis on large enterprises, which concentrated production in a few centers and thus reduced the likelihood of diffused production. The early postwar expectation that spatial disparities could be eliminated in a short period of time at an early stage in the socioeconomic development of a country invariably encountered difficulties due to the low level of economic development in these countries. The experiences of the socialist countries show clearly that a viable regional policy demands the implementation and coordination of sectoral and regional policies, and its success depends upon the level of economic development, the initiative, and the type of decision-making at various levels of the planning process.

What actually happened in the postwar period in the socialist countries was that the early stages of the postwar economic development had to rely, in most countries, on existing industrial facilities and available labor that in the first place were already heavily polarized, mostly in a few urban concentrations. Development policy emphasizing sectors and branches, where a neglect of regional policies existed, logically gave priority to areas with a maximum availability of facilities (many had increased production by the use of shifts), many of which could quickly be enlarged and modernized, thus further adding, at least in the initial period, to increased concentrations of production and population. Considerable investments concentrating on the extracting industries and on building industrial facilities were made in underdeveloped and lagging regions (the principle of balanced-even development), but due to the fact that they had a longer activation period, both in the actual physical building of factories and in educating their workers, their contribution to the

over-all economic growth and distribution of economic activities was
initially of medium- or long-term importance only.

In summary, more-developed regions with previous industrialization and polarization continued to advance, but with new production
facilities being dispersed throughout the countryside, including the
underdeveloped regions, their advantage seemed to disappear. Still,
locational and cost factors and the earlier starting point in both
economic and noneconomic activities were decisive when meeting
increased competition and offered a long-term advantage. At the
same time, however, it should be pointed out that, by the time the
first stage of sectoral and branch emphasis was generally completed,
it had brought about the desired diversification in a variety of productive forces and had spread to many medium-size towns. The
great emphasis on sectoral and branch policies had succeeded in
bringing basic socioeconomic structural changes to the socialist
countries.

PATTERNS OF LOCATIONAL DISTRIBUTION

The principles of location decisions as they apply broadly to
the countries of Southeast Europe were discussed in Chapter 7. A
discussion of the actual locational distribution pattern of economic
activities brought about by the postwar policies in the socialist
countries as well as in Greece are the concern in the following
analysis. Special attention in these discussions will be given to the
previously mentioned notion of growth poles (development poles) and
centers and to the various types of effects (e.g., trickling-down land
polarized) this policy has on spatial organization in various countries
of Southeast Europe.

Again, as has been emphasized repeatedly in this book, the
basic pattern was set by the concentration established during various
historical developments, by the availability of natural resources, and
simply by the geography of the region. The early polarization had
taken place in long-established urban concentrations and along interregional and international traffic arteries. As new industrial activities
developed throughout the countries of Southeast Europe, polarization
often increased—at least in the early stages of economic growth—but
economic activities also spread along certain interregional and international axes. Much of this development was related to specific
policies influencing locational distribution, especially the dispersion
of newly built industries and the control, or more often absence of
control, of migration into large urban concentrations. The developments

in the five countries of Southeast Europe make it clear that the actual
location of industries is not based on any specific location theory.
Decisions are based strictly on the enterprise's internal economies
and as Mihailović made it clear "location is accepted such as it is
and is later investigated whether it served as a growth pole in the
region . . . it is subsequently evaluated on its own merits. . . ."

The discussion begins with developments in the country where
the most radical changes exist in the spatial distribution of economic
activity since the prewar period.

Bulgaria

Bulgaria's developmental policies, perhaps influenced by its
small size and homogeneity, aims at a balanced (even) development,
thus hoping to avoid congestion of economic activities and population
concentration and at the same time aiming at dispersion over as
many economically viable parts of the country as feasible.[9] Basically,
it has followed a trend of dispersed locational policies following some
initial polarized developments in the Sofia-Pernik-Kremikovtsi region,
heavy and service industries in Sofia, with iron and steel in the traditional and nearby prewar center of Pernik and the new development
of Kremikovtsi. This dispersed policy gave greatest emphasis to
the development in small- and medium-size towns and villages along
two axes in the most fertile part of the country, the Thracian plains
and the Danubian Plateau region. Presently, attention is being focused
on development in certain underdeveloped and lagging regions, all
located on the periphery of the country.[10] It is the hope of Bulgarian
planners that by a policy of well-selected growth centers a scientific
solution to the full integration of the underdeveloped and lagging
regions of the country can be found.

Bulgaria's policy of dispersed location of its productive forces
was first initiated some ten years ago, and this process culminated
in a special meeting of the Central Committee in March, 1970, when
decisions were made on basic long-term policies affecting the territorial distribution during the next fifteen to twenty years.[11] The
changes were initiated in 1962, when it was decided that a policy of
dispersion of industrial activities to nearly 100 villages was to begin.
Altogether, "In the course of ten years, 677 industrial enterprises
have been set up in middle sized and small towns."[12] In 1964, for
example, new industrial enterprises were located in twenty-five
smaller towns, and certain industries were forced to move from
Sofia to smaller towns. The moves that followed prolonged discussions

and disagreements between members of the Economic Institute of the Academy of Science and the State Planning Committee are closely related to the previously mentioned discussions about the unity of functions between administrative and economic regions. These moves became necessary in the mind of Party leaders when the locational concentration reached a very high degree: 53 percent of the country's industrial production was concentrated in nine towns, with 20 percent in Sofia alone and with the greatest additional concentrations in Plovdiv, Varna, Ruse, Burgas, Pleven, and Stara Zagora. Because of specific governmental policies initiated in the 1960s, economic activities affecting the location of new industries, the expansion of those existing, and through the control of migration expansion into major urban concentrations, economic activities spread along the east-west axes through the Thracian Plain to the Black Sea ports of Varna and Burgas and to the Danubian Plateau region. It was concentrated by design largely in small- and medium-size towns and villages. This emphasis on "even distribution of industry throughout the country and not solely in certain areas" favored towns and even villages with a population as small as 0,000 to 4,000.[13]

The far-reaching decision to follow a dispersed policy of locational distribution for the growth of Bulgaria's productive forces was explained earlier, it became urgent, due to the need to improve the economic conditions of the rural and underdeveloped areas of the country and to slow down the wave of migration from the villages to the industrial centers, thus breaking the excessive growth of a few cities and meliorating the serious housing and other municipal problems. More recently (Plenum of March, 1970), specific policies were promulgated on specific assistance to the less-developed parts of the country—the districts of Smolyan, Kardzhali, Silistra, Razgrad, and Blagoevgrad. The Plenum made special mention that "labor resources are not fully utilized in these districts . . . districts which have lagged behind in the past." Bulgarian planners have stressed on numerous recent occasions that the achievements in building a developed socialist society must be followed up with a new stage in territorial planning—meaning the "fullest dispersion of all productive forces among the regions of the country."* Bulgaria's territorial planning envisions

----

*Professor Bradistilov, a member of the Economic Institute of the Academy of Sciences, explained this territorial structure as being "the result of the interaction of mainly two groups of socio-economic factors. The first encompasses the level of development of production forces and their branch structure. The second includes

greater emphasis on the Black Sea and Danube areas. Both of the areas also would make easier the furthering of Comecon trade and the closer integration between Bulgarian and Soviet economic planning.

Greece

Economic growth in Greece thus far is clearly concentrated in the Athens-Piraeus and to a lesser degree Thessaloniki areas. Only recently and in part under government sponsorship, an axis development is being encouraged, with a number of growth or development poles north from the Athens-Piraeus superconcentration* to Thessaloniki envisioned.[14] (See Figure 14). New industries that agree to locate along this axis or other potential developmental areas (industrial districts, as they are called in Greece) are being granted a 30-percent reduction in turnover tax (on certain islands as high as 40 percent). A six-percent wage tax for all enterprises in the Athens area serves as a disincentive to investments. According to Greek planners, industrial-development priority growth zones are to be in Volos in Thessaly, in Iraklion and Khania on Crete, and in the

---

the means of production and the form of ownership of capital goods and, on this basis, the specific economic laws which arise." His main argument for a new stage in territorial planning is explained in Dobri Bradistilov, "A New State and New Problems of Territorial Planning, Ikonomicheska misul (May, 1970), where figures are also cited showing the radical restructuring of the Bulgarian economy: e.g., between 1948 and 1968 over 1,750,000 active men and women left agriculture; the labor resources engaged in farming declined from 81.9 percent at the initial period to 30 to 39.1 percent; and the number of people engaged in industry, construction, and transport rose from 743,000 to 2,469,500 in twenty years. He also cited the migration and urbanization processes demanding dispersed territorial planning, with the number of cities with a population in excess of 100,000 rising from 2 to 5 and Sofia already over one million, with the prospect of doubling its population in the next few years.

*Greater Athens alone has 29 percent of the total population of the country (1961). It has more than 50 percent of the manufacturing industries, accounting for roughly 42 percent of the employment and 57 percent of the value in manufacturing industries in 1961 and produced over one-third of the GNP of the country.

towns of Pátrai, Kávalla, and Préveza.* The projected axes development in Greece is also being encouraged to spread to the west, to
Pátrai, and ultimately along the west coast north to Arta, offering a
connection to Italy and to Western Europe. The Athens-Lárisa-
Thessaloniki axis ultimately will be expanded to Kávalla in Thrace.
Most of this development is in its initial stages, though Pátrai,
Lárisa, and Kávalla are certainly promising growth centers with a
nuclei of economic and noneconomic activities present. The planned
emphasis on such an axis development presupposes greater initiative
by the government. And, indeed, the latest governmental measures
are all directed toward an increased regional development emphasis
and integration of potential regional resources.

Romania

During the early postwar period a policy of concentrating on
existing strong nuclei was generally followed in Romania (see Figure

---

*Two large industrial complexes, Aluminium of Greece and
Esso-Pappas, were both established before 1967. Aluminium of
Greece is the largest Greek corporation and the second-largest
exporter of manufactured goods. It has a capacity to transform
bauxite into 465,000 tons of alumina and produces 150,000 tons of
aluminium per year. Its 1971 exports amounted to $60 million. It is
estimated that Greece in 1971 had bauxite deposits of 71 million tons.
Greek industrial production rose by 9 percent a year since 1963,
with the output of electricity doubling since 1966. Other important
exports with good possibilities for future expansion are nickel ($46
million exports in 1970); the Esso-Pappas complex at Thessaloniki
specializes in petrochemicals and also built a large oil refinery; in
addition, Hellenic Steel in Thessaloniki produced 340,000 tons of of
plate from hot roll coils imported mainly from Japan. Other industries
recently developed or modernized include the promising textile industry. (Greece is the only European country that produces all its cotton
needs.) It earned $34 million through exports in 1970. The electronic
industry also has a considerable growth potential. And in part, at
least, the promise for further industrial expansion is Greece's
association with the Common Market and its stable labor supply in
terms of absence of strikes since the new government seized power.
For details, see "The Two Faces of Greece," The Economist, July
31, 1971.

14). In 1938, 70 percent of the total Romanian industrial production
was concentrated in six locations that employed 60 percent of the
industrial labor force. These six centers, forming an east-west and
north-south axis, were: the city of Bucharest (with 30 percent of the
total value of industrial production), the Prahova Valley with Ploiesti
as its center, Braşov, Hunedora-Deva, Reşiţa, and Timişoara.[15]
(See also the discussion on p. 63.) Raising the economic level, especially in terms of the share in the industrial production of the country, became the major goal of postwar planners. Therefore, important postwar investment was directed toward improvement of the
economic position of less-developed regions.* Table 5 presents a
summary of the regional changes between 1950 and 1970.

New industries were located in regions well provided with
natural resources and ample labor, such as Moldavia, Oltenia,
Maramureş, and Dubraja, in addition to the older development centers
of Reşiţa and Hunedoara (iron and steel works). Today, many new
centers have been created in addition to several axes developments,
largely based on the availability of important natural resources
(petroleum, natural gas, and to a lesser degree agricultural products)
along the southern and eastern Sub-Carpathian region (Craiova-
Piteşti-Tirgoviste-Cîmpina-Ploieşti and Oneşti-Moineşti-Bacău).
These developments are based on growth centers and growth poles
specializing in the production of petrochemical products in the southern Sub-Carpathian region and chemicals and electrical power in the
eastern Sub-Carpathians. A central axis development is based on the
cities of Braşov, Sibiu, Cluj, and Tîrgu Mureş, with numerous special
industrial centers concentrating on mechanical construction, textiles,
wood processing, and extraction. A western axis is based on the prewar center in Hunedoara-Deva-Reşiţa and now includes an axis
development to Timişoara and Arad in the west to Alba Julia in the
east on the Mureş River. A number of individual centers have
important industrial developments, i.e., Lugoj, east of Timişoara,
and Sebeş, south of Alba Julia. This axis development with its
numerous small industrial centers bases its production on deposits
of ferrous minerals and coal. Important iron and steel works,
mechanical construction, engineering plants, and so on are located
in this region. Numerous other growth poles and centers have been

---

*For details, see the author's study "The Problem of the Under-
developed Regions in Southeast Europe: A Comparative Analysis of
Romania, Yugoslavia and Greece," Annals of the Association of
American Geographers, LVII (December, 1967), 637-66.

TABLE 5

Romania: Regional Changes, 1950–70
(in percent)

Region	Population 1966	Total Investment			Industrial Output				
		1950-59	1960-65	1966-70	1950	1955	1960	1965	1970[a]
Advanced regions	31.5	48.8	40.0	37.4	62.7	60.8	60.9	58.3	61.5
Growth area: Sub-Carpathian	44.0	38.3	43.8	49.8	20.7	21.9	23.2	26.2	24.5
Underdeveloped areas	24.5	13.2	16.2	12.8	16.6	17.3	15.9	15.5	14.0

[a]Estimated figures, calculated by author from official statistics.

<u>Source</u>: Direcţia centralā de statisticā, <u>Anuarul statistic al R.S.R. 1969.</u>

planned or actually have been started all over the country. The Galati-Brăila iron metallurgy development of the 1960s is the largest.

In spite of the dispersion of the industrial development and a policy of restricting migration into the capital city of Bucharest, a few urban concentrations have developed.[16] Bucharest's population increased from 640,000 in 1939 to over 1.5 million in 1968, amounting to 8 percent of Romania's total population in 1968, with one fifth of the value of the country's industrial production concentrated in the capital. Romania also followed a policy of encouraging a variety of economic acitivities in widely dispersed medium-size towns and villages with the result that many of those grew relatively fast and their activities show already important spread-effects. Between 1950 and 1970, fifty new cities were incorporated and all show rapid population increases, but with the absence of super concentrations (Bucharest is the exception) the problem was a less-serious one.* Still, in 1968, for example, eighteen towns, representing 8 percent of the total number of towns, produced nearly one half of the total industrial output of the country.

Albania

Albania is going through a typical polarization development in its capital, Tiranë, and in a few other settlements in the interior and along the Adriatic coast (Durrës, Vlorë on the coast and Shkodër, Elbasan, and Korcë, to mention just a few) which have both industrial

---

*Lucija Gheorghitza, "Principles and Trends with Regard to Industrial Location and Regional Spatial Planning," International Planning Workshop, 1969, Proceedings and Selected Papers (Ljubljana: The Urbanistic Institute of SR, Slovenia, American-Yugoslav Project in Regional and Urban Planning Studies, 1969), p. 58 (mimeographed), noted that in view of the fact that "the value of land held by industry was not taken into consideration because the terrain belonging to the State was considered 'free of charge.' Within recent years this has led to industrial use of some important and very fertile agricultural areas." The author also mentioned that "the concentration of some industries with high noxious emissions and the lack of efficient technical means to neutralize them has occasionally led to the increase of air and water pollution, thus raising problems for the population's health, the productivity of the agricultural land and the quality of the hydrologic resources."

and often agrarian activities concentrated in the same places (see
Figure 14). The socioeconomic structural changes going on in isolated
Albania are typical for a very low level of development; a policy of
equalization simply was not feasible. Mihailović made the interesting
observation that even though polarization of industrial activities in
Albania has taken place under socioeconomic conditions different
from those of capitalism, the same tendencies have appeared as those
in a capitalistic society. He draws the conclusion from the example
of Albania "that polarization is not just a product of the spontaneous
interplay of market forces but is a law that cannot be changed by the
socialist system either."[17]

Yugoslavia

In Yugoslavia, development was more complicated, in part due
to the greater diversity in the country, including its multi-ethnic
makeup (see Figure 6). In part, this was due to the great differences
in the level of economic development between the advanced regions
located north of the Sava and Danube rivers and those south of it,
generally encompassing the republics of Slovenia and Croatia (though
both republics have considerable territory classified as underdeveloped) and the autonomous province of Vojvodina (see Figure 14).[18]
Table 6 presents an over-all view of the changes between 1947 and
1969. Those parts of Yugoslavia considered in 1919 as more developed
were the first with some industrial activity while still part of the
Austro-Hungarian Monarchy. They are still today among the more-
developed parts of the country, while the so-called underdeveloped
regions, most of which had been for a long time part of the Ottoman-
Turkish state, with few exceptions—parts of Serbia and Bosnia—still
remained underdeveloped. As a result of historical developments,
basic spatial patterns of economic activity and population concentration had changed only slowly by the outbreak of World War II.

The locational distribution of economic-industrial activities
has greatly spread since the war.* The territorial distribution of

---

*Ekonomska Politika, September 20, 1971, published a com-
pilation of the 100 largest industrial concerns in Yugoslavia: 70 percent
of these industries are located in the more-advanced regions of the
country (Slovenia, Croatia, northern Bosnia, Vojvodina, and greater
Belgrade); 62 percent of these are in ten cities (in order of employment: Belgrade, Zagreb, Niš, Skopje, Zenica, Sarajevo, Ljublana,

TABLE 6

Yugoslavia: Distribution of Industrial Investments Between
Underdeveloped and Advanced Republics, Selected Years, 1947-69
(in percent)

Location	1947	1953	1958	1960	1965	1969
Total	100.0	100.0	100.0	100.0	100.0	100.0
Underdeveloped republics	19.3	38.5	21.2	25.0	29.0	30.2
Serbia,[a] Croatia, Slovenia	80.7	61.5	78.8	75.0	71.0	69.8

[a]Serbia includes here Serbia Proper (Inner Serbia) and Vojvodina.

Source: Jugoslovenka Investiciona Banka, Investicije 1947-1958 (Belgrade, 1959); communication received from Investiciona Banka, October 15, 1965; and Statistički Godišnjak SFRJ, 1970.

productive forces spread from the regional capitals to medium-size towns throughout all republics, but in addition showed highly polarized tendencies in Belgrade and Niš. The beginnings of an axis development in the lower Morava Valley between Belgrade-Smederovo and Niš and also along the international route that passes from Budapest through Subotica and Novi Sad to Belgrade, with a highly polarized development in Novi Sad, are clearly visible.* Slovenia's development is marked by a strong industrial dispersion originally made possible by a well-developed infrastructure. Croatia had three polarized developments at the end of World War II, expressed in both economic activities and population concentrations—Zagreb, Rijeka and Split.[19] There also are a number of potential growth poles and centers: on the Adriatic coast (Dubrovnik, Šibenik, Zadar), in certain hinterland regions (Sinj, Knin), on the important Rijeka-Zagreb axis (Karlovac), a number of long-established centers in the lagging regions of Slavonia (Varaždin, Osijek, Vinkovci), and Slavonski Brod on the Zagreb-Belgrade international highway. Numerous other towns played a more important role as market-administrative and military centers before World War II. They have never regained their economic and administrative functions as important market centers.[20]

As a result of these developments, one can clearly observe in Yugoslavia two basic developments: one is the spread effect from polarized developments concentrated in a few larger urban concentrations, expressed in the slow development of important axes, though

---

Kragujevac, Novi Sad, Osijek) and it is interesting that four of these ten cities are in the underdeveloped parts of the country. Comparing these figures with the total industrial employment in Yugoslavia in 1969, 35 percent of the total industrial employment is located in the 100 largest industrial enterprises. This process of concentration has been especially accelerated since the reforms of 1965 with uneconomical small enterprises being absorbed by large firms—both industrial and commercial (banking, foreign trade, etc.).

*The excellent infrastructure dating from the time when most of the region north of Belgrade (Vojvodina) was part of the Dual Monarchy serving a large economic region could actually have supported a dispersed economic development, but, due to the international boundary erected as a result of World War I, several potential development centers lost their markets. As a result, one today finds Novi Sad as the only outstanding center with a high degree of polarization and several depressed cities and their hinterland. A number of cities, however, have specialized industries, e.g., Bačka Palanka, Pancevo, Sombor, Zrenjamin.

greatly expanded in the last twenty years (Ljubljana [from Italy] and Maribor [from Austria] to Zagreb, Rijeka to Zagreb and in the south through the Morava-Ibar valleys to Niš, as well as the extension of the Hungarian axes over Novi Sad to Belgrade), the other is increased economic activities in a large number of medium-size centers, more confined in the southern, underdeveloped part of the country than in the northern, more-developed part, with the exception of some real dispersion in the most-developed republic, Slovenia.

Economic activities in the underdeveloped regions also vary greatly. In Bosnia and Herzegovina, they are concentrated in Sarajevo, but a number of growth poles have assumed economic importance, e.g., Banja Luka, Skopje is certainly the center for development in Macedonia, and since the earthquake of 1963 has shown a growing tendency toward encompassing both economic activity and population. Developments have spread south to the old town of Titov Veles along the important Vardar route, but other growth centers are slow to assume important economic roles. The pull effect of Skopje is simply too overwhelming. Montenegro and Kosovo have received considerable investment in the postwar period, but with the exception of Titograd, the capital of Montenegro, and Priština, the capital of Kosovo, no other large town has as yet shown any real developmental potential, though Nikšić in Montenegro and lately Kosovska Mitrovica, Prizren, and Pec in Kosovo have received considerable aid for developing local industries.

Finally, a few words should be said about two basic concepts of development prevailing in Yugoslavia about which much has been written. These are the development concepts based on two geographic regions proposing to concentrate major economic resources. They are the concentration along the main interior valleys of the Sava, Danube, Morava, and Vardar rivers, generally known as the "Danube concept," and an industrial and service (tourism) development concentrated along the Adriatic coast, centered in Split and known as the "Adriatic concept." Kosta Mihailović was the proponent of the Danubian concept, but at the same time he envisioned the development of a few select growth centers in the underdeveloped interior regions, such as Bosnia, western Serbia, Kosovo, and Montenegro, and the development of the Adriatic coast mainly for services and tourism.[21] The late Professor Rudolf Bićanić and also Josip Roglić are strong proponents of the Adriatic concept, proposing the development of a number of growth poles along the coast, with Split becoming the major development pole. Absolutely necessary for the success of this concept is a modern rapid highway connecting Split with Karlovac and Zagreb, which it is ultimately hoped will be connected via Maribor

with the European-Austrian highway system, already partially completed between southern Germany and Vienna and south towards Graz,
with a continuation to the Po Valley and the planned major Italian
highway system.[22] Bićanić defined the purpose of the maritime
orientation in the development of Yugoslavia as "an inclusion of
Yugoslavia into the universal division of labor by way of the sea. . . .
It is therefore not to be seen as the development of some 'coastal
belt' of subsidiary, tertiary significance. . . . The maritime orientation signifies a connection with the world, an international exchange
of goods and services as a prerequisite to the viability of a modern
developed nation."[23] The main worry of the proponents of the Adriatic
concept was the possibility of too much orientation of the Danubian
concept towards Comecon. In Bićanić's view, the whole future of
Yugoslavia lay in orienting its economy toward the sea, thus partici-
pating in the West's division of labor.

The solution to this controversy of two basically opposite concepts of economic development was typical of Yugoslavia. A compromise was reached using parts of both concepts. The joint hydroelectric power development on the Danube with Romania (known in
Yugoslavia as Djerdap) and the completion of the Bar to Belgrade
railroad and a new highway connecting Titograd with the key interior
cities in Kosovo of Mitrovica and Priština satisfied the Danubian
concept, though the new highway was also of importance for connecting
Greece with the Adriatic coast and Central Europe.* The development
of the aluminium kombinat at Titograd and Sibenik and the proposed
steel works at Split** satisfied the Adriatic concept. A modern highway between between Zagreb and Karlovac, the first step for faster
service connecting the coast with the Croatian interior (Rijeka and
Split with Zagreb), is being assisted by a loan from the IBRD. The
Croatian section of the new highway to Maribor has been completed
and the Karlovac-Zagreb highway is now under construction.

It must again be emphasized that there never was a unified

---

*Attention must also be drawn to the study sponsored by the
United Nations Development Program, "Regional Plan for the South
Adriatic Region." This detailed study has now been completed
(covering an area from the island of Hvar to the Albanian border) and
a new study has been initiated, continuing north from Hvar to Rijeka.

**Certainly the building of a new steel plant in Split cannot be
defended from an economic point of view.

regional policy of economic development in Yugoslavia, but compromises throughout the postwar period characterize locational
development policies. The decentralization emphasizes the role of
the republics, but free-market forces are already making their mark
on locational policies and creating new links irrespective of administrative boundaries. The use of the fuel and power resources of
Kosovo by the new steel plant in Skopje is a good example of these
new links. The problem of an optimal location policy in respect to
resources and industrial plants still remains unsolved in Yugoslavia.[24]
It is much simplified in the other countries of Southeast Europe. The
absence of strong national tendencies permits a more-unified approach
to locational policies, and, in addition, locational policies of important
industrial activities are basically treated centrally in Albania, Bulgaria, Greece, and Romania, though, as Hamilton pointed out, "as
yet there is no comprehensible and rigorous body of location theory
incorporating the principles [nine principles]."[25] Locational policies
are based on a compromise between those advocating concentration
and those advocating dispersion, and such a compromise is essential
"where highly articulate national minorities and a historical legacy
of regional differentials in infrastructure as in Yugoslavia" exist.[26]

THE COMPARATIVE APPROACH TO
REGIONAL PLANNING

Emphasis on a regional approach to planning, meaning both
social and economic planning, came to the forefront in all of the
countries of Southeast Europe during the 1960s, with varying intensity.
Awareness that massive unequal spatial development resulting in
serious imbalances could affect the economic growth of individual
countries became widespread. Much theoretical work has gone into
the problem of regional development, including the study of locational
decisions, the application of the growth-pole theory, and the problem
of superconcentration of population.[27]

The problems of concern here deal with the approach to the
strategy of regional planning, as practiced by the five countries
under consideration. This is based on the assumption that an emphasis on regional development policies, the introduction of a regional
component for over-all national planning policies, the disaggregation
of national into regional plans, and the recognition of the interrelationship between national and regional development is essential for a
successful national developmental strategy. Inasmuch as great spatial
differences exist within four of the five countries of Southeast Europe
(Albania is uniformly underdeveloped, but with great diversity in its

geographical regions), the key contribution of a comprehensive regional policy will be felt first by areas poorly integrated into the national space economy and areas with a low level of development (the under-developed or depressed areas). All efforts must be directed toward maximizing their total national contribution. That a two-way relation-ship—interdependency or interaction—must encompass every avenue and implication of sectoral and regional growth is obvious. Regions themselves, as Kuklinski and others have pointed out rather con-clusively, must not only participate in the benefits of national eco-nomic and social development, but must themselves act as self-generating units in a development policy.[28]

The increased attention given to integrating underdeveloped areas into the national space economy is evidence of the concern of national leaders. The varied emphases on decentralization of impor-tant decisions associated with planning policies is the most outward manifestation (this is true in both the socialist and capitalist coun-tries). These policies of decentralization effect different planning decisions, for different sectors or for a different region, away from the single layer of decision-making—from one Party bureaucracy to greater participation by the people and/or their economic organiza-tions—and, finally, transfer of vital decision-making functions from a single center to two or more centers.

The recent realization in all countries of Southeast Europe that regional policies form an integral part of the socioeconomic develop-ment of the whole country was, in part, brought about by the stage of economic development of the individual economies, a greater sophistication in all economic activities, and increasing economic ties with foreign countries. The introduction and emphasis on regional policies is also based on a desire to stop or at least slowdown the further trend toward centralization within the government apparatus and the overconcentration in the capitals of Bucharest, Sofia, Athens, and Tiranë. Such a policy is closely related to the growing desire of the inhabitants of individual regions to participate in the decisions affecting their livelihood, including socioeconomic planning.

The following analysis will summarize the major developments and features of a regional development strategy of the individual countries of Southeast Europe. Inasmuch as various aspects of this strategy have already been discussed in earlier sections of this book, especially in the analysis of the over-all development strategy in Chapter 5, the purpose of the following discussion will be to point up the major aspects of the development strategy as it relates to regional development only. It also should be stressed that the literature on this topic, especially as it refers to developments in Yugoslavia, is considerable. For this reason, footnoting has been held to a minimum. The interested reader is referred to the selective bibliography at the end of the book.

Yugoslavia

In Yugoslavia, the emphasis on a rigid, centralized, sector- and branch-oriented planning policy was slowly transformed beginning in 1952, first by greater attention being given to the most under-developed regions of the country and later by the transfer of important decisions from the federal to the republican and commune level and even to individual enterprises.[29] This had an important bearing on the whole spatial structure of the national economy. The multi-national character of the country forced planners and politicians at an early stage to give added attention to the regional problem, though this meant mostly to the officially determined underdeveloped regions.[30] This often brought the more-developed and underdeveloped regions into conflict regarding locational and investment priorities, and the condemnation of the so-called political factories in certain underdeveloped regions became a rallying cry for the more-advanced republics in Yugoslavia prior to the economic reform of 1965.

The problem of the underdeveloped regions of the country was one of rising expectations resulting from promises that more attention would be given to the underdeveloped regions.[31] These areas presented an extremely grave problem, since neither industrialization within the country as a whole nor within the region was able to improve their specific situation, including the absorption of the surplus population. This development was brought about by the low priority given to investments in infrastructure (attention to this problem was not increased until the 1960s), made possible in view of an earlier policy of moving job opportunities (industry, construction, and services) to the people of the underdeveloped areas. Such a policy of creating local job opportunities saved investment in transport, but in the long run it seriously undermined a policy creating efficient economic opportunities by establishing noncompetitive, high-cost productive facilities. In addition, such a policy of dispersed development was also influenced by the ethnic structure of the country and seriously hampered interregional migration. It contributed to substantial capital transfer from the developed regions of the country, as well as tied up scarce capital.

The bankruptcy of these policies was substantially responsible for the demands of economic reform of 1965. While still emphasizing aid to the underdeveloped regions, the regional policy now stresses the development of a series of potential growth poles and centers, including the encouragement of interregional migration, though the important interregional (interrepublic) cooperation still leaves much to be desired. The previously mentioned sizable emigration to foreign countries from some areas has resulted in this problem being a manageable one.

Yugoslavia commonly delineates four levels of planning: the federation, the republic, the commune, and the enterprise. Its broad indicative social plan on the federal level, as well as on the republic level, must be approved by legislative bodies and "are implemented through the different instruments of the economic system." Its policy of decentralization in vital aspects of decision-making is based on "social ownership of the means of production, on the principle of self-management of the working people in the production and distribution of the social product by working organizations and the social community."[32] With the initial introduction of self-management of the enterprise (1950), economic instruments slowly replaced administrative instruments of planning and are now constantly being refined. Broad federal guidelines now influence regional development processes.*

The emphasis was first on integrated developments in each region, with the main vector of change the amount of allocation of investments centered around a core of some kind of heavy industry in each republic as the growth pole. While the Yugoslav model now calls for emphasis on productivity and cost advantages in new

---

*Among the most important administrative instruments available are: tax policy—the turnover tax is of importance in bringing the demands for goods to the level of available supply; foreign-trade control and currency regulations; budgets on various administrative levels (federal, republic, and communal), though it is becoming of less importance in planning as a larger amount of the national income is redistributed by the state budget; and credits, aid, and subsidies, though they have a reduced impact. Allocation of credit is of importance with regard to investment policies. For details, see Rudolf Bićanić, Problems of Planning East and West (The Hague: Mouton & Co., 1967), pp. 58-62.

investments, most integrated industrial complexes actually were planned in the period of the 1950s, following the Soviet model of sectoral and branch priorities. Recent reforms stress a development strategy with "strict sector and locational priorities to exploit regional potentials in order to achieve a large measure of regional specialization according comparative advantages in production for both home and overseas markets."[33] A policy of this nature will ultimately influence the adjustment of population densities in relation to the economic potential of individual regions, and interregional migration should contribute to an equalization in the standard of living. What impact the large foreign labor migration will have when and if these people return home is still very unclear.

The changes in the whole planning philosophy marks a clear-cut reduction of the role (fiscal) of the federation. Federal financing of the armed forces, the federal administration and security, and the guaranteeing of the unity of the market as specifically charged in the constitution is basically the only role the central government has left. The federal government still makes a number of so-called supplementary grants to the less-developed regions (Montenegro, Kosovo, Macedonia, Bosnia, and Herzegovina) based on earlier commitments, e.g., the Skopje steel works, the Bar to Belgrade railroad, and the joint Yugoslav-Romanian Danubian hydroelectric power development (Djerdap). The financing of the final part of the Bar to Belgrade railroad is now being undertaken by public subscriptions and possible foreign loans. In 1971, these grants amounted to 7.2 percent of the total budget, but it is expected that these expenditures will be phased out during the next few years, and no new commitments are expected.

Generally the federal government is decreasing its economic role, including the contribution to special organizations such as the Fund for the Development of Underdeveloped Regions, the Fund for Financing Exports of Ships and Equipment, federal payments of "anticipated interests" on construction of tourist projects, etc. Some of the funds of the federation have already been distributed among the republics, but the problems are not easily solved. With the federal treasury being divided, the republics must assume many obligations formerly carried out by the federal government. The individual republics will have to carry a much-heavier burden, but the implementation of these policies depends on interrepublic agreements.

The greater regional emphasis and decentralization in the decision-making processes in multinational Yugoslavia has continuously raised the serious question of regional loyalties vs. national needs, and regional vs. national priorities. And this has occurred while a largely decentralized economic policy has contributed without doubt to a more balanced economic growth at the same time it has raised some serious economic and political questions as expressed in the recent upheavals in Croatia, which forced a reorganization in the top echelons of the Croatian as well as Yugoslav state and party organs.

The upheavals in Croatia affect every republic in Yugoslavia. Because the demands made by the Croatian leadership were not only strongly backed by its people but also by the Croatian Party Leadership (though a minority dissented from these policies), and, in addition, found varied support by Party leaders in other republics (Slovania, Macedonia, and the autonomous provinces of Kosovo and Vojvodina), they rallied powerful centralist forces, e.g., the Army and the Veterans organizations, and criticized the Croatian Party leadership under the slogan of nationalism, anti-state, and even separatist activities. When Tito himself followed this line, the Croatian government and Party leadership was forced to resign. Since that time a fairly large number of party officials in various communes and enterprises (Managers) were forced out of their positions or to acknowledge their mistakes. What was surprising in the Croatian development was not the dissatisfaction of a broad group of its populace (even the university students took the initiative), but the fact that this demand for change reached into the highest party circles (members of the Presidium, the government of the republic, and representatives at the parliament in Belgrade). It was the new generation of Communists including the highest Party officials who rebelled against Belgrade's policies. That they moved too rapidly and had too high hopes of overt support from the other republics is without question and is even acknowledged by those in favor of their demands. Greater political sophistication by the Croatian Party leadership probably could have averted the catastrophe of November-December, 1971, and no one at the present time can with any amount of certainty forecast the long-term impact of the Croatian upheavals. Hopefully, the impact on the economic and political development of the country will be only a passing one.*

So much for the actual development. What were the basic issues? While Croatia is responsible for 33 percent of Yugoslavia's industrial

---

*Background for these discussions was obtained by the author during a longer stay in Yugoslavia during the summer of 1971 and a shorter visit during February, 1972.

production and 27 percent of its GNP, it was allowed to retain only 18 percent of its capital assets. This was considered in Croatia a form of economic exploitation and even high Croatian party officials regarded this contrary to the principle of "equality of nationalities." The recent developments in Croatia were no sudden development, but were, rather, the reaction to resistance to the implementation of the 1965 reform, especially as it referred to the contemplated reforms of foreign trade, banking, and the allocation of foreign currency among the different republics. On the other hand, it must also be noted that the Croatian dissatisfaction (to a lesser extent duplicated in Macedonia, Kosovo, and Slovenia) was only a continuation and perhaps new form of nationalism prevalent for such a long time in this republic. The recent dissatisfaction can be traced directly to the decision of the January, 1970 Plenum of the Croatian Central Committee when it agreed to concentrate its struggle on promoting "Croatian national interests on the basis of the 'natural right' of every Yugoslav nation to dispose of its resources and of its own realized surpluses."

An important issue raised at the recent conflict is specifically connected with the question of the allocation of foreign currency among the republics. Croatia was able to retain only 7 percent of the country's foreign exchange earnings, even though it earned over 70 percent of Yugoslavia's tourist revenue and a large part of its export revenue and foreign workers' transmittals (altogether Croatia in 1970 earned 32.9 percent of Yugoslavia's convertible currency). A compromise has been considered for some time, and was finally approved whereby Croatian firms will be allowed to retain up to 20 percent of their foreign currency earnings instead of only 7 to 10 percent as at present. Tourist establishments will be allowed to keep up to 42 percent.*

The basic reason why the contemplated reforms, including the question of the allocation of foreign currency, plays such an important role, especially for Croatia, is the fact that Croatia contributes such a large number of its citizens to Yugoslav foreign workers. Fully 47 percent of all Yugoslav foreign workers in 1971 came from Croatia and the impact of this large number of able-bodied workers leaving their home is of considerable importance to the whole economic and political fabric of the republic. It is not only that a large part of the

---

*Data used in these discussions came from official statistics and various reports published by Radio Free Europe, Research, during 1971 and early 1972.

remittances are being made by people from Croatia and only a small part of these foreign currencies remains within the republic, but even of greater importance for the whole economy of the republic is the need for these foreign currencies earned by its people in foreign lands to enable the government to raise the standard of living, to provide additional jobs, and thus entice its people to remain in the republic or return home. The fact that its own people work in foreign countries and thus create the need for bringing non-Croatian workers from the underdeveloped regions of the country to replace the lost Croatian manpower also plays a considerable role in the developments.

Greece

Greece,* with its overconcentration of almost all economic activity in the greater Athens area, which is the main cause of under-development in most of the remainder of the country, completely lacked a national planning policy until the late 1960's.[34] The need for an annual plan, including attention to regional problems, became obvious by the middle of the decade. The Economic Development Plan for Greece, 1968-72, for the first time gives specific emphasis to regional development policies, but the lack of detailed regional studies, including feasibility studies for industrial investment, which must serve as the basis for any over-all plan, is still generally lacking. It also must be remembered that the economic plans for Greece are essentially "indicative plans for the private sector of the economy" on the macrolevel without setting a parameter of action for individual enterprises, with the exception of a few large and very specific proj-ects. Nevertheless, it must be made clear that the government can and does initiate projects that it deems of importance to national development. The government also decides on priority growth zones, usually underdeveloped or lagging areas of the country with a growth potential. Studies now have been initiated by the Ministry of Coordi-nation and the planning services pointing to such potential growth centers. The 1973-77 draft plan favors "regional development by adopting a strategy of development poles thus hoping for a rapid and effective mobilization of our national potential as a whole."**

——————————

*See Appendix Tables 1 and 8.

**The recent reorganization (fall, 1971) of the whole planning apparatus, including a very extensive reorganization of the country's administrative structure, established a new Ministry of Government

It also should be mentioned that the Hellenic Industrial Development Bank, founded in 1964 as the central state agency for promoting private investments in Greece, has now been merged with several development and financing organizations, e.g., the Industrial Development Corporation and the Tourist Credit Organization. With its increased functions, it has become the main state agency to accelerate the development of the economy and implement industrial expansion. It now is wholly owned by the Greek government and by charter must give priority to enterprises outside the Athens-Piraeus region.

In the socialist countries of Romania and Bulgaria, socioeconomic planning generally follows the Soviet model, emphasizing all economic and social aspects, and is directed toward sectoral and branch growth. Such a procedure included a decision concerning apportionment of both productive and unproductive investments, aiming at a policy of equalization, including harmonizing social interests throughout all regions. This policy obviously strengthened the central decision-making bodies and placed the integration of underdeveloped regions into the national economies within the general planning priorities. A specific regional development policy as such does not exist in either of the two countries, though general references are often made to the "more harmonious development of the production forces," to "see a more rational distribution of the productive forces," to give "greater attention to the territorial distribution of productive forces," and so on.[35]

Romania

In Romania, a more-active policy of decentralization made itself felt in the middle 1960s.[36] The introduction of industrial centrals as large, integrated units, serving as organs to facilitate better management of the economy and to decentralize the functions of the former ministerial directorates while at the same time encouraging enterprises to draft their own plans, was initiated by the National Party Conference in 1967. The actual implementation of some of these reforms remained unsatisfactory, as the repeated criticism by the Romanian leadership referring to the absence of initiative seemed to indicate.[37] In spite of the various planning

---

Policy combining various policy-making and economic-planning functions. Details affecting planning functions are at the time of this writing not available. See also the note on p. 163.

reforms, little, beyond some generalities, was said about a regional emphasis of their sectoral and branch plans. The furthest Party leaders went in emphasizing regional policies—and there are few differences from earlier statements on the same topic—is best expressed by Ceausescu's statement on the 1971-75 five-year plan in his speech on the occasion of the fiftieth anniversary of the Romanian Communist Party on May 7, 1971.[38]

> In this five-year period we will carry on the rational re-
> partition of production forces, the sustained development
> of the less industrialized counties—providing for them
> annual industrial production increases of 20 to 26 percent.
> The policy of social and economic development of all
> regions of the country is of essential importance for the
> general increase of the living standard of the people.

The functions and organizational structure of the State Planning Committee (Comiteitul de Stat al Planificării) has undergone considerable changes during the 1960s, including the addition of a Directorate of Territorial and Local Planning, which coordinates the work of county and local planning bodies (a similar office is found in other bodies concerned with planning). Each economic ministry, the industrial centrals, enterprises, banks, special state committees, and government organizations, including the county and municipal councils, all have their own planning organs. But from the available information, it is not too clear how much real power of initiative these various planning bodies really have, or if they are simply organs of the State Planning Committee and the Party.

Planning proposals are supposed to flow upward from the enterprise through the ministries to the State Planning Committee, according to the principal of "democratic centralism." This is the thrust of the directives adopted on October 5 and 6, 1967, by the Plenum of the Central Committee of the Romanian Communist Party. They were designed to remedy excessive centralism of planning, which has resulted in the improvisation of plans from the top without proper regard for the capacities of the enterprises to meet various aspects of the plan. But the fact remains that very little has changed in the planning mechanics or the level of the decision-making processes.

One way the Romanians are trying to bring regional viewpoints into the planning processes is the increased authority given to individual enterprises, though there is a question as to how much these local viewpoints are really considered in the final preparation of the sectoral and branch plans. Each year, however, the regime feels it is worthwhile for the workers to "debate" the next year's plan. It is possible that some actual changes may be incorporated in the plan as a result of enterprise observations or objectives, but in general the purpose of the "debate" is to create a feeling among the workers of participation in the planning process and to encourage them to greater efforts to meet the planned goals. The same is true for the discussions at various local government organizations, e.g., the county and municipal councils.

There is obviously a difference in the disaggregation of national plans to meet specific regional needs, or in the preparation of a unified plan by branches and sectors, and their transmission through various hierarchial layers to the enterprise. The basic problem in improving planning in Romania is its emphasis on giving greater attention to "the relation between the central plan and the enterprise autonomy. In the opinion of the Romanian Communist Party, improvement of planning should strengthen the role of the plan as the major instrument for directing socioeconomic development . . ."[39] As was pointed out earlier in the discussion, the basic principles and mechanics of Romanian planning objectives have not been changed; they simply have been modified and improved, and in this process enterprises received some sort of greater participatory role. But a real initiative is doubtful, and this also holds true for any real local and regional planning initiative by local governmental organizations. The initiative rests still with the State Planning Committee, and the broad outline of national goals is sketched within the responsible sections of the Central Committee apparatus. This includes the specific tasks assigned to the economy, e.g., specific goals for total output, total investment proportion to consumption, regional distribution of investment, and major new industry. The latter, together with the type of investments, is decisive in influencing regional projects, including their territorial distribution.

Bulgaria

Based on all available evidence,* the reform movement of the 1960s in Bulgaria was somewhat more successful in establishing

---

*This evidence includes, besides the generally available literature, some very perceptive reports compiled by Radio Free Europe, Research and also is based on discussions by the author during his three visits to Bulgaria in the 1960s and 1970.

procedures aiming at a better integration of national plans (annual economic plans) or, as they have been referred to, as "unified plans for socioeconomic development" with territorial aspects of planning and management. The various discussions of the 1960s culminated in decisions made at the Plenum of the Central Committee in March, 1970 (see the earlier discussions in this chapter) creating "a unified system of management for the development of territorial location of productional forces," which included a system of forecasts on the development of individual territorial units and the setting-up of "unified plans for the socio-economic development of these units."[40] The March Plenum also created a General Directorate for the Territorial Location of Production Forces, which was attached to the State Planning Committee, and district (okrug) planning commissions, originally created in May, 1963, were "to be organizationally strengthened by including in them the necessary number of highly qualified specialists and by changing their statutes."[41] Planning is still of a centralized type, but plans now are more regionally integrated, with greater dependence on local needs based on feasibility studies that emphasize possible concentrations and specializations.

In addition to the closer integration of national plans with regional needs (certainly not disaggregation of national plans), the March discussions also gave considerable attention to the problems of individual districts and especially the underdeveloped lagging areas. It is obvious from the economic geography of Bulgaria that the least-developed parts of the country lack national resources and often are deficient in infrastructure. Therefore, the implementation of decisions demanding the expansion of productive forces into the less-developed parts of the country, considering the decisions of earlier Party congresses, which emphasized concentration and specialization of production; e.g., the organization of agro-industrial complexes (1969) will not be an easy one for the planners and has some inherent contradictions.[42] The whole aspect of territorial planning in Bulgaria is in a state of flux, but all evidence points toward a greater scientific approach in the locational distribution of productive forces and in a closer integration of national sectoral and branch plans with regional requirements.

Emphasizing dispersion based on regionally integrated plans goes hand in hand with a planned pattern of urbanization largely directed against the excessive urbanization developing as a result of the policies of the 1950s. Such a policy has brought restrictive measures in the migration of people to certain large urban concentrations. It has brought the reallocation of certain industrial complexes into smaller towns. For example, a policy of restricting capital investments in the most-advanced and populated districts is now followed and modernization and reconstruction will be emphasized. On the other hand, obvious deficiencies exist. Little planning has been going on in Bulgaria on improvements in intercity transport or transport between concentrated and high-density settlements and the surrounding rural countryside. With so many small settlements in close contact with larger towns, the development of so-called peasant-workers would mean a great improvement in the Bulgarian situation.* In spite of its excellent over-all infrastructure, the intercity or city-rural transportation aspects of many regions are extremely deficient. Bulgarian planners and transportation specialists are well aware of this deficiency.[43]

In summary, one can conclude that Bulgaria's centralized planning policies, based on sectoral and branch priorities, were modified and relaxed all throughout the 1960s, but, while the centralized planning apparatus remained in full charge of all important planning decisions, a closer coordination with regional needs, especially with regard to the territorial location of productive forces, was established and further emphasized by important decisions in early 1970. It is still too early to evaluate these developments as they are actually implemented (sometimes the outsider has serious doubts as to whether decisions actually are being implemented) and only time will tell what their impact is. Actually, the Soviet Union between 1957 and 1965 gave some priority to a regional approach in planning by organizing territorial economic councils that received control over major industrial and construction enterprises (sovnarkhozy). They were subordinated to the republic governments and, through them, to the All-Union Councils of Ministers.[44] Bulgaria followed its lead, though when the Soviet Union abandoned this approach, Bulgaria evidently quickly followed. Developments clearly indicated that a truly regional approach in planning simply did not go hand in hand with a policy of autarchy.[45]

Albania

Albania only recently instituted planning reforms of its highly centralized sectoral and branch planning system, calling for extensive decentralization of power within its administrative agencies.[46]

---

*Taking the lagging district of Silistra as an example, most small settlements are less than 50 kilometers from the important industrial center of Ruse, which has been cited as having serious housing shortages. In the Sofia region, a distance of 25 to 35 kilometers from the city makes commuting to work impossible due to the lack of transportation.

SUMMARY

The discussions in the preceeding pages on the underlying philosophy and approach to the spatial organization of economic activity in Southeast Europe stressed the importance of a comprehensive and integrated regional development policy, of special importance for countries with great spatial disparities and those with multinational societies. The broad aims of such policies in the countries under discussion are very similar, though the characteristics of specific policies differ markedly, depending on the needs of individual countries, the basic model followed in their planning policies, and on certain institutional and political factors. The integration of sectoral and regional policies is considered essential in long-term national economic plans and must be based on a series of well-studied and long-term objectives, such as technological and economic trends, population growth, and educational objectives.

In more than one way, Yugoslavia and Bulgaria have made the greatest structural changes in their economies, including the spatial (territorial) distribution of their productive forces. Yugoslavia is the only socialist country without a Soviet-type centralized planning apparatus and has gone furthest in decentralizing its decision-making processes to the regional and commune level with respect to all aspects of its development strategy. Based on available data and observations, it also has probably done more work in urban planning than any other of the socialist countries. Every country of the area today follows more-scientific methods in the study of the territorial distribution of its productive forces, emphasizing growth centers and axes development and aiming ultimately at a widespread dispersion or "evenness" in the distribution of its economic activities.*

The greatest deficiencies in such a policy are decisions based on insufficient scientific data, the lack of quantitative and other scientific methods available for evaluating the trade-off between the attainment of the goal of national integration and the goal of economic efficiency of a particular project, as well as communication and information exchanges between different layers of government, from a local to a national level.[47] Every country now has begun to give this aspect, which is of such importance to any modern society,

---

*Both Romanian and Bulgarian leaders refer regularly to the industrialization of countries and provinces not having industries thus far.

considerable attention, but the research in this area must constantly face inadequate and unavailable statistical and other basic information when discussing regional or geographical subareas within a country.

It is clear from the preceding discussions that important changes in the implementation of national development policies in all five countries of Southeast Europe have been initiated during the last few years. While these changes, with the exception of those in Yugoslavia, have not altered the basic long-term development strategy, they have taken cognizance of deficiencies in the planning apparatus and of the importance of regional aspects in the national development strategy.

Although there are basic differences both in the scope and the approach to regional development policies of these countries—based in part on historical, political, and socioeconomic developments, and in part on their size and location with regard to neighboring influences— as past discussions have shown, there are also common factors of similarity in their goals and policies. The growing awareness of regional aspects of economic development, including the recognition of regional forces, has been brought about largely by the failure of earlier policies. While these policies have resulted in increasing spatial distribution of economic activity, at the same time they have produced agglomerations in the larger cities and polarizations, rather than the hoped for dispersion among many medium-size potential growth poles, thus creating a promised more "even" development within the respective countries. In addition, the recognition that most underdeveloped areas in individual countries have only slightly improved their relative position with regard to the more-developed areas, including neglecting their interregional linkages, in spite of considerable capital investment (this was especially true in Yugoslavia), led to the realization by the central authorities that present methods of planning, or, in the case of Greece until recently, the lack of planning, needed some change.

It also has been obvious that, with increased sophistication of economic activity, regional forces must play a more important role in influencing national policies, in addition to simply improving the decision-making processes. Some of the planning policies of the countries of Southeast Europe, Romania and Bulgaria specifically, follow a policy of centralization in the administration of economic policies, but also at various degrees of decentralization of economic operations. In Yugoslavia, the demise of central-planning authorities, for example, increased the responsibilities of local authorities and the pursuit of nearly all regional development policies is now the responsibility of a variety of political, economic, and social authorities, all on the regional and local level. In Greece, an awareness of the need to exploit regional potentials, largely brought about by the superconcentration in the Athens-Piraeus area, has led to the assumption of greater planning responsibilities by central authorities and the preparation of rather detailed regional planning studies.*

Earlier, it was emphasized that while no country in Southeast Europe had truly integrated regional development policies, a regional development strategy emphasizing the disaggregation of national sectoral and branch plans, with emphasis on a policy of dispersion of major productive forces in broad growth zones or axes, is receiving increased attention in Bulgaria, Greece, and Romania and in some of the Yugoslav republics. Such a national development strategy, regionally integrated, to be successful must encourage interregional labor mobility, partly to adjust to uneconomic population densities, while at the same time equalizing interregional standards. It also has been suggested for some countries that abandoning their least-developed areas without any or only little developmental potential might be the best long-term solution. On the other hand, it is obvious that even if such a policy should be feasible from an economic point of view, political constraints would act as a major deterrent. Recent large-scale emigration from underdeveloped areas in northern Greece, however, has literally emptied wide regions of any economic activity.

Finally, it is clear that regional policies are not only concerned with the integration of underdeveloped and lagging regions in the space economy of the country. While their problems very often overshadowed

---

*This statement is based on meetings with members of the Regional Development Service and the Ministry of Coordination, both in 1966 and 1970, and on correspondence and material received since that time.

other equally important considerations, it must be stressed that they
form only one aspect of the country's developmental policies. Other
problems in need of regionally oriented development policies, and only
a few are mentioned here from a long list, are: the restructuring of
rural areas, often lacking centrally located development centers;
lagging or depressed areas with stagnating economic activity, including
outdated industries and infrastructure; the problem of superconcentration of economic activities and population in a few cities and towns;
the problem of border regions where boundaries divide geographic
entities, e.g., the development of the Danube region, the border regions
in the Pannonian Basin, the agricultural potential of the lower Maritsa-
Merica (Turkish name) -Evron (Greek name) region, and the agricultural-
irrigation-navigation potential of the Vardar-Axios region. The impact
of the recent outward migration of large numbers of the most-pro-
ductive working ages in certain regions of Greece and Yugoslavia
(especially Croatia), leading to a deterioration in the population structure and a marked decline in economic activity, demands most urgent
study. The whole problem of structural imbalances in the spatial
distribution of economic activities demands a variety of regional
policies, though it has long been understood that the complete abolition
of spatial inequalities is neither possible nor desirable.

REGIONAL COOPERATION

One development often overlooked in the discussions, but of
increasing importance in the development strategy of the countries of
Southeast Europe and mentioned thus far only in a cursory way, are
regional cooperation efforts between individuals or a group of countries of Southeast Europe and also with neighboring countries including
the Soviet Union.* All the countries of the area in the past few years

---

*Excluded from the following discussions are cooperative schemes,
mostly special trade arrangements between individual Southeast Europe
countries and others. One example that is worth mentioning, however,
is the increasing industrial cooperation between Yugoslavia and Poland.
Poland in 1971 had more cooperative arrangements with Yugoslavia
than with its own Comecon partners. Some of these special trade
arrangements are already on a hard-currency basis. Poland is desperately in need of modern technology, which Yugoslavia, far ahead
in the achievement of licenses and Western capital, especially for
consumer goods, is anxious to supply. Such cooperation includes the
production in Poland of the Fiat 125 and small tractors, especially

have expressed a greatly increased interest in various forms of economic cooperation, including joint-development schemes. Such cooperation ranges all the way from the joint Romanian-Yugoslav hydroelectric scheme on the Danube, to joint-promotion efforts for tourist attractions between Yugoslavia, Bulgaria, Greece, and Turkey, to cooperative schemes encouraged between Comecon members. Cooperation is bilateral or multilateral and goes far beyond simply cooperation in foreign trade.[1]

The emphasis on and the size of regional cooperation in the field of economic and cultural contacts and joint-development schemes depends heavily on the political climate in the area, especially the Soviet's attitude toward reducing tension. The political cooperation is restricted for the moment to a few moves toward establishing diplomatic relations between Albania and Greece—for the first time bringing about a de facto recognition of the present boundary between the two states by establishing trade and cultural links—and Romanian and Bulgarian initiatives to improve greater political cooperation in the area and to reducing tensions.[2]

Political as well as economic cooperation greatly depends on great-power relations, but especially on Soviet interest in the area with regard to reducing tensions. Strategically, Southeast Europe has increased in importance, especially since the Soviet Union's entry into the Mediterranean and the various aspirations of the great powers— the Soviet Union, the United States, and China—are most strongly reflected in block-free Yugoslavia. Romania's drive for a "zone of peace" and later for the establishment of a "zone free of nuclear weapons," including a proposal for a "permanent Balkan conference," thus far has led to no noticeable response from its neighbors.[3] Russia's periodic emphasis on reducing tensions can always best be observed in Bulgaria's desire for a rapprochement with Yugoslavia. The polemical dispute about Macedonia, however, with Yugoslavia's demand for Bulgarian recognition of the existence of a "separate Macedonian nationality," acts as a real deterrent, especially with regard to improvements in Yugoslav-Bulgarian relations.[4]

Regional cooperation between the countries of Southeast Europe, as mentioned earlier, has been greatly increased during the last few

---

designed for the small Polish and Yugoslav farms, the only two socialist countries with large private farming. For details, see London Economist, December 11, 1971.

years. As a matter of fact, hardly any month goes by without the
announcement of a new cooperative agreement. Table 7 and Figure 15
present samples of the most-important cooperative schemes now
undertaken or actually on the planning boards. Table 7 does not
provide a complete listing of all schemes, but rather shows the type
of ongoing cooperation among the countries of the area. This cooperation can be grouped according to type as follows:

1. Broad interregional and/or governmental schemes. These
include joint tourist promotion, extension or new projects for improving the infrastructure of border areas across political barriers,
bilateral economic cooperation (Vardar-Axios flood control, irrigation,
and transport schemes), sometimes with the aid of international
financing.

2. Bilateral and multilateral economic cooperation focused on
specific projects. These cooperative projects concerned new or
improved means of transport for the purpose of facilitating the movement of minerals or fuel (building of highways, canals, and railroads).
They also included the building of industries such as the steel and
iron works with Soviet financing in Bulgaria; the joint development of
timber resources with Bulgarian manpower in Komi SSR; the joint
construction by Bulgaria, Hungary, and the Soviet Union of the calcinated
soda plant in Bulgaria: a joint Bulgarian-Soviet cellulose plant in the
Soviet Union.[5] Arrangements have been concluded between the Comecon countries and also with Yugoslavia, e.g., facilitating the transport
of the rich iron ore from the Ljublja mine (limonite with a high-quality
iron content) to Romania, which ultimately should go to the nearby
Sava River port of Orahova and by barge to the Smederevo steel plant
and on the Danube to Romania.[6]

3. Joint investments for the exploration and exploitation of
minerals. In addition to Soviet-Bulgarian cooperation in the exploration
for petroleum in Bulgaria, only one other project is known—Romanian-
Yugoslav explorations for petroleum in the Banat.

4. Special trading and investment arrangements. These include
the possible expansion of the Yugoslav Free Zone in the port of
Thessaloniki (originally established in 1929) as well as the establishment of a free zone for Bulgaria.[7] Also included are the expansion of
the already numerous arrangements between Yugoslavia and Western
countries for production of certain goods (mostly consumer goods)
under foreign licenses and lately the encouragement for outright
investment in the Yugoslav economy. This latter possibility is also
under discussion between Romania and some Western industries.

TABLE 7

Regional Cooperation in Southeast Europe

Type of Cooperation	Albania	Bulgaria	Greece	Romania	Yugoslavia	Soviet Union	Other
Broad Interregional and/or Governmental Schemes							
Joint tourist promotion		x	x		x		Turkey
Vardar River (Axios) scheme with initial UNDP financing: flood control, irrigation, navigation			x		x		
Project Trigun (Slovenia, Carinthia, Udine, Friuli, Croatia-Istria) cooperation in tourism, roads, economics, etc.					x		Italy, Austria
Arrangements for free border traffic between Slovenia and Italy; Austria and Hungary; Croatia and Hungary; Serbia and Hungary; Macedonia and Bulgaria		x			x		Italy, Austria Hungary
Bilateral and Multilateral Economic Cooperation							
Cultural exchanges	x				x		
Bar-Belgrade railroad: proposed financial contribution for final stage by Romania and Hungary[a]				x	x		Hungary
Oil pipelines: Adriatic line (preliminary agreement with Hungary), Bakar to Yugoslav-Hungarian border at Bokov, to continue to Czechoslovakia; construction begin 1972, completed 1975[a]					x		Czechoslovakia, Hungary
Pipeline Constanta to Cernavoda and shipment by boat to Pančevo				x	x		
Gas pipeline on Romanian territory for delivery of natural gas from Soviet Union to Bulgaria		x		x		x	
Power (electric) line from Soviet Union to Bulgaria through Romania		x		x		x	

Type of Cooperation	Albania	Bulgaria	Greece	Romania	Yugoslavia	Soviet Union	Other
Hydroelectric project at Islaz-Somovit on Danube: in planning stage between Romania and Bulgaria[a]		x		x			
Electric power line from Craiova (Romania) to Boichinovci (Bulgaria) to connect national power system; completed		x		x			
Timber resources in Komi SSR		x				x	
Calcinated soda plant in Bulgaria; completed		x				x	Hungary
Cellulose plant (joint construction) in Soviet Union		x				x	
Soviet investments in Kremikovti iron and steel works		x				x	
Iron-ore shipments from Yugoslav Ljubija mine to Romania (long-term financial arrangements for financing navigability for Sava River to reduce transport costs)[a]				x	x		
International highway, Nis-Dragoman-Sofia; completed		x			x		
Pipeline, Thessaloniki-Skopje (natural gas)[a]			x		x		
Hydroelectric project on Danube between Yugoslavia and Romania, few km from Iron Gates power station; under discussion				x	x		
Joint Investments for the Exploration and Exploitation of Minerals							
Soviet-Bulgarian exploration in gas and petroleum fields in Danubian Plateau		x				x	
Romanian-Yugoslav explorations in the Banat				x	x		

(continued)

235

TABLE 7 (continued)

Type of Cooperation	Albania	Bulgaria	Greece	Romania	Yugoslavia	Soviet Union	Other
Special Trading and Investment Arrangements							
Free Zone in Thessaloniki; Yugoslavia to be enlarged and Bulgaria under consideration		x	x		x		
Various Western investments in Yugoslav industries					x		U.K., U.S. Fed. Republic of Germany, etc.
Regional International Complexes Between Comecon Countries							
Proposed complexes: Black Sea area-Bulgarian ports and hinterland (Burgas, Varna) with USSR lower Danube region		x x		x		x x	
Regional Cooperation Mentioned (not at present under discussion)							
Bulgaria and Greece: joint exploitation of minerals (lead and zinc ore) in the border regions		x	x				
Joint hydroelectric power schemes in border areas on Struma, Mesta, Arda, and Maritsa rivers		x	x				
Yugoslav (Macedonian) free border traffic with Greece			x		x		
Highway branch south of Austrian European road south of Graz to connect with Yugoslav highway from Split-Karlovac-Zagreb-Maribor					x		Austria

[a]Negotiations commenced.

Sources: various Radio Free Europe research reports, 1969-71; issues of Viata Economica (Bucharest); reports in Rabotnichesko Delo, as translated by U.S. Embassy in Sofia; Pre-Investment News, U.N. Development Program; lecture by Professor E. B. Valev of Moscow University at Geographical Institute, University of Zagreb, January, 1967; various reports of London Economist and Züricher Zeitung; reports in Agerpress International Service (Burcharest), Joint Translation Service (Belgrade).

FIGURE 15

REGIONAL COOPERATION IN SOUTHEAST EUROPE

Legend:
- International highways
- Proposed highways
- Railroads
- Railroad under construction
- Oil pipelines
- Gas pipelines
- Proposed pipeline
- Gas and oil exploration
- Hydro-electric station
- Hydro-electric station (proposed)
- Electric power cable
- × Zinc-lead mines
- Irrigation project

Not specifically mentioned here, but of obvious importance, is the association agreement between Greece and the Common Market and the recently established cooperation between Yugoslavia and the Common Market.[8]

5. Regional international complexes.[9] The establishment of such complexes was first raised by Soviet and Bulgarian geographers and certain planners, and, though no formal implementation or even discussions have ever been held and political obstacles make their large-scale implementation extremely doubtful at the present time (Romania has consistently shown its objections to this type of planning), some of the recently agreed regional cooperation schemes of international complexes in the Black Sea and lower Danube region follow the original proposals.[10]

The question of joint enterprises between the Soviet Union and Comecon members is a touchy one (see the problem with Romania, discussed in Chapter 5). Romania's 1971-75 economic plan directives, however, seem to modify its earlier position. The latest directives specifically stated that "one must take into consideration the realization of joint investments designed to meet raw material needs as well as the establishment of mixed enterprises of a production or commercial nature."[11] It was made clear, however, that the organization of joint enterprises must have the unanimous consent of its members.[12]

On the whole, it can be said that, with the exception of Albania, all the countries of Southeast Europe either have established greatly increased economic cooperation or such is under consideration. Bulgaria and the Soviet Union have gone furthest in this type of regional economic cooperation, extended now to joint planning in a number of productive branches. The territorial emphasis on certain priority growth zones on the Black Sea coast and along the lower Danube, the latter thus far a typical border region with a considerably lagging development, points to the direction of increased Bulgarian-Romanian economic cooperation. Marinov's previously mentioned thesis for the need of the development of international complexes based on the Black Sea and the lower Danube regions is thus clearly in the background of these discussions.[13] Joint Romanian-Bulgarian-Soviet planning within Comecon for the over-all development of such complexes has recently begun. Joint Bulgarian-Soviet planning and even actual production has started, as evidenced in the newly built petrochemical concern in Burgas and the construction and partial completion of a huge thermal power plant near Varna, based on Donbas coal now shipped from the new Crimean port at Don Uzlow. Bulgaria has pushed for some time for the joint development with Romania of hydroelectric

plants on the Danube. Marinov suggested a total of four such plants,
the Somovit-Izlaz the first one, which could result in considerable
economic benefit to the whole lower Danube region. With the completion of the Romanian-Yugoslav hydroelectric project, discussions
have now started between Romania and Bulgaria for a joint Romanian-
Bulgarian Danube power plant and also for a second Romanian-Yugoslav
plant. As mentioned earlier, political, not economic, factors seem
to be the real deterrent for increased Romanian-Bulgarian regional
economic cooperation.

Yugoslavia's willingness for greater economic cooperation with
the Comecon countries always must be balanced against both its
internal and external political need for avoiding too great a reliance
on Comecon trade (cooperation with Romania naturally is favored).
Greece and Bulgaria are cautiously moving toward greater regional
cooperation, though at the moment there is more talk than action.
Nearly all the initiative came from Bulgaria. However,[14] Yugoslavia
has moved far ahead in opening its borders with neighboring countries.
Its various republics, especially Slovenia, Croatia, Serbia (Vojvodina),
and Macedonia, for economic and national reasons, have encouraged
the elimination of the negative impact of borders by initiating border
talks for greater freedom of border traffic for its citizens with its
neighbors. Italy, Austria, and, to a lesser degree, more recently
Hungary, offer good examples of what can be accomplished by easing
or even abolishing border restrictions. This was in good part brought
about by Yugoslavia's opening its borders to encourage tourism, and
also by doing away with all restrictions for the travel of its own citizens.*

It is then clear that regional cooperation in its broadest sense
plays an increasingly important economic role, obviously affecting
political relations. Its effect is both of long-term short-term impact.
It gives individual regions and border areas, as well as others, an increasing stake in the development of a truly integrated national development strategy. It improves the leverage of many lagging regions, especially those located along international borders. Regional cooperation
initiated thus far shows the direction of future economic developments.
It affects the choice of growth poles and centers, as well as axes
development. It is the most significant development coming out of the
area in the last few years and augers well for future cooperation in

---

*The easing of border restrictions was followed by the joint
building of bridges, highways, and motels at key border crossings
with Italy and Austria.

the area. Southeast Europe offers a multitude of potential cooperative development schemes, affecting both national and regional interests, avoiding the pitfalls of the autarkic developments of the earlier post-war years. Their impact* is evident on underdeveloped, lagging, and developed areas, with the prospect of ultimately having some sort of regional economic integration, by the furtherance of existing axes development, by prospective large-scale bilateral and multilateral financing in the construction of pipelines, the building of international highways connected and cooperating electric power network, and . improvements in the navigability of a number of key rivers (Danube, Sava, Morava, Vardar-Axios, and Maritsa-Merv, including Turkey in these considerations).

The future possibilities for regional cooperation in Southeast Europe for the most part are not even on the drawing board, but the beginnings of international cooperation in this area, with its history of long-neglected opportunities, provides great challenge for the people. It gives those interested in the future peaceful development of the area and all those interested in international cooperation a ray of hope in an otherwise bleak outlook of internal rivalries and big-power intrigues. The five countries of Southeast Europe, by their example, could show to their people as well as to the rest of the world the way to accomplish rapid economic growth based on close regional economic cooperation without losing their own identity in an area of great geographic, socioeconomic, and political differences.

---

*The Romanian-Yugoslav hydroelectric development of the Danube offers a good example of the multiplier effect of a single regional cooperative scheme. The necessity of building an entirely new transport infrastructure—highways, railroads, and an electric network to reach Djerdap on the Yugoslav side—opened up the whole underdeveloped area of northeast Serbia. Not only will it offer a new and more direct route between Belgrade and Bucharest, but it opens an area for economic exploitation (forestry and minerals), as well as for recreation. Unfortunately, no regional development plan, to the best of the author's knowledge, exists for this underdeveloped area, planning which certainly should have gone hand in hand with the building of the joint Danube hydroelectric project and the resettlement of several thousands of people necessitated by the raising of the level of the Danube River.

ABBREVIATIONS USED IN THE NOTES

1. Am. Eco. Rev.   American Economic Review

2. Annals-AAG   Annals of the Association of American Geographers

3. East Eur. Qua.   East European Quarterly

4. Eco. Bu. Eu.   United Nations, Economic Bulletin for Europe

5. Eco. Su. Eu.   United Nations, Economic Survey of Europe

6. Geo. Rev.   Geographical Review

7. OECD   Organization for Economic Cooperation and Development

8. Reg. Sc. Assoc. Papers   Regional Science Association, Papers

9. RFER:EE   Radio Free Europe Research-Eastern Europe

10. Série de Geographie   Revue Roumaine de Geophysique et Geographie, Série de Géographie

11. UNRISD   United Nations Research Institute for Social Development

12. ZfW.   Zeitschrift für Wirtschaftsgeographie

NOTES TO CHAPTER 1

1. The author has drawn freely in this and other parts of this book from his own writings: "Regional Synthesis: An Introduction," in George W. Hoffman, ed., Eastern Europe: Essays in Geographical Problems (London and New York: Methuen and Praeger Publishers, 1971), pp. 1-33; "Regional Development Processes in Southeast Europe: A Comparative Analysis of Bulgaria and Greece," ibid., pp. 431-83; "Eastern Europe," in George W. Hoffman, ed., A Geography of Europe (3d ed.; New York: The Ronald Press, 1969), pp. 431-524; "The Problem of the Underdeveloped Regions in Southeast Europe: A Comparative Analysis of Romania, Yugoslavia and Greece," Annals-AAG, LVII (December, 1967), 637-66; The Balkans in Transition, Searchlight Book No. 20 (Princeton: D. Van Nostrand, 1963); and, with Fred Warner Neal, Yugoslavia and the New Communism (New York: The Twentieth Century Fund, 1962).

2. Jack C. Fisher, Yugoslavia—A Multinational State (San Francisco: Chandler Publishing Co., 1966), p. 19.

3. The late German historian Fritz Valjevac called it a Bindeglied, Kulturbrücke, or Völkerbrücke. See Fritz Valjevac, "Die Eigenart Südosteuropas in Geschichte und Kultur," Südosteuropa Jahrbuch, I (1956), 54-55.

4. Ibid.; and Richard V. Burks, "Social Forces and Cultural Change," in Robert F. Byrnes, ed., The United States and Eastern Europe, (Englewood Cliffs, N.J.: Prentice-Hall, 1967), p. 82.

5. For details of the routes, see André Blanc, Géographie des Balkans (Paris: Presses Universitaires de France, 1965), pp. 33-35; and George W. Hoffman, "Thessaloniki: The Impact of a Changing Hinterland," EastEur.Qua., II (March, 1968), 1-27.

6. For details of the physical geography of the area, including reference maps, see Hoffman, "Eastern Europe," pp. 431-44.

7. Ian M. Matley, "Traditional Pastoral Life in Romania," The Professional Geographer, XXII (November, 1970), 311-16. The central position of Transylvania (which means "the country beyond the woods") and its importance in the historical geography of Romania is best described by Tiberiu Morariu, "The Position of Transylvania

within the Unitary Territory of Romania," Série de Géographie, XIII, 1, (1969), 14-23.

8. Em. Condurachi, Rumanian Archaelogy in the 20th Century, Bibliotheca Historica Romania No. 3 (Bucharest: Publishing House of the Academy of the Rumanian People's Republic, 1964); and Constantin Daicoviciu and Miron Constantinescu, eds., Brève histoire de la Transylvanie, Bibliotheca Historica Romaniaé Monographies III (Bucharest: Éditions de L'Académie de la République Socialiste de Roumanie, 1965).

9. Hoffman, "Thessaloniki," pp. 12-14, esp. map on p. 13.

10. Josip Roglić, "The Geographical Setting of Medieval Dubrovnik," in Norman J. G. Pounds, ed., Geographical Essays on Eastern Europe, Indiana University Publications, Russian and East European Series, Vol. XXIV (Bloomington: Indiana University Press, 1961), pp. 141, 159.

11. George W. Hoffman, "Die Agrarentwicklung der Vojvodina seit 1945," Wissenschaftlicher Dienst Südosteuropa, XII (July-August, 1963), 123-30.

12. Ibid., p. 123.

13. Günther Erich Rothenberg, The Austrian Military Border in Croatia 1522-1747 (Urbana: University of Illinois Press, 1960); and Rothenberg, The Military Border in Croatia in the 19th Century (Albuquerque: University of New Mexico Press, 1963).

14. Orme Wilson, Jr. "The Belgrade-Bar Railroad: An Essay in Economic and Political Geography," in Hoffman, Eastern Europe, pp. 365-93.

15. For a more detailed description, see Margaret Reid Shackleton, Europe, A Regional Geography (7th ed.; New York: Frederick A. Praeger, 1964), pp. 137-47.

16. Hoffman, "Thessaloniki."

17. Roglić, "Medieval Dubrovnik," p. 562

18. Josip Roglić, "O geografskon položaju i ekonomskom razvoju Jugoslavije" [The Geographical Position and Economic Development of Yugoslavia], Geografski Glasnik, XI-XII (1950), 11-24,

discusses in some detail the meaning of the term "Balkan" and its use by various European writers of the ninetieth and twentieth centuries. See also the most recent work by Roglić "Die Gebirge als die Wiege des Geschichtlichen Geschehens in Südosteuropa," Colloquium Geographicum, Argumenta Geographica, Festzeitschrift Carl Troll, Band 12 (Bonn: Ferd. Dümmlers Verlag, 1970), pp. 225-39.

19. Three works by Traian Stoianovich discuss the domestic and foreign trade in Southeast Europe: with Georges C. Haupt, "Le mäis arrive dans les Balkans," Annals (Economics, Sociétés), XVII (1962), 84-93; "The Conquering Balkan Orthodox Merchant, The Journal of Economic History, XX (June, 1960), 234-313; and a more general study, A Study in Balkan Civilization (New York: Alfred A. Knopf, 1967).

20. Stoianovich, "Balkan Orthodox Merchant," p. 282.

21. William H. McNeill, Europe's Steppe Frontier 1500-1800 (Chicago: The University of Chicago Press, 1964), pp. 202-10.

22. Ibid., pp. 205-6.

23. Ibid., p. 221.

24. Stoianovich, "Le mäis," pp. 84-93.

25. McNeill, "Europe's Steppe," p. 185.

26. For a series of essays dealing with various developments in this period, see Charles and Barbara Jelavich, eds., The Balkans in Transition (Berkeley and Los Angeles: University of California Press, 1963).

27. Arthur J. May, "Trans-Balkan Railway Schemes," The Journal of Modern History, XXIV (December, 1952), 352-67.

28. L. S. Stavrianos, The Balkans Since 1453 (New York: Rinehart and Co., 1959), pp. 339-63.

NOTES TO CHAPTER 2

1. Quote from Kosta Mihailović, Regional Development in Eastern Europe: Experience and Prospects, UNRISD/70/C.49, GE 70-18044 (Geneva: UNRISD Programme IV—Regional Development, August, 1970).

2. Nicolas Spulber, The State and Economic Development in Eastern Europe (New York: Random House, 1966), p. 62.

3. Ibid.

4. Nicolas Spulber, "Changes in the Economic Structures of the Balkans, 1860-1960," in Charles and Barbara Jelavich, eds., The Balkans in Transition (Berkeley and Los Angeles: University of California Press, 1963), p. 347.

5. Mihailović, Regional Development, pp. 12-13.

6. Much of the basic information used in Chapters 2 and 3 were taken from the following publications: Economic Development in S.E. Europe (London: Political and Economic Planning, Oxford University Press, January, 1945); Hermann Gross, "Die Industriali- sierungspolitik der Südosteuropäischen Staaten bis zum zweiten Weltkrieg," Südosteuropa Jahrbuch, IX (1969), 35-45; Frederick Hertz, The Economic Problem of the Danubian States (London: Victor Gollancz, 1947); L. Pasvolsky, Economic Nationalism of the Danubian States: A Study in Economic Nationalism (Washington, D.C.: The Brookings Institution, 1928); Paul N. Rosenstein-Rodan, "Problems of Industrialisation of Eastern and South-Eastern Europe," The Economic Journal, LIII (June-September, 1943), 202-11; Spulber, Economic Development; Spulber, "Changes in the Economic Structures," pp. 346-75; and the various economic reports of the League of Nations.

7. David Mitrany, The Land and the Peasants in Rumania (1917-1921) (London and New Haven, Conn.: Yale University Press for the Carnegie Endowment for International Peace, 1930), p. 571.

8. Spulber (Economic Development, p. 24) also commented on the energy wasted in transforming these backward provinces into modern states "by each of these small units in building a top-heavy bureaucracy and police and military organization."

9. For details, see Traian Stoianovich, "Land Tenure and Related Sectors of the Balkan Economy 1600-1800," The Journal of Economic History, XIII (Fall, 1953), 398-411.

10. Jozo Tomasevich, Peasants, Politics, and Economic Change in Yugoslavia (Stanford, Cal.: Stanford University Press, 1955), p. 172.

11. For a brief and excellent summary of Montenegro, see L. S. Stavrianos, The Balkans Since 1453 (New York: Rinehart and Co., 1959), p. 237. For a more intimate picture of Montenegro, see the two books by Milovan Djilas, Montenegro (New York: Harcourt, Brace and World, 1963), and Land Without Justice (New York: Harcourt, Brace and World, 1958).

12. Quote is from Economic Development in S.E. Europe, p.25.

13. Paul N. Rosenstein-Rodan, Agricultural Surplus Population in Eastern and Southeastern Europe (London: Royal Institute of International Affairs, 1943), Table I (mimeographed).

14. Herhard Schacher, Der Balkan und seine Wirtschaftlichen Kräfte (Stuttgart: Ferdinand Enke, 1930), pp. 150-62.

15. Adamantios Pepelasis, "Country Case Studies: Greece," in Adamantios Pepelasis, Leon Mears, and Irma Adelman, eds., Economic Development (New York: Harper, 1961), p. 509.

16. Rosenstein-Rodan, Agricultural Surplus Population, p. 1.

17. Spulber, "Changes in the Economic Structures of the Balkans," p. 358.

18. Sergije Dimitrijević, Das Ausländische Kapital in Jugoslawien vor dem Zweiten Weltkrieg (Berlin: Rütten and Loenig, 1963); translated from the original in "Strani kapital u privredi bivše Jugoslavije," Ekonomska Biblioteka, IV. Mining in Yugoslavia was, for example, geared for exporting mostly in raw or concentrated form close to 75 percent of the production of zinc, lead, bauxite, copper, antimony, chrome, pyrites, and magnesite.

19. Ibid., pp. 200-201.

20. F. E. Ian Hamilton, Yugoslavia: Patterns of Economic Activity (New York: Frederick A. Praeger, 1968), p. 94.

21. Dimitrijević, Das Ausländische Kapital, pp. 156-61.

22. For detailed figures, see Annuaire statistique de la grèce, 1939. For a critical analysis of Greece's interwar economic policies, see Adamantios Pepelasis, "Socio-Culture Barriers to Economic Development in Greece" (unpublished Ph.D. dissertation, Department of Economics, University of California, Berkeley, 1955), pp. 95-106.

23. In the period 1928-50, Athens' population increased by 40 percent and Sofia's by 20 percent. See F. W. Carter, "Population Migration to Greater Athens," Tijdschrift voor econo. en soc. Geografie, LIX (March-April, 1968), 100-105.

NOTES TO CHAPTER 3

1. Stjepan Lovrenović, Ekonomska politika Jugoslavije [Economic Politics of Yugoslavia] (Sarajevo: Izdavačko preduzeće "Veselin Masleša," 1963), p. 80. In Yugoslavia, between 10 and 12 percent of the budgetary receipts in 1938-39 were used for servicing foreign loans.

2. Kosta Mihailović, Regional Development in Eastern Europe: Experience and Prospect, UNRISD/70/C.49, GE 70-18044 (Geneva: UNRISD [Programme IV—Regional Development], August, 1970), p. 12.

3. One of the best studies written by a man with close ties to his people was by the late Rudolf Bićanić, "Kako živi narod. Zivot u pasivnim krajevima" [How People Live. Life in the Passive Regions.], trans. by Stephen Clissod (Zagreb, 1936) (unpublished manuscript).

4. F. E. Ian Hamilton, "The Changing Pattern of Yugoslavia's Manufacturing Industry 1938-1971," Tijdschrift voor econo. en soc. Geografie, LIV (April, 1963), p. 916.

5. Ibid., p. 96. The author uses the employment-capacity of industry by regions and the distribution by individual factories to obtain figures indicating the degree of manufacturing activities. A compilation of addresses of industrial plants in 1938 underline the localization and concentration in certain areas. See also, Dimitrije Misić, Ekonomika Industrije F.N.R.J. [Industrial Economics of Yugoslavia] (Belgrade: Naučna knjiga, 1957).

6. George W. Hoffman, "The Problem of the Underdeveloped Regions in Southeast Europe: A Comparative Analysis of Romania, Yugoslavia and Greece," Annals-AAG, LVII (December, 1967), 643, 644-47.

7. Mihailović, Regional Development, pp. 11-12.

8. Ibid., p. 12.

NOTES TO CHAPTER 4

1. Leszek A. Kosiński, "Changes in the Ethnic Structure in East-Central Europe, 1930-1960," Geo. Rev., LIX (July, 1969), 388-402.

2. Nicolas Spulber, The State and Economic Development in Eastern Europe (New York: Random House, 1966), p. 47. Spulber's figures are for all countries of East-Central and Southeast Europe. They are estimated, based on statistical data available to the author, for the countries of Southeast Europe.

3. The interested reader is referred to three excellent studies discussing the Soviet Model and its workings: Charles K. Wilber, The Soviet Model and Underdeveloped Countries (Chapel Hill: University of North Carolina Press, 1969), pp. 3-133; Nicolas Spulber, The Economics of Communist Eastern Europe (New York: The Technology Press of M.I.T. and John Wiley & Sons, 1957), pp. 282-305; and John M. Montias, "The Soviet Economic Model and the Underdeveloped Countries," in Nicolas Spulber, ed., Study of the Soviet Economy, Russian and Eastern European Series, Vol. XXV (Bloomington: Indiana University Press, 1961), pp. 57-82.

4. Wilber, Soviet Model, p. 6.

5. Ibid.

6. Thomas M. Poulsen, "Administrative and Regional Structure in East-Central and Southeast Europe," in George W. Hoffman, ed., Eastern Europe: Essays in Geographical Problems (London and New York: Methuen and Praeger Publishers, 1971), p. 229.

7. Nicolas Spulber, "Economic Modernization," in Robert F. Byrnes, ed., The United States and Eastern Europe (Englewood Cliffs, N.J.: Prentice-Hall, 1967), p. 72.

8. F. E. Ian Hamilton, "The Location of Industry in East-Central and Southeast Europe," in Hoffman, Eastern Europe, p. 174; F. E. Ian Hamilton, Yugoslavia: Patterns of Economic Activity (New York: Frederick A. Praeger, 1968); George W. Hoffman and Fred Warner Neal, Yugoslavia and the New Communism (New York: The Twentieth Century Fund, 1962); F. E. Ian Hamilton, "Planning: The Spatial Development of Industry of East Europe: The Principles and Their Impact," Economic Planning (Montreal) (March, 1970), pp. 4-6.

9. F. E. Ian Hamilton, "Aspects of Spatial Behavior in Planned Economies," Reg.Sc.Assoc.Papers, XXV (1970), 83-84.

10. Spulber, Economics, p. 283. For a more detailed discussion, see pp. 282-85.

11. Ibid., p. 284.

12. Spulber, Economic Development, pp. 45-49, 76-78.

13. Hoffman and Neal, Yugoslavia, pp. 86-91, 95-99.

14. Paul N. Rosenstein-Rodan, "Problems of Industrialisation of Eastern and South-Eastern Europe," The Economic Journal, LIII (June-September, 1943), 203. For an excellent analysis, see Andrzej Brzeski, "Two Decades of East European Industrialization in Retrospect," East Eur.Qua., III (March, 1969), 1-14. For a critical assessment, see Kosta Mihailović, Regional Development in Eastern Europe: Experience and Prospect, UNRISD/70/C.49, GE 70-18044 (Geneva: UNRISD [Programme IV—Regional Development], August, 1970), pp. 27-28.

15. Paul N. Rosenstein-Rodan, Agricultural Surplus Population in Eastern and Southeastern Europe (London: Royal Institute of International Affairs, 1943), Table I (mimeographed).

16. Spulber (Economics, pp. 166-206) discusses these in considerable detail.

17. Ibid., p. 190, lists fifteen, including oil exploitation, air transport, wood exploitation, natural-gas exploitation, metallurgy, oil equipment, ship building, and uranium mining.

18. Spulber, Economic Development, p. 47. It should be noted that Romania fought with the German army and only at the end of the war reversed its policies and was forced then to pay reparations to the Soviet Union. It remained a constitutional monarchy until December 30, 1947.

19. Much has been written about the problem of the underdeveloped regions of Yugoslavia and for this reason only a selective list of references is presented here: George W. Hoffman, "The Problem of the Underdeveloped Regions in Southeast Europe: A Comparative Analysis of Romania, Yugoslavia and Greece," Annals-AAG, LVII (December, 1967), 637-66; Kiril Miljovski, "Underdeveloped Areas and the Conditions for their Development," (paper presented at Yugoslav-American Conference, Indiana University, 1964) (mimeographed); Asen Simičiev, Development of the Economically Underdeveloped Regions of Yugoslavia, Study No. 35 (Belgrade: Medunarodna Politika, 1970); and Borisav Srebić "Policy, Method and Basic Results of Developing the Underdeveloped Areas in Yugoslavia," Ekonomist (English edition) (1969), pp. 113-27.

20. Mihailović, Regional Development, p. 30.

21. Hoffman and Neal, Yugoslavia, p. 399.

22. See the critical analysis of the Greek postwar economic problem in Richard M. Westebbe, "Greece's Economic Development: Problem and Prospects," International Development Review, VIII (March, 1966), 11-16. Three studies are presented here, giving an excellent picture of the postwar developments in Greece: Wray O. Candilis, The Economy of Greece 1944-1966: Efforts for Stability and Development (New York: Frederick A. Praeger, 1968); D. J. Delivanis, "Marshall Plan in Greece," Balkan Studies (Thessaloniki), VIII (1967), 333-38; and William Hardy McNeill, Greece: American Aid in Action 1947-1956 (New York: The Twentieth Century Fund, 1957).

NOTES TO CHAPTER 5

1. For a summary of the basic features of a centrally planned economy, see the compilation of terms and explanation in Alan A. Brown and Egon Neuberger, eds., International Trade and Central

Planning: An Analysis of Economic Interactions (Berkeley and Los Angeles: University of California Press, 1968), pp. 405-14; and also Egon Neuberger's discussions and Benjamin N. Ward's commentary "Central Planning and Its Legacies: Implications for Foreign Trade," ibid., pp. 349-76, 377-83. Neuberger, in his contribution, suggests a list of key elements of the Soviet-type system, (pp. 351-52).

    2. V. I. Lenin, Collected Works Vol. VI (Moscow: Co-operative Society for Foreign Workers in the Soviet Union, 1936), p. 113; also Politische Ökonomie (East Berlin) (1959), p. 533.

    3. A great deal has been written on this topic. The author's interpretation of the key factors of the development strategy of the 1950s and 1960s draws heavily on the following works: Maurice Ernst, "Postwar Economic Growth in Eastern Europe (A Comparison with Western Europe)," in New Directions in the Soviet Economy, in Studies prepared for the Subcommittee on Foreign Economic Policy of the Joint Committee, Congress of the United States, Pt. IV: The World Outside (Washington, D.C.: U.S. Government Printing Office, 1966), pp. 875-916; Michael Gamarnikow, Economic Reforms in Eastern Europe (Detroit: Wayne State University, 1968); Economic Developments in Countries of Eastern Europe: A Compendium of Papers, Submitted to the Subcommittee on Foreign Economic Policy of the Joint Economic Committee, Congress of the United States (Washington, D.C.: U.S. Government Printing Office, 1970); Nicolas Spulber, The Economics of Communist Eastern Europe (New York: The Technology Press of M.I.T. and John Wiley & Sons, 1957), and The State and Economic Development in Eastern Europe (New York: Random House, 1966). The various volumes of the United Nations, Economic Bulletin for Europe and the Economic Survey of Europe, as well as the research reports published by Radio Free Europe are an invaluable source for anyone interpreting the developments in the socialist countries of Europe.

    4. The literature on Comecon (CMEA) is abundant. The author has found the following most helpful in the analysis: John P. Hardt, "East European Economic Development: Two Decades of Interrelationships and Interactions with the Soviet Union," in Economic Developments in Countries of Eastern Europe, pp. 5-40; Michael Kaser, COMECON: Integration Problems of the Planned Economies (London: Oxford University Press, 1965); R. E. H. Mellor, COMECON: Challenge to the West, Searchlight Book No. 16 (New York: Van Nostrand Reinhold Co., 1971); and Henry Schaefer, "What Role for Comecon?," RFER:EE, Economics/1, April, 1970, p. 123.

5. Hardt, "Economic Development," pp. 10-11.

6. Ivo Crkvenčić, "The Effects of Industrialization on the Local Distribution of Manpower in Croatia," The Effects of Industrialization on the Agricultural Population in the European Socialist Countries, Symposium of Hungarian Academy of Sciences, Institute of Geography, October 18-22, 1967 (Budapest, 1967), pp. 18-28; Joel M. Halpern, "Yugoslav Peasant Society in Transition—Stability in Change," Anthropological Quarterly, XXXVI (July, 1963), 156-82 and "Peasant Culture and Urbanization in Yugoslavia," Contributions to Mediterranean Sociology: Mediterranean Rural Communities and Social Change, Acts of the Mediterranean Sociological Conference, J. G. Peristiany, ed., (Athens, July, 1963), pp. 289-311; Vladimir Klemencič, "Sozialgeographische Probleme der Arbeiter Bauern-Strukturen unter besonderer Berücksichtigung der Situation in Jugoslawien," Münchner Studien zur Sozial-und Wirtschaftsgeographie, Band 4: Zum Standort der Sozialgeogeographie (1969), pp. 75-82.

7. Harry G. Shaffer, "East Europe: Varieties of Economic Management," East Europe, XIX (1970), 21.

8. Ernst, "Postwar Economic Growth," p. 889.

9. Hardt, "Economic Development," p. 8.

10. Spulber, Economic Development, p. 76.

11. United Nations, "Economic Development in Romania," Eco.Bu.Eur., XXIII (1961), p. 57. This and the following discussions leaned heavily on this United Nations study, specifically pp. 55-60.

12. For details of the economic organization see ibid., pp. 57-60.

13. Ibid., p. 58.

14. For the discussions on Romania, the author has found the following publications of special value: Emilian Dobrescu, The Structure of Romanian Economy (Bucharest: Meridiane Publishing House, 1968); George W. Hoffman, "The Problem of the Underdeveloped Regions in Southeast Europe: A Comparative Analysis of Romania, Yugoslavia and Greece," Annals-AAG, LVII (December, 1967), 637-49; Gustav Holzmann, "Strukturwandel der rumänischen Wirtschaft," ZfW., VI (1962), 40-46; John M. Montias, "Unbalanced Growth in Rumania," Am.Eco.Rev., LII (May, 1963), 562-71; John M. Montias, Economic Development in Communist Rumania (Cambridge, Mass.:

MIT Press, 1967); Vasile Rausser, "Sotsialisticeskaya Industrializa-tziya i eyo posledstviya v razvitii narodnogo khozyaystva RNR" [Socialist Industrialization and Its Consequences in the Development of the National Economy of the Rumanian People's Republic], Revue, Roumaine Sciences Sociales, Seria Science Economique, VIII (1964), 239-56; and Christache Stan, "Industrialisation et Urbanisation en Roumaine," Série de Géographie, XIII (1969), 129-43.

15. State farms and collectives cultivated 71 percent of the arable land in 1961 as compared to 28 percent in 1957. See "Economic Development in Romania," pp. 19, 21.

16. Montias, "Unbalanced Growth," pp. 20, 23.

17. R. V. Burks, "The Politics of Economic Reform in Bulgaria and Romania," paper presented at Research Conference on Economic Reform in Eastern Europe, University of Michigan, November, 1970, pp. 50-51 (mimeographed).

18. For the discussions on Bulgaria, the following publications are of special value: Liliana Brisby, "Bulgaria's Economic Leap Year," World Today, XVI (January, 1960), 35-46; J. F. Brown, Bulgaria Under Communist Rule (New York: Praeger Publishers, 1970); Government of Bulgaria, The Industrialization of the People's Republic of Bulgaria: Its Nature, Present State and Prospects, United Nations, Industrial Development Organization, International Symposium on Industrial Development, ID/CONF. 1/G.52, July 10, 1967 (Athens, 1967); Kristov T. Todor, Geografija na Promÿslenosta v B'lgarija [Industrial Geography of Bulgaria] (Sofia: Drzavno Izdatelstvo, Nauka I Izkustvo, 1962); Todor D. Zotschew, "Wandel und Wachstum der Bulgarischen Volkswirtschaft," Bulgarische Jahrbücher, I (1968), 239-62; and United Nations, "Economic Development in Bulgaria," Eco.Su.Eur. (Geneva, 1961), Ch. VI, pp. 16-44.

19. "Economic Development in Bulgaria," Ch. VI, p. 38, publishes a table of the distribution of gross fixed investments. The statistical data in this report served as a basis for the discussions in this section.

20. Novo Vreme (translated), October, 1959, p. 21.

21. The following publications have served as background for these discussions: William E. Griffith, Albania and the Sino-Soviet Rift (Cambridge, Mass.: MIT Press, 1963); Nicolas C. Pano, The People's Republic of Albania, Integration and Community Building in Eastern Europe, Jan F. Triska, ed. (Baltimore: The Johns Hopkins

Press, 1968); Harilla Papajorgh, The Development of Socialist Industry and Its Prospects in the People's Republic of Albania (Tiranë: The State Publishing House, 1962); Hans Joachim Pernack, "Die albanische Wirtschaftspolitik nach dem Zweiten Weltkrieg," Estratto da Shejzat, XIII (October-December, 1969), 1-21; Stavro Skendi, Albania, East-Central Europe Under the Communist, series published for the Mid-European Studies Center, Inc. (New York: Frederick A. Praeger, 1956); and United Nations, "Economic Development in Albania," Eco. Su.Eur. (Geneva, 1961), Ch. 6, pp. 1-15.

22. Investments during the Second Five-Year Plan (1956-60) allocated 18.3 percent to agriculture and 44.1 percent to industry and mining. J. Simeon, "Die wirtschaftliche Entwicklung Albaniens, Bulgariens and Rumäniens nac dem Zweiten Weltkrieg," Osteuropa Wirtschaft, II (1957), 127.

23. Hoffman, "Underdeveloped Regions," pp. 649-66; Benjamin N. Ward, "Capitalism vs. Socialism: A Small Country Version," in Gregory Grossman, ed., Essays in Socialism and Planning in Honor of Carl Landauer (Englewood Cliffs, N.J.,: Prentice-Hall, 1970), pp. 58-85.

24. For developments to 1961, the reader is referred to George W. Hoffman and Fred Warner Neal, Yugoslavia and the New Communism (New York: The Twentieth Century Fund, 1962). The literature on Yugoslav's economic development problems is very plentiful, therefore only a few very selected publications are cited here. The following were most useful: Rudolf Bićanić, "Problematika jedinstva privrede u Jugoslaviji" [Problems of the Unity of the Economy of Yugoslavia], Zbornik Pravnog Fakulteta u Zagrebu, Spomenica prof. Rudolfu Bićaniću, XIX (1969), 302-16; Rudolf Bićanić, "Economics of Socialism in a Developed Country," Foreign Affairs, XXXXIV (July, 1966), 633-50; Joseph T. Bombelles, Economic Development of Communist Yugoslavia 1947-1964 (Stanford, Cal.: The Hoover Institute on War, Revolution and Peace, 1968); J. T. Crawford, "Yugoslavia's New Economic Strategy: A Progress Report," in Economic Developments in Countries of Eastern Europe, pp. 608-34; F. E. Ian Hamilton, Yugoslavia: Patterns of Economic Activity (New York: Frederick A. Praeger, 1968); Wayne S. Vucinich, ed., Contemporary Yugoslavia: Twenty Years of Socialist Experiment (Berkeley: University of California Press, 1970); and Benjamin N. Ward, "Yugoslavia," in Adamantios Pepelasis, Leon Mears, and Irma Adelman, eds., Economic Development (New York: Harper & Bros., 1961), pp. 523-62. Very useful are the various reports by Dennison I. Rusinow, written for the American Universities Field Staff and published since 1964. The United Nations publishes

regularly reports on Yugoslavia, both in the Surveys and the Bulletin; the same goes for the OECD (Economic Surveys). See also the very useful study by The Economist (London), "Another Way. A Survey of Yugoslavia," August 21, 1971.

25. Hoffman and Neal, Yugoslavia, p. 211.

26. Rudolf Bićanić, Problems of Planning—East and West (The Hague: Mouton and Co., 1967), p. 60.

27. Hoffman and Neal, Yugoslavia, pp. 166-67. The quote within the quote is from Boris Kidrić, "From State Socialism to Economic Democracy," Yugoslav Review, February, 1952, pp. 6, 14.

28. Hoffman and Neal, Yugoslavia, p. 212.

29. Quote is from Crawford, "Yugoslavia's New Economic Strategy," p. 611.

30. Dennison I. Rusinow, "Understanding the Yugoslav Reform," World Today, XXIII (February, 1967), 71-79.

31. Hoffman and Neal, Yugoslavia, pp. 347-56.

32. Joseph Berliner, Soviet Economic Aid (New York: Frederick A. Praeger, 1958), p. 33; also Hoffman and Neal, Yugoslavia, pp. 340-345. Greece in the period 1945-64 received Soviet aid to the amount of $84 million, according to Leo Tansky, "Soviet Foreign Aid to the Less Developed Countries," in New Directions in the Soviet Economy, p. 974.

33. Crawford, "Yugoslavia's New Economic Strategy," pp. 613-15.

34. Yugoslav Survey (English edition), V (April-June, 1964), pp. 2505-12.

35. The literature on the developments in Greece in the aftermath of the civil war are plentiful; only a few are cited, having served for basic reference purposes: Wray O. Candilis, The Economy of Greece 1944-1964: Efforts for Stability and Development (New York: Frederick A. Praeger, 1968); Bernard Kayser, "La Grèce Moderne: La péninsula hellénique," in l'Encyclopaedia Universalis (1971), pp. 1071-77; Bernard Kayser, Géographie Humaine de la Grèce (Paris: Presses Universitaires de France, 1964); William Hardy McNeill, Greece: American Aid in Action 1947-1956 (New York: The Twentieth

Century Fund, 1957); Andreas G. Papandreou, A Strategy for Greek
Economic Development, Research Monograph No. 1 (Athens: Center
of Economic Research, 1962); Adamantios Pepelasis, "Greece," in
Pepelasis, Leon Mears, and Irma Adelman, eds. Economic Development,
pp. 500-522; Harry J. Psomiades, "The Economic and Social Transfor-
mation of Modern Greece," Journal of International Affairs, XIX (1965),
194-205; and Irwin T. Sanders, "Greek Society in Transition," Balkan
Studies, VIII (1967), 317-32. See also "Structural Changes in the
Economy," Economic Bulletin (Commercial Bank of Greece), LXV
(July-September, 1970), 5-15; and the very excellent study, "A Survey:
The Two Faces of Greece," Economist (London), July 31, 1971. The
OECD publishes regularly the Economic Surveys on Greece, and much
statistical data is available in the various United Nations publications
e.g., Survey and Bulletin.

36. Pepelasis, "Greece," p. 518; and George W. Hoffman,
"Regional Development Processes in Southeast Europe: A Comparative
Analysis of Bulgaria and Greece," in George W. Hoffman, ed. Eastern
Europe: Essays in Geographical Problems (London and New York:
Methuen and Praeger Publishers, 1971), pp. 443-51.

37. Certain sections of these discussions are taken from the
author's contribution in Hoffman, ed., Eastern Europe, pp. 431-83.
Ministry of Coordination, The Five Year Programme of the Economic
Development of Greece, 1960-1964 (Athens, 1964).

38. Benjamin N. Ward, Greek Regional Development, Research
Monograph No. 4 (Athens: Centre for Economic Research, 1962).

39. Pepelasis, "Greece," pp. 520-21.

40. Ernst, "Postwar Economic Growth," p. 905. Ernst's
study excludes Yugoslavia from its considerations.

41. John Michael Montias, "Producer Prices in a Centrally
Planned Economy—The Polish Discussion," in Gregory Grossman,
ed., Value and Plan (Berkeley: University of California Press, 1960),
pp. 64-65.

42. Vladimir Treml, "Politics of Libermanism," Soviet Studies,
XIX (April, 1968), 567-72. See also the discussions by Hardt, "Economic
Development," pp. 27-28.

43. Gamarnikow, Economic Reforms, p. 12.

44. Gregory Grossman, "Economic Reform: The Interplay of Economics and Politics," in R. V. Burks, ed., The Future of Communism in Europe (Detroit: Wayne State University, 1968), p. 113.

45. Burks, "The Politics of Economic Reform," pp. 47-105.

46. Ibid., p. 2.

47. Shaffer, "East Europe," p. 35; and Lubomir A. Dellin, "Bulgarien," in Hermann Gross, ed., Osteuropa-Wirtschaftsreform, Dokumente und Kommentare zu Ost-Europa-Fragen, Band VIII (Bonn: Atlantic Forum, 1970), pp. 75-89.

48. The National Conference of the Romanian Communist Party adopted in December, 1967, "Measures for Perfecting the Management and Planning of the National Economy" (Agerpress, December 6, 1967). Also see Harry Trend, "Some Aspects of Current Economic Policies in Rumania," RFER:EE, Rumania/6, 3-13-70; Burks, "The Politics of Economic Reform"; and Dellin, "Bulgarien," pp. 92-93.

49. Montias' publications provide, without doubt, the most thorough analysis of the Romanian development; see, e.g., "Unbalanced Growth in Rumania," and Economic Development. Also, Claus D. Rohleder, "Rumänien,"in Gross, ed., Osteuropa-Wirtschaftsreformen, pp. 91-111.

50. Gregory Grossman, "Economic Reforms: A Balance Sheet," Problems of Communism, XV (November-December, 1966), 44; and Grossman, "Interplay," pp. 110-11.

51. Grossman, "Balance Sheet," p. 44.

52. Grossman, "Interplay," p. 111. The author here also cites the positive effects, such as social mobilization, high rates of investment and massive if crude capital formation.

53. Nicolas Spulber, "Economic Modernization," in Robert F. Byrnes, ed., The U.S. and Eastern Europe. (Englewood Cliffs, N.J.,: Prentice-Hall, 1967), p. 74.

54. Benjamin Higgins, "The Scope and Objectives of Planning for Underdeveloped Regions," Proceedings of the First Interamerican Seminar of the Definition of Regions for Development Planning (Rio de Janeiro: Comisión de Geografía, Instituto Panamericano de Geografía e Historia, 1969), p. 56.

55. Burks, "The Politics of Economic Reform," p. 1.

56. John M. Montias, "Economic Nationalism in Eastern Europe: Forty Years of Continuity and Change," Journal of International Affairs, XX (1966), p. 69.

57. "Decentralization Underway in Albania," RFER:EE, Albania, 4-21-66.

58. "Tenth Plenum Against Excessive Centralism," RFER:EE, Albania, 7-15-71.

59. The literature analyzing Yugoslav developments is abundant; the following is of special value: S. Pejovich, "Planning and the Market in Yugoslavia," paper presented at the Research Conference on Economic Reform in Eastern Europe, University of Michigan, Ann Arbor, November, 1970 (mimeographed); the United Nations Surveys for 1965 (Pt. I, Ch. 2, pp. 99-102), for 1966 (Ch. 1, pp. 58-65), for 1967 (Ch. 1, pp. 93-98), for 1968 (Ch. 1, pp. 72-76), and for 1969 (Pt. II, Ch. 2, pp. 149-52); Crawford, "Yugoslavia's New Economic Strategy," pp. 615-33; and the excellent summary prepared by the editors of The Economist, "Another Way," August 21, 1971.

60. Eco.Su.Eu., I (1965), p. 57.

61. Shaffer, "East Europe," pp. 27-28.

62. Grossman, "Interplay," p. 114.

63. R. V. Burks, "The Political Implications of Economic Reform," paper presented at Research Conference on Economic Reform in Eastern Europe, University of Michigan, Ann Arbor, November, 1970, pp. 61-62 (mimeographed).

64. Grossman, "Interplay," p. 125.

65. Ibid., p. 121.

66. Burks, "Political Implications," p. 6.

67. Quote is from Grossman, "Balance Sheet," p. 54.

68. The 1965 reform grew out of the The Resolution on the Basic Guidelines for Further Development of the Economic System in 1964. The literature discussing the situation that led to the reform,

and the Reform itself, is tremendous. The following are the most perceptive: K. Dzeba and M. Beslac, Privredna reforma, Što i zašto se mijenja [Economic Reform, What and Why They Change] (Zagreb: Novinarska izdavačka kuća Stvarnost, 1965); Bićanić, "Economics of Socialism"; the reports by Rusinow for the American Universities Field Staff; Deborah Milenkovitch, Plan and Market in Yugoslav Economic Thought (New Haven, Conn.: Yale University Press, 1971); Fred Warner Neal and Winston M. Fisk, "Economics and Politics," Problems of Communism, XV (November–December, 1966), pp. 28-37; Benjamin N. Ward, "Political Power and Economic Change in Yugoslavia," Am.Eco.Rev., LVIII (May, 1968), 568-79.

69. Pejovich, "Planning," p. 10.

70. Ibid. Pejovich comments that "some vestiges of administrative control of the economy are still present in Yugoslavia, such as administrative investments in less developed areas, price controls, various informal channels of administrative interference, etc."

71. Borba, October 27, 1970, as translated in Joint Translation Service, No. 5771, speaks even of a higher figure, amounting to 824,000, with 425,000 in Germany. But this figure includes 200,000 in non-European countries. Also, RFER:EE, Yugoslavia, 6-23-70 and 7-9-70, published two articles on this critical problem for Yugoslavia: "Greater Economic Freedom Urged for Yugoslav Workers Returned from the West," and Slobodan Stankovic, "Yugoslav Workers in the West." A very good analysis of this problem is by Ernest Bauer, "Die jugoslawischen Gastarbeiter in Westeuropa," Der Donauraum, XV (March-April, 1970), pp. 140-51.

72. Crawford, "Yugoslavia's New Economic Strategy," pp. 618-23.

73. For these statistics and those for earlier years, see the country reports published by OECD at intervals of approximately eighteen to twenty-four months, the last one published at the time of the writing of this book was for November, 1970.

74. Zdenko Antić, "Foreign Investments in Yugoslavia Expanding," RFER:EE, Communist Area, 8-5-70. Also, see Miodrag Sukijasović, Foreign Investment in Yugoslavia (Belgrade and New York: The Institute of International Politics and Economics and Oceana Publications, 1970).

75. Two studies discuss this problem from a different point of view: Benjamin N. Ward, The Socialist Economy: A Study of

Organizational Alternatives (New York: Random House, 1967), pp. 182-257; and Pejovich, "Planning," whose analysis "the fundamental role of property rights structures as a specification of the set of opportunity choices about resource use."

76. Reference is made to three recent publications; Burks, "The Politics of Economic Reform"; Dellin, "Bulgarien"; and Brown, Bulgaria. Of invaluable aid are the discussions published by RFER and the United Nations Economic Surveys of Europe.

77. Dellin, "Bulgarien," pp. 83-84; and Brown, Bulgaria, 167-70.

78. Dellin, "Bulgarien," p. 76.

79. Ibid., p. 77.

80. R.N., "Bulgarian Trade with Developed Non-Communist Countries," RFER:EE Background Report: Bulgaria, 10-15-69; Michael Costello, "Self-Interest Versus Orthodoxy: A Study of Bulgaria's Relationship with the Federal Republic of Germany," RFER:EE, Background Report: Bulgaria, 5-4-70.

81. R.T., "International Tourism—A Matter of Concern to the Bulgarian Regime," RFER:EE, Bulgaria/7, 2-19-70; Georgi Evtimov, "Entwicklung des Fremdenverkehrs in der Volksrepublik Bulgarien," in Karl Ruppert and Jörg Maier, eds., Der Tourismus und seine Perspektiven für Südosteuropa, "WGI"-Berichte zur Regionalforschung, Heft 6, "Südosteuropa-Studien," No, 17 (Munich: Eigenverlag der Sudosteuropa-Gesellschaft, 1971), pp. 157-62.

82. Dellin, "Bulgarien," p. 84; also, J. F. Brown, "Reforms in Bulgaria," Problems of Communism, XV (May-June, 1966), 17-21.

83. Steve Larabee, "The Reorganization of the State Economic Associations in Bulgaria," RFER:EE, Bulgaria, 2-1-71.

84. R.N., "The July Plenum: Economic Considerations," RFER:EE, Bulgaria, 8-22-68; also Dellin, "Bulgarien," pp. 84-87. Zhivkov's report at the July Plenum was published in Rabotnichesko Delo, July 25-27, 1968, and translated by the U.S. Embassy in Sofia, Bulgaria.

85. Novo Vreme, No. 10, 1968, as translated by the U.S. Embassy in Sofia.

86. Radio Free Europe, Research, published during 1969 and 1970—a series of reports discussing these developments and analyzing their impact on the economy and its institutions.

87. Dellin, "Bulgarian"; and Dellin, "Bulgarian Economic Reform—Advance and Retreat," Problems of Communism, XX (September-October, 1970), pp. 44-52.

88. M. Savov, "Cooperation Among the Socialist Countries and the Development of our Economy," Ikonomicheska Misal, No. 7 (1962), as translated in RFER:EE, Press Survey Bulgaria, October 20, 1969; other Radio Free Europe reports discussing Bulgarian-Soviet economic relations are: "More on Bulgarian-Soviet Economic Relations," RFER:EE, Bulgaria, 6-2-69; "Bulgarian-Soviet Economic Relations," RFER:EE, SR, Bulgaria, 5-28-69; Henry Trend, "Joint Sector Planning— A Form of Supranational Planning," RFER:EE, Bulgaria, 10-2-69.

89. R.N., "Bulgaria to Build a Third Metallurgical Combine," RFER:EE, Bulgaria, 26-11-60; "Construction of Atomic Power Station Began," RFER:EE, SR, Bulgaria, 9-3-70; "Bulgarian-Soviet Agreements and 1971-75 Plan Coordination," RFER:EE, SR, Bulgaria, 9-3-70; Henry Trend, "Recent Developments in Soviet Bulgarian Economic Integration—a Soviet Blueprint for Comecon?," RFER:EE, BR, Bulgaria, 7-3-70.

90. "Bulgarisch-sowjetische Vereinbarungen und Planungskoordinerung für 1971-75," Osteuropäische Rundschau, XVI (October, 1970), p. X/35.

91. Vitali Tadzher, "The Agrarian-Industrial Complex, a New Form of Economic Organization," Kooperativno selo (translated from the Bulgarian), October 31, 1970, pp. 1-2; R. N., "Central Committee Decision on Reorganization of Bulgarian Agriculture," RFER:EE, SR, Bulgaria, 5-13-70; "Giant Agricultural-Industrial Complexes Formed," RFER:EE, SR, Bulgaria, 1-15-69; "Agro-Industrielle Komplexe umstritten," Osteuropäische Rundschau, XVII (1971) V/36. Burks, "The Politics of Economic Reform," p. 47, draws the conclusion that the safety and assistance of the Soviet Union permitted the organization of these uneconomical complexes, which at the same time permit a reduction in rural-urban migration and better central control of industrial centers. See also "Central Committee Plenum on Territorial Planning," RFER:EE, SR, Bulgaria, 3-5-70.

92. Called "Unified plan for socioeconomic development," it was approved by the National Assembly on December 16, 1970. R.N., "The Bulgarian Economic Plan for 1971," RFER:EE, Bulgaria, 1-22-71.

93. Burks, "The Politics of Economic Reform," pp. 46, 47.

94. Numerous writers discussed the problem of Romanian-Soviet relations, only a few are cited here: R. V. Burks, "The Rumanian National Deviation: An Accounting," in Kurt London, ed., Eastern Europe in Transition (Baltimore: The Johns Hopkins Press, 1966), pp. 93-116; Burks, "The Politics of Economic Reform," Stephen Fischer-Galati, "Rumania and the Sino-Soviet Conflict," in London, ed., Eastern Europe in Transition, pp. 261-75.

95. Kaser, COMECON, pp. 91-92.

96. Ibid., pp. 93-94.

97. Ibid., p.94.

98. Ibid., p. 104.

99. "Draft Directives of the Central Committee of the Rumanian Communist Party on the Perfecting of Management and Planning of the National Economy in Keeping with the Conditions of the New State of Rumania's Socialist Development," as translated in RFER:EE, Press Survey: Rumania, December 20, 1967.

100. Quote is from Montias, Economic Development in Communist Rumania, p. 54.

101. Ibid., p. 164. Henry Schaefer, "Rumania's Economic Turn to the West Since the Ninth Party Congress," RFER:EE, Background Report, Rumania, August 28, 1969.

102. Quote is from Burks, "The Politics of Economic Reform," p. 50. A new Institute for Trade Research and a State Inspectorate General for Quality Control of Export Products was organized.

103. Rohleder, "Rumänien," p. 93.

104. "The Statute on the Industrial Central," Buletinul Oficial, No. 47, Pt. I, April 2, 1969, as translated in RFER:EE, Press Surveys, Bulgaria, 7-8-69. A sizable number of writings dealing with the centrals were translated by RFER.

105. Robert R. King, "The Party and the Implications of Technology," RFER:EE, Rumania, 3-22-71.

106. "The New Profit-Sharing System," RFER:EE, SR, Romania, 2-24-70; "New Measures Concerning the Economic Reform," RFER:EE, SR, Romania, 7-8-70.

107. Harry Trend, "Some Aspects of Current Economic Policies in Rumania," RFER:EE, Rumania/6, 3-13-70, p. 51.

108. Ibid., pp. 52, 57-58.

109. Burks, "The Politics of Economic Reform," pp. 68-85. The information here was taken largely from reports published by Radio Free Europe, e.g., "Economic Cooperation and Trade with Comecon, 1971-75," RFER:EE, SR, Romania, 9-9-70; "Targets in Rumanian Foreign Trade," RFER:EE, SR, Romania, 8-26-70.

110. Henry Schaefer, "Rumania's Economic Turn to the East," RFER:EE, Romania, 4-3-71, pp. 22-26.

111. Dan Morgan, "Romania Stresses Self-Help As It Faces Flood Damage," International Herald Tribune (European edition), June 11, 1970.

112. Robert R. King, "Rumania Reasserts its Foreign Policy Position," RFER:EE Rumania, 5-6-71.

113. For the background to the conflict, see Griffith, Albania and the Sino-Soviet Rift.

114. "Albania's 1969 Plan Fulfillment and the 1970 Plan," RFER:EE Communist Area, Albania, Economy, 3-2-70.

115. "Elements of Albanian 'Model' of Economic Reform," RFER:EE, Albania, Economics, 11-3-69.

116. "Tenth Plenum Against Excessive Centralism," RFER:EE, Communist Area, Albania, 7-15-70; "Intensification of Decentralization in Albania," RFER:EE, Albania, 8-18-70.

117. Ibid., p. 2.

118. Ibid., p. 3.

NOTES TO CHAPTER 6

1. Harvey S. Perloff et al., Regions, Resources and Economic Growth (Baltimore: The Johns Hopkins Press, 1960).

2. Antoni R. Kuklinski, Trends in Research on Comprehensive Regional Development, UNRISD/69/C.2/Rev.1, GE 68-15133 (Geneva: UNRISD, June, 1968), p. 4; Andrezj Wróbel, in a recent paper, defined development as an "innovating process leading to structural transformation of social systems." Andrezj Wróbel, "Theories and Models of Regional Development: A Critical Examination," paper presented at IGU Commission on Regional Aspects of Economic Development, colloquim on Regional Inequalities of Development (Rio de Janeiro, April, 1971), p. 10 (mimeographed).

3. Comisión de Geografía, Instituto Panamericano de Geografía e Historia, Proceedings of the First Interamerican Seminar on the Definition of Regions for Development Planning (Rio de Janeiro, 1969), p. 322.

4. Wróbel, "Theories and Models."

5. Tormond Hermansen, "Information Systems for Regional Development Control," Regional Science Association, Papers, XXII (1968), p. 120, considers "planning like decision-making, consists of processing input information which is transformed into different output information. However, in contrast to decision-making, planning is of a preparatory character and therefore does not imply, to the same degree, a commitment to action. While decision-making is of a discrete character, it is more convenient to view planning as a continuous process."

6. Rudolf Bićanić, "The Planner and the Politician," lecture delivered at Conference Internationale de Futurilles, Paris, April, 1965, p. 1 (mimeographed). For a brief summary of the various stages in development planning, see the discussions in Tormond Hermansen, Interregional Allocation of Investments for Social and Economic Development: An Elementary Model Approach in Analysis, report No. 70.4 (Geneva: UNRISD, 1970), pp. 14-15.

7. Rudolf Bićanić, Problems of Planning—East and West (The Hague: Mouton & Co., 1967), pp. 14-20, summarizes the views of both sides.

8. The term, as defined in ibid., p. 20, expresses "the objective technological or functional qualities inherent in certain economic activities which make them suitable for planning."

9. Ibid., pp. 20-21 discusses these points in some detail.

10. Tormond Hermansen, Spatial Organization and Economic Development—The Scope and Task of Spatial Planning, UNRISD/69/C.68, GE 69-23863 (Geneva: UNRISD, July, 1969), p. 1.

11. Derwent Whittlesey, "The Regional Concept and the Regional Method," in Preston E. James and Clarence F. Jones, eds., American Geography Inventory and Prospect (Syracuse, N.Y.: Syracuse University Press, 1954), pp. 19-68; Kazimierz Dziewoński, "Théories de la Région Économique," in M. Omer Tulippe, ed., Mélanges de Géographie (Gembloux: Editions J. Duculot, 1967), pp. 545-57; also the writings on theory and terminology of Economic Regionalization by Hans Bobek ("Some Remarks on Basic Concepts in Economic Regionalization," pp. 17-24), Kazimierz Dziewoński ("Concepts and Terms in the Field of Economic Regionalization," pp. 25-30), and George W. Hoffman ("Development of Regional Geography in the United States"), all in Miroslav Macka, ed., Economic Regionalization, Proceedings of the 4th General Meeting of the Commission on Methods of Economic Regionalization of the IGU (Brno, Czechoslovakia, September, 1965).

12. Niles M. Hansen, French Regional Planning (Bloomington: Indiana University Press, 1968), pp. 3-25; also A. R. Kuklinski, "Regional Development, Regional Policies and Regional Planning: Problems and Issues," Regional Studies, IV (1970), pp. 269-70.

13. Kuklinski, "Regional Development," p. 270.

14. Kuklinski, Trends, p. 8. See also the discussions in Bićanić, Problems of Planning, pp. 57-68.

15. Some writers even feel that there does not exist such a thing as a theory of economic development; J. Hillhorst, "Regional Development Theory: An Attempt to Synthesize," in Multidisciplinary Aspects of Regional Development (Paris: Development Centre of the OECD, 1968), p. 21.

16. D. F. Darwent, "Growth Poles and Growth Centers in Regional Planning—a Review," Environment and Planning, I (1969), pp. 5-32; Niles M. Hansen, "Development Pole Theory in a Regional Context," Kyklos, XX (1967), pp. 709-27; Hansen, Criteria for a Growth

Center Policy, UNRISD/71/C.33, GE 71-7452 (Geneva: UNRISD, April, 1971); Hillhorst, "Regional Development Theory"; Albert O. Hirschman, The Strategy of Economic Development (New Haven, Conn.: Yale University Press, 1958); and Kuklinski, "Regional Development . . ." op. cit.

17. Tormond Hermansen, Development Poles and Development Centres in National and Regional Development—Elements of a Theoretical Framework for a Synthetical Approach, UNRISD/69/C.77, GE 69-26981 (Geneva: UNRISD, December, 1969), pp. 50-53.

18. François Perroux, "La notion de pôle de croissance," L'économie du XXe siècle (2d ed.; Paris: Presses Universitaires de France, 1964), pp. 142-53, originally published in Economie Appliquée, Nos. 1-2 (1955); Hirschman, Strategy, esp. Ch. 10.

19. Kuklinski, "Regional Development," pp. 270-72.

20. Gunnar Myrdal, Economic Theory in Underdeveloped Regions (London: Duckworth, 1957).

21. Hillhorst, "Regional Development Theory," p. 24.

22. Benjamin Higgins, in "The Scope and Objectives of Planning for Underdeveloped Regions," in Proceedings of the First Interamerican Seminar on the Definition of Regions for Development Planning (Rio de Janeiro: Comisión de Geografía, Instituto Pan Americano de Geografía e História, 1969), pp. 48-49, discusses five possibilities that could lead to backwash effects.

23. Hermansen, Development Poles, pp. 50-56, gives an excellent summary of the "theories of geographical incidence and transmission of economic development." This discussion has been most useful for its precision and brevity. See also the discussions in William Alonso, Industrial Location and Regional Policy in Economic Development, Center for Planning and Development Research Working Paper No. 74 (Berkeley, Cal.: Institute of Urban and Regional Development, February, 1968).

24. For a discussion of Rosenstein-Rodan's "balanced growth" theory, see Ch. 4 and 8. Paul N. Rosenstein-Rodan, "Problems of Industrialization in Eastern and Southeastern Europe," The Economic Journal, LIII (June-September, 1943), 202-11.

25. Kuklinski, "Regional Development," pp. 271-72.

26. Ibid., p. 272.

27. Several sources discussing the concepts of growth poles and centers have already been cited; see especially footnote 16 of this chapter. A few additional sources for background reference are cited here: J. R. Lasuen, "On Growth Poles," Urban Studies, VI (June, 1969), pp. 137-61; Morgan D. Thomas, "Growth Pole Theory: An Examination of Its Basic Concepts," (Seattle: University of Washington) (mimeographed); and a valuable reference, D. E. Keeble, "Models of Economic Development," in Richard J. Chorley and Peter Haggett, eds., Models in Geography (London: Methuen Publishers, 1967), pp. 281-87.

28. François Perroux, "Economic Space: Theory and Applications," reprinted from Quarterly Journal of Economic, LXIV (February, 1950) in John Friedmann and William Alonso, eds., Regional Development and Planning: A Reader (Cambridge, Mass.: MIT Press, 1964), pp. 21-36.

29. Ibid., p. 27.

30. Higgins, "Scope and Objectives," p. 60.

31. Ibid., p. 60.

32. Hermansen, Development Poles, pp. 36-50, summarizes the central-place theories of spatial organization and the relation between central-place theories and theories of localized poles of development. See also the original references: August Lösch, The Economics of Location, translated by William Wolgom and W. F. Stolper (New Haven, Conn.: Yale University Press, 1954); Walter Christaller, Central Places in Southern Germany, (Englewood Cliffs, N.J.: Prentice-Hall, 1965); and "Das Grundgerüst der räumlichen Ordnung in Europa," Frankfurter Geographische Hefte, XXIV (1950). See also the discussions in Hermansen, Spatial Organization, pp. 24-40.

33. Jacques Boudeville, Problems of Regional Economic Planning (Edinburgh: University Press, 1966).

34. Wróbel, "Theories and Models," p. 8.

35. Higgins, "Scope and Objectives," p. 61.

36. These discussions are summaries, quoted from Lasuen, "On Growth Poles," p. 159, footnote 43.

37. Hermansen, Spatial Organization, p. 76.

38. Ibid., p. 77.

39. Hermansen, Development Poles.

40. Darwent, "Growth Poles," p. 13, further elaborates "that the most important normative questions of regional economic development, those concerned with the regional allocation of investments in both time and space, can be given some clearer direction if this intuitive notion is adopted."

41. Alan Gilbert, "Growth Poles—The Instant Solution to Regional Problems?," paper presented at IGU Commission on Regional Aspects of Economic Development, colloquim on Regional Inequalities of Development (Rio de Janeiro, April, 1971), pp. 12-13 (mimeographed). Gilbert's study critically analyzes the relationship of growth poles to the solution of regional problems.

42. Mens en Ruimte, "A Summary of Regional Development in Western Europe—Experiences and Prospects," provisional working paper (Geneva: UNRISD, December, 1969), pp. 30-32.

43. John R. Friedman, Regional Development Policy—A Case Study of Venezuela (Cambridge, Mass.: MIT Press, 1966); R. P. Misra, Regional Planning—Concepts, Techniques, Policies and Case Studies (Mysore India: The University of Mysore Press, 1969); and Z. Pioro, "Growth Poles and Growth Centres in Regional Policies in Tanzania," report prepared for UNRISD (Geneva: UNRISD, August, 1969).

44. See the discussions summarizing the problem in Hermansen, Development Poles, pp. 74-75, and the paper by M. Penouil, "Growth Poles in Underdeveloped Regions and Countries," paper prepared for the Expert Group on Growth Poles and Growth Centres (Geneva, May, 1969) (mimeographed).

NOTES TO CHAPTER 7

1. A. R. Kuklinski, "Regional Development, Regional Policies and Regional Planning: Problems and Issues," Regional Studies, IV (1970), 275.

2. V. M. Gokhman and L. N. Karpov, "Growth Poles and Growth Centres," in A Review of the Concepts and Theories of Growth Poles and Growth Centres, UNRISD/70/C.6, GE 70-24266 (Geneva: UNRISD, November, 1970), pp. 193-205. See also the discussions about the recently organized industrial/agricultural complexes in Bulgaria in Chapters 5 and 8.

3. John R. Friedman, "A Conceptual Model for the Analysis of Planning Behaviour," Administrative Science Quarterly, XII (1967), 12; Kuklinski, "Regional Development," p. 275; and Tormond Hermansen, Spatial Organization and Economic Development—The Scope and Task of Spatial Planning, UNRISD/69/C.78, GE 69-23863 (Geneva: UNRISD, July, 1969), pp. 2-5.

4. Ibid., p. 3.

5. F. E. Ian Hamilton, "Aspects of Spatial Behavior in Planned Economies," Reg.Sc.Assoc.Papers, XV (1970), 83-105.

6. Ibid., pp. 97-98. See also Egon Neuberger, "Libermanism, Computopia and Visible Hand: The Question of Informational Efficiency," Am.Eco.Rev., LVI (1966), 131-44.

7. For a detailed discussion of this problem, see Richard V. Burks, Technological Innovation and Political Change in Communist Eastern Europe, memorandum RM. 6051 (Santa Monica, Calif.: Rand Corporation, August, 1969). A number of thoughts expressed by the author have been summarized in the following discussions.

8. Rudolf Bićanić, Problems of Planning—East and West (The Hague: Mouton & Co., 1967), p. 85, comments that decentralization in the socialist countries simply represents a correction and not a basic change "in the mechanism of monocentric planning," and that it means transfer "from one center to other centers, be it in a spatial sense (from capital to region) or in a functional sense (from a central planning body to various bodies)."

9. "Intensification of Decentralization in Albania," RFER:EE, 8-18-70.

10. Burks, Technological Innovation, p. 42, stressed "that pluralization and the democratization of the polity are (not) necessarily one and the same." While the process of democratization may very well be desired by the population, pluralization of a Communist polity "may take place without the establishment of either parliamentary government or a multi-party system."

11. Ministry of Coordination, Economic Development Plan for Greece 1968-72 (Athens, December, 1967), pp. 7-8.

12. Ibid., p. 8.

13. George W. Hoffman, "Regional Development Processes in Southeast Europe. A Comparative Analysis of Bulgaria and Greece," in George W. Hoffman, ed., Eastern Europe: Essays in Geographical Problems (London and New York: Methuen and Praeger Publishers, 1971), Table 11.1, p. 437, and also pp. 465-68.

14. Benjamin Ward, "Political Power and Economic Change in Yugoslavia," Am.Eco.Rev., LVIII (May, 1968), 574-76.

15. M. George Zaninovich, "Party and Non-Party Attitudes on Social Change," in R. Barry Farrell, ed., Political Leadership in Eastern Europe and the Soviet Union (Chicago: Aldine Publishing Co., 1970), pp. 294-334, examines various aspects of Communist Party members' value, as opposed to that of non-Party individuals, stressing social characteristics or attributes and values of societal change, and testing these themes against a set of situational attributes. Other studies discussing these issues are Burks, Technological Innovation, and by the same author "The Communist Politics of Eastern Europe," in James N. Rosenau, ed., International Politics and Foreign Policy (New York: The Free Press, 1969), pp. 275-303. Bogdan Denitch, "Mobility and Recruitment of Yugoslav Leadership: The Role of the League of Communists," (New York: Bureau of Applied Research, Columbia University, 1971) (mimeographed, draft); and "Political Cultures and Social Mobility in Yugoslavia," paper presented at Seventh World Congress of the International Sociological Association in Varna, Bulgaria, September, 1970 (mimeographed). See also M. George Zaninovich, "Delineating Political Cultures in Multi-Ethnic Settings: The Yugoslav Case," draft paper, April, 1971 (mimeographed). As is to be expected, the literature on this topic is most extensive for Yugoslavia. Gary K. Bertsch and M. George Zaninovich, "Centralization vs. Decentralization in Yugoslav Political Society," paper presented at American Political Science Association, September, 1971 (mimeographed).

16. Kosta Mihailović, Regional Development in Eastern Europe: Experiences and Prospects, UNRISD/70/C.49, GE 70-18044 (Geneva: UNRISD, August, 1970), p. 118. Throughout this study, the author used examples for explaining the specific problem of Yugoslavia. Polls and opinion and attitudinal studies are available on numerous topics in Yugoslavia. They are still largely unavailable for the other countries of Eastern Europe.

17. Zaninovich, "Attitudes," p. 334. For an excellent analysis and summary of objectives and characteristics of behavioral research in political geography, see the discussions in Roger E. Kasperson and Julian V. Minghi, The Structure of Political Geography (Chicago: Aldine Publishing Co., 1969), pp. 301-18.

18. Aleksander Bajt, "Decentralized Decision Making Structure in the Yugoslav Economy," Economics of Planning (Oslo), VII (1967), 73-85, discusses the problems of the decentralized decision-making structure of Yugoslavia.

19. Janusz A. Ziółkowski, Methodological Problems in the Sociology of Regional Development, UNRISD/69/C.2, GE 69-609 (Geneva: UNRISD, January, 1969).

20. Ibid., pp. 4-5.

21. Peter F. Sugar, "External and Domestic Roots of Eastern European Nationalism," in Peter F. Sugar and Ivo I. Lederer, eds., Nationalism in Eastern Europe, Vol. I (Seattle: University of Washington, Far Eastern and Russian Institute Publications on Russia and Eastern Europe, 1969), pp. 3-54. The literature on "nationalism" is horrendous, and Sugar's article has an excellent selection.

22. Rude Petrović, Prostorna determinacija teritorijalnih jedinica u kommunalnom sistemu Jugoslavije [Spatial Delimitation of Territorial Units in the Communal System of Yugoslavia], Studie i Monografije, Knjiga 1 (Sarajevo: Ekonomski Institut Universiteta u Sarajevu, 1962), p. 28.

23. P. Sicherl, "Regional Aspects of Yugoslav Economic Development and Planning," in Multidisciplinary Aspects of Regional Development (Paris: OECD Development Centre, 1968), p. 163.

24. The makings of location decisions for industries in East European countries are generally applicable for decisions in the general economic sphere. F. E. Ian Hamilton, among geographers, has written most on these problems: "The Location of Industry in East-Central and Southeast Europe," in Hoffman, ed., Eastern Europe, pp. 199-201; "Planning: The Spatial Development of Industry of East Europe: The Principles and Their Impact," Economic Planning (Montreal), (March, 1970), pp. 4-6; and "Models of Industrial Location," in Richard J. Chorley and Peter Haggett, eds., Models in Geography (London: Methuen Publishers, 1967), pp. 361-424.

25. Thomas M. Poulsen, "Administration and Regional Structure in East-Central and Southeast Europe," in Hoffman, ed. Eastern Europe, p. 228. Professor Poulsen's valuable contribution has served as a most useful background for the discussions here.

26. Ibid., 230-50, esp. Tables 1, 2, 3.

27. Victor Tufescu and Constantin Herbst, "The New Administrative-Territorial Organization of Romania, 1968," Série de Géographie, XIII (1969), 25-37. Also, the valuable study by Ronald A. Helin, "The Volatile Administrative Map of Rumania," Annals-AAG, LVII (September, 1967), 481-502.

28. Helin, "The Volatile Administrative Map of Rumania."

29. Poulsen, "Administration," pp. 239-40.

30. Kazimierz Dzieweński and Stanislaw Leszczycki, "Geographical Studies of Economic Regions in Central-Eastern Europe: Problems and Methods," Problems of Economic Regions, Geographical Studies No. 27 (Warsaw, 1961), p. 81.

31. Abraham Melezin, "Soviet Regionalization," Geo. Rev., LVIII (1968), 593-621; also Richard E. Lonsdale, "The Soviet Concept of the Territorial-Production Complex," Slavic Review, XXIV (September, 1965), 466. The term "territorial production complex" denotes a functionally organized area within which economic activities are sufficiently interrelated as to form a single integrated unit. The unity of the "territorial production complex" is thus based on economic relationships or "linkages" rather than on a condition of economic homogeneity. The major contributions to the investigations of economic regionalization in Bulgaria have been by Christo Marinov, Ikonomichesko Raionirance Na NR Bulgaria [Economic Regionalization of Bulgaria] (Sofia: Bulgarian Academy of Sciences, 1963); Dobri Bradistilov, "Efektivnost na teritorialnata organizatsiya na proizvodstvoto," [Effectiveness of the Territorial Organization of Production], translated by A. Bráčkov, Novo Vreme, XLIV (1968), 56-67.

32. Poulsen, "Administration," p. 241.

33. The literature discussing the impact of the administrative map on the economic and political developments of individual countries is still small, though a few penetrating studies have appeared. A few examples are: Jack C. Fisher, "The Yugoslav Commune," World Politics, XVI (1964), 418-41; Eugen Pusić, Lokalna Zajednica [The

Local Community] (Zagreb: Narodne Novine, 1963); Petrović, Prostorna
Determinacija; Kazimierz Dziewoński "Theoretical Problems in the
Development of Economic Regions (Within One Country)," Reg.Sc.
Assoc.Papers, X (Zürich Congress, 1962), 51-60.

34. Over many years, the U.N. Economic Commission for Europe
has presented very useful empirical data and analyses of planning and
institutions in the socialist countries. Much of the information used
in this manuscript is taken from these analytical reports. See especially United Nations, "The European Economy in 1968," Economic
Survey of Europe 1968, Ch. 2, and Economic Survey of Europe in 1969,
Pt. I: "Structural Trends and Prospects in the European Economy."

35. Bićanić, Problems of Planning, p. 58, also mentions so-
called neutral instruments, those contributing to the effectiveness of
the planning techniques. The following discussions lean heavily on
Section IV of Bićanić's discussions.

36. J. T. Crawford, "Yugoslavia's New Economic Strategy:
A Progress Report," Economic Developments in Countries of Eastern
Europe: A Compendium of Papers, submitted to the Subcommittee on
Foreign Economic Policy of the Joint Economic Committee, Congress
of the United States (Washington, D.C.: U.S. Government Printing
Office, 1970), pp. 623-630.

37. Economic Survey of Europe 1968, p. 99 (iv).

38. United Nations, Department of Economic and Social Affairs,
"Problems of Regional Development and Industrial Location in Europe,"
in John R. Friedman and William Alonso, eds., Regional Development
and Planning: A Reader (Cambridge, Mass.: MIT Press, 1964), p. 405.

39. Hamilton, "The Location of Industry," p. 175; and Hamilton,
"Planning."

40. J. Hillhorst, "Regional Development Theory: An Attempt to
Synthesize," in Multidisciplinary Aspects of Regional Development
(Paris: Development Centre of the OECD, 1968), p. 30.

41. Criteria used in different countries include the rate of
profit, the index of profitability, and rentability—total cost/total
revenue or total income/fixed and variable assets. For Yugoslavia,
see the discussions by F. E. Ian Hamilton, Yugoslavia: Patterns of
Economic Activity (New York: Frederick A. Praeger, 1968), pp. 111-13.
Hamilton explains the word "rentability" (rentabililet or rentabilnost

in Serbo-Croatian), which is related to the French word rentabilité, which, loosely translated, means "profitability." It is felt, however, that the literal translation, "rentability," is a more satisfactory interpretation since it avoids the pitfall of equating "profitability" in the capitalist sense (economic profit of a project in isolation) with "rentability," which denotes a balancing of the least investment and production costs of the project itself with the least cost of the macro-economic and macrogeographic situation of the project within the total system of the social and economic structure of the state. "Rentability," therefore, is a broader concept than "profitability." (Ibid., p. 114, footnote 14.)

42. Hamilton, "The Location of Industry," p. 206.

43. Ibid., p. 195. Hamilton discusses, in Yugoslavia, problems of vested interests and behavior in Yugoslav location planning, cf. pp. 138-53, 235-40, 251-52, 282-83, 292-93, 350-62.

44. Hamilton, "Planning," p. 4. The author discusses here two locational solutions that are apparent and in accord with two variable environmental situations. His analysis, however, applies to all the socialist countries of East-Central and Southeast Europe.

45. Hamilton, "The Location of Industry," pp. 200-201.

46. Ibid., pp. 202-4.

47. For a valuable contribution, see Alan Pred, "Behaviour and Location," Lund Studies in Geography, B: Human Geography, 27 (1967).

48. Remarks to Orme Wilson, Jr. "The Belgrade-Bar Railroad: An Essay in Economic and Political Geography," in Hoffman, ed., Eastern Europe, pp. 390-91.

49. See the discussions in Hamilton, "The Location of Industry," p. 201; and Bajt, "Decentralized Decision Making Structure."

NOTES TO CHAPTER 8

1. Antoni R. Kuklinski, "Goals in Regional Policies and Objectives in Regional Planning," UNRISD/68/C.48/Rev. 1, GE 70-6604,

paper prepared for presentation March, 1970, pp. 1-2 (mimeographed).
Perhaps it should be noted here that when speaking of "development,"
as distinct from "growth," both economic and social developments are
included.

2. Kosta Mihailović, Regional Development in Eastern Europe:
Experiences and Prospects, UNRISD/70/C.49, GE 70-18044 (Geneva:
UNRISD, August, 1970), p. 61.

3. Ian Abjiyev, "Agrarian-Industrial Complexes—New Stage
in Development of Bulgarian Agriculture," World Marxist Review,
(December, 1970), 76-81.

4. Lloyd Rodwin, "Choosing Regions for Development," in John
R. Friedman and William Alonso, eds. Regional Development and
Planning: A Reader (Cambridge, Mass.: MIT Press, 1964), p. 40.
While Rodwin's discussions do not specifically refer to the countries
of Southeast Europe, his statement with reference to the growth potential of lagging regions (underdeveloped has been added by the author),
can be applied without question.

5. William Alonso, Industrial Location and Regional Policy in
Economic Development, Center for Planning and Development Research,
Working Paper No. 74 (Berkeley: Institute of Urban and Regional
Development, February, 1968), p. 1.

6. Mihailović, Regional Development, p. 53.

7. Alica Wertheimer-Baletić, "Regionalne demografske
implikacije zaposljavanja u inozemstvo" [Regional Demographic
Implications of Employment Abroad], Ekonomski pregled, XXI (1969),
703-21. The author cites figures showing the great imbalances in
this emigration; e.g., Slovenia's population as part of Yugoslavia's
total population amounted to 8.6 percent (1961 census) while its total
emigration was 15.1 percent; in Croatia this disproportion is even
greater, 22.4 against 50.1 percent. In Bosnia and Herzegovina it is
small—17.7 against 22.1 percent—while in the remaining republics,
the emigration is always smaller than the ration of the emigration to
total population.

8. Mihailović, Regional Development, p. 30.

9. Philippe Bernard, Growth Poles and Growth Centres in
Regional Development. Vol. III: "Growth Poles and Growth Centres
as Instruments of Regional Development and Modernization with

Special Reference to Bulgaria and France," Report No. 70.14 (Geneva: UNRISD, 1970), pp. 29-61.

10. Ibid., pp. 52-58.

11. RFER:EE, Bulgaria/10, "CC Plenum of Territorial Distribution of Production Forces," March 20, 1970; Misho Mishev, "The Development of Productive Forces in the Bulgarian People's Republic and the Problem of Labor Resources" (Translated from the Bulgarian), Novo Vreme, V (May, 1970), 80-91.

12. According to Rabotnichesko Delo, March 10, 1970, as quoted in "CC Plenum of Territorial Distribution of Productive Forces," p. 3, "in the course of 10 years, 677 industrial enterprises have been set up in middle-sized and small towns."

13. Quote is from Bernard, Growth Poles, p. 53. Seven towns have been named that in 1966 restricted in-migration of both populations and productive forces.

14. George W. Hoffman, "The Problem of the Underdeveloped Regions in Southeast Europe: A Comparative Analysis of Romania, Yugoslavia and Greece," Annals-AAG, LVII (December, 1967), 659-61; Dimitra Katochianos, "Planning the Development of the National Network of Urban Centers (Athens Ministry of Co-ordination, Center of Planning and Economic Research, National Physical Planning Service, October, 1967) (mimeographed); "Location of National Industry within a Wider Economic Context," working paper, International Symposium on Industrial Development, United Nations Industrial Development Organization, ID/CONF/L/G/63, Summary, July 1,1967 (mimeographed).

15. Hoffman, "Underdeveloped Regions," pp. 644-49; David Turnock, "The Pattern of Industrialization in Romania," Annals-AAG, LX (March, 1970), 540-59.

16. A. Iancu, "Imbunătătirea repartizării teritoriale a industrie" [Improving the Territorial Distribution of Industry], Lupta de clasa, seria V-a (October, 1966), 11-23; Vintilă Mihăilescu, "Die Wirtschafts-regionen Rumäniens," Série de Géographie, XIV (1970), 197-207; and Christache Stan, "Industrialisation et urbanisation en Roumainie," Série de Géographie, XIII (1969), 129-43.

17. Mihailović, Regional Development, pp. 42-43. As an example, the population of Tiranë increased from 11,000 in 1923 to

25,000 at the outbreak of World War II and reached close to 170,000 in 1969.

18. The problems of the Yugoslav underdeveloped regions have been much covered in the postwar literature, therefore only a few key sources are given: F. E. Ian Hamilton, Yugoslavia. Patterns of Economic Activity (New York: Frederick A. Praeger, 1968), Ch. 16; Rudolf Bićanić, "The Problem of Underdeveloped Regions of Yugoslavia" (unpublished paper, Zagreb, 1965), p. 12; Branko Colanović, Development of the Underdeveloped Areas of Yugoslavia, Studies, No. 9 (Belgrad: Medunarodna politika, January, 1966); Asen Simitciev, Development of the Economically Underdeveloped Regions of Yugoslavia, Studies, No. 35 (Belgrad: Medunarodna politika, 1970); Kosta Mihailović, "On the Yugoslav Experience in Backward Areas," in E. A. G. Robinson, ed. Backward Areas in Advanced Countries (New York: Macmillan, 1969), pp. 256-75; Kosta Mihailović, Nerazvijena područja Jugoslavije [Underdeveloped Regions of Yugoslavia] (2d ed.; Belgrade: Druge Izdanje, 1970).

19. Stanko Zuljić and Stjepan Zdunić, "Redosljed općina SR Hrvatske s obzirom na stupanj razvijenosti" [The Ranking of Communes in Croatia with Regard to Their Level of Development], Ekonomske Studije, VI (1967), 55-89; Veljke Rogić, "Fizionomska i funkcionalna regionalizacija Hrvatske" [Physiognomic and Functional Regionalization of Croatia], Zbornik VI kongresa geografov FNRJ V Ljubljani 1961 (Ljubljana, 1962), pp. 279-88.

20. Wertheimer-Baletić, "Regionalne Demografske"; Hamilton, Yugoslavia, pp. 331-36, 339-57; Igor Vrišer, "Centralna naselja v Jugoslaviji" [Central Places in Yugoslavia], Ekonomska revija, 4 (1968), 395-430, with maps; and "The Urbanization in Yugoslavia," unpublished paper (Ljubljana, 1971).

21. Kosta Mihailović, "Regionalni aspekt privrednog razvoja" [Regional Aspects of Economic Development], in Problemi regionalnog privrednog razvoja, Savez ekonomista Jugoslavije, Ekonomska biblioteka, 18 (Belgrade, 1962), pp. 11-47.

22. Josip Roglić, "Die Wirtschaftsgeographischen Beziehungen des Jugoslawischen Küstenlandes mit den östlichen Bundesländern Österreichs," Österreichische Osthefte, IV (March, 1962), 111-22, and "Litoralizacija i njeno značnje [Littoralization and its Significance], Pomorski zbornik, 4, Pt. 2, (Zagreb, 1966), 679-708.

23. Rudolf Bićanić, "O jadranskoj koncepciji ekonomskog razvoja Jugoslavije" [On the Adriatic Conception of Economic Development of Yugoslavia], Pomorstvo (Rijeka) (1964), 38-39.

24. See the discussions in Hamilton, Yugoslavia, and Hamilton, "Planning: The Spatial Development of Industry in East Europe: The Principles and their Impact," Economic Planning (March, 1970), pp. 4-6.

25. Hamilton, Yugoslavia, p. 200.

26. Ibid.

27. Numerous studies have been published by individuals and were already cited. The most useful for this study were published by the Development Centre of the OECD and the UNRISD. The following individual studies have been most valuable: Multidisciplinary Aspects of Regional Development (Paris: OECD Development Centre, 1968), and especially the study by Hilhorst, "Regional Development Theory: An attempt to Synthesize," pp. 21-34; OECD, The Regional Factor in Economic Development: Policies in 15 Industrialized OECD Countries (Paris: OECD, 1970).

28. Kuklinski, "Goals in Regional Policies," p. 2.

29. Material referring to economic planning in Yugoslavia, planning policies, and especially the changes brought about by the massive decentralization are amply covered in the literature. Therefore, only a few very selective items can be cited here, those generally discussing the latest changes: Deborah Milenkovitch, Plan and Market in Yugoslav Economic Thought (New Haven Conn.: Yale University Press, 1971); Rikard Stajner, "The System of Planning," Yugoslav Survey, XII (February, 1971), 15-30; Jaroslav Vanek, "Economic Planning in Yugoslavia," in Max F. Millikan, ed., National Economic Planning, paper presented at a Conference of the Universities-National Bureau Committee for Economic Research (New York: Columbia University Press, 1967), pp. 379-407; and M. Sokolović, "New Plan—A Policy of Common Interest," Yugoslav Life, XVI (November, 1971), 1.

30. For an excellent discussion, see Rudolf Bićanić, "Planner and the Politician," paper presented at Conférence Internationale de Futuribles, Paris, April, 1965 (mimeographed).

31. For a discussion of this problem, especially in connection with the building of the Belgrade-Bar Railroad, see Orme Wilson, Jr., "The Belgrade-Bar Railroad: An Essay in Economic and Political Geography," in George W. Hoffman, ed., Eastern Europe: Essays in Geographical Problems (London and New York: Methuen and Praeger Publishers, 1971), pp. 365-84, also the comments by Guide C. Weigend, pp. 385-89, and the remarks on pp. 390-93.

32. The literature discussing Yugoslavia's implementation, aims, goals, and principles of self-management is abundant. Some were cited earlier. For a good summary of the developments until 1961, see George W. Hoffman and Fred Warner Neal, Yugoslavia and the New Communism (New York: The Twentieth Century Fund, 1962); International Labour Office, Workers' Management in Yugoslavia (Geneva, 1962); and numerous articles in scholarly journals.

33. Hamilton, Yugoslavia, pp. 353-54.

34. An OECD report published in 1965 classified Greece as "developed Athens" and the remainder as "lagging or underdeveloped." See Angus Maddison, Alexander Stavrianopoulos, and Benjamin Higgins, Technical Assistance and Greek Development, Development Centre Studies, No. 6 (Paris: OECD, October, 1965). For details, see also Hoffman, "Undeveloped Regions," pp. 659-65. An interesting case study is Ernestine Friedl, "Migration and Decision-Making: A Greek Case," in George Devos, ed., Adaptation, Adjustment and Culture Change (forthcoming). Finally, see also "The Two Faces of Greece," The Economist, July 31, 1971.

35. These statements are taken from various issues of Scinteia and from public statements by the leaders of Romania and Bulgaria.

36. Reference is made to the earlier discussions in Chapters 5 and 7. The conclusions in two articles by Hoffman, "Undeveloped Regions," pp. 641-49, and Turnock, "Pattern of Industrialization," basically remain valid. The literature discussing details on plant location is very meager, but from discussions in Romania, especially in 1970, the picture described becomes quite clear.

37. RFER:EE, Rumania/21, "1971-75 Economic Plan Revised Upward," December 11, 1970, pp. 13-14.

38. Scinteia, May 8, 1971.

39. M. Berghianu, "Planning, the Main Strategic Instrument in Social Construction," Lupta de Clasa, No. 7 (1971). Berghianu is

chairman of the State Planning Committee and a member of the Party's Central Committee Executive Committee.

40. RFER:EE, Bulgaria/10, "CC Plenum of Territorial Distribution of Production Forces," March 20, 1970, p. 9.

41. Ibid.

42. Abjiyev, "Agrarian-Industrial Complexes"; and also Vitali Tadzher, "The Agrarian-Industrial Complex, a New Form of Economic Organization" (translated), Kooperativno selo, October, 1970.

43. Statement by Pencho Kubadinski at the Central Committee Plenum in November, 1968, as cited in Rabotnichesko Delo, November 28, 1968, and quoted in RFER:EE, Bulgaria/10, March 20, 1970; and RFER:EE, Bulgaria BR/26, "CC Plenum Discusses the Role and Activities of the People's Councils in Bulgaria," December, 1968.

44. For details, see United Nations, Secretariat of the Economic Commission for Europe, Economic Survey of Europe in 1962, Pt. 2 and Economic Planning in Europe (Geneva, 1965), Chapter 6, pp. 5-10.

45. Mihailović, Regional Development, p. 134, points out that there was no evidence of a single study explaining the effects of sovnarkhoz. Its abrogation, according to the author, was certainly not accepted with any enthusiasm. Rudolf Bićanić, Problems of Planning—East and West (The Hague: Mouton and Co., 1967), p. 50, comes to the conclusion that "since most of the economic ministries were abolished in the USSR in 1957 . . . this, along with more general reasons, has led to a constant tension between the operational administrative agencies, the Economic Councils and the planning agencies. In October 1965, decentralization along territorial lines was abolished, economic administration by ministries was reintroduced, and centralized planning was strengthened again." Bićanić commented further that "the mishap of the system of territorially decentralized planning in the USSR was due more to the battle between the half-hearted attempt at decentralization and the resistance of centralistic state bureaucracy which put obstacles to every attempt at independent decision, outside its own circles."

46. RFER:EE, Albania: Economics, "Elements of Albania 'Model' of Economic Reform," November 3, 1969; "Intensification of Decentralization in Albania," RFER:EE, Albania: Government, August 18, 1970; and RFER:EE, "Decentralization Coupled with Rejuvenation," Albania/7, October 30, 1970, pp. 1-2.

47. Tormond Hermansen, "Information Systems for Regional Development Control," Reg.Sc.Assoc.Papers (Budapest), XII (1968), pp. 107-40, gives this problem of information systems his special attention by surveying useful analytical approaches and conceptual frameworks by analyzing "questions related to how information systems for regional development control should be designed, established, operated and expanded."

NOTES TO CHAPTER 9

1. Kosta Mihailović, Regional Development in Eastern Europe: Experience and Prospects, UNRISD/70/C.49, GE 70-18044 (Geneva: UNRISD, August, 1970), pp. 75-79; F. W. Carter, "Bulgaria's Economic Ties with Her Immediate Neighbors and Prospects for Future Development," East European Quarterly, IV (1971), 209-24 and "La cooperation economique dans les Balkans," L'Information Géographique, XXXIII (1969), 157-65.

2. "Belebung der Balkanpolitik," Züricher Zeitung, July 10, 1971, p.1; RFER:EE, Rumania/20, "Rumania and the Balkans," October 11, 1971; Slobodan Stankovic, "Yugoslav Appraisal of Rumanian Balkan Initiative," RFER:EE, "Yugoslavia: Foreign Relations," July 23, 1970.

3. This drive has been going on since 1958. For an interpretation of Romania's position, see Stephen Fisher-Galati, The New Romania (Cambridge, Mass.: MIT Press, 1967), p. 69; "Rumania and the Sino-Soviet Conflict," in Kurt London, ed., Eastern Europe in Transition (Baltimore: The Johns Hopkins Press, 1966), pp. 261-75; and various Radio Free Europe reports.

4. RFER:EE, Bulgaria/22, "Bulgaria's Balkan Policy: The Search for Rapprochment," December 10, 1970.

5. Harry Trend, "Joint Rumanian-Soviet Investments and Joint Enterprises," RFER:EE, Rumania/17, September 18, 1970.

6. H. Husedzinovic, "What to Do with the Iron Ore Surplus from the Ljubija Mine," Borba, August 27, 1969, p. 4, as reported in RFER:EE, Economics/8, September 16, 1969.

7. RFER:EE, Bulgaria/7, Bulgaria Proposes Bold Plan for Economic Co-Operation with Greece," March 8, 1971.

8. Rudolf Bićanić, "Jugoslawiens Stellung in der Weltwirtschaft und das Auslandskapital in Jugoslawien," lecture at annual meeting of Südosteuropa Gesellschaft, Munich, December 2, 1967 (mimeographed). Professor Bićanić discusses here in some detail Yugoslavia's position in international economic relations, including its relationship with the Common Market and Comecon.

9. Christo Marinov, Socialisticjeski mezhdunarodni kompleksi i raioni [Socialist International Complexes and Regions] (Varna: D'rzhavno Izdatelstvo, 1965).

10. Ibid., 108-30.

11. Trend, "Joint Rumanian-Soviet Investments," p. 6.

12. This new form of cooperation was evident in the recently concluded Romanian-Chilean joint stock enterprise; see RFER:EE, Background Report/16, "Rumanian-Chilean Joint Stock Enterprise, September 7, 1970.

13. Marinov, Kompleksi.

14. "Bulgaria Proposes Bold Plan."

STATISTICAL APPENDIX

APPENDIX TABLE A.1

Economic Development of Southeast Europe, 1939-69

Indexes	Albania Prewar[a]	Albania 1950's[b]	Albania 1960's[c]	Bulgaria Prewar	Bulgaria 1950's	Bulgaria 1960's
1. Area (sq. miles)	11,101	11,101	11,101	39,824	42,822	42,729
2. Population (thousand's)	1,070	1,507	1,964	6,292	7,667	8,400
3. Percent of total population in towns of 2,000 +	15.9	22.0	33.2	21.4	33.6	46.5
4. Natural increase in population per 1,000	16.9	23.7	25.4	8.0	9.8	7.2
5. Death rate per 1,000 population	17.8	14.8	8.6	13.4	8.6	8.1
6. Birth rate per 1,000 population	34.7	38.5	32.2	21.4	18.4	15.3
7. Infant mortality per 1,000 live births	100.0	87.0	80.0	138.9	66.3	32.2
8. Illiteracy (over 10 yrs. of age)	75.0	28.0	30.0	31.4	13.5	12.5
9. Students graduated from institutions of higher education	n.a.	240	1,666	1,223	5,860	7,781
10. Proportion of active population in:						
Manufacturing, mining, construction	5	15	22	8	19	33
Agriculture, forestry, fishing	85	75	58	80	64	45
Trade, services, other activities	10	10	20	12	17	22
11. Cultivated land as percent of total land	10.2	15.7	17.1	43.2	40.9	41.1
12. Population density per sq. mi. agricultural land	233	310	403	285	358	370
13. Fertilizers used (kg./hectare of arable land)	0.1	10.0	17.0	1.0	16.0	79.0
14. Tractors for agricultural use (1.5 liters and above)	28	1,332	5,321	3,200	17,000	42,000
15. Physicians per 1,000 population	0.1	0.4	0.5	0.5	1.2	1.4
16. Road density (miles per sq. miles of territory)	n.a.	n.a.	0.173	0.305	0.373	0.420
17. Railroad density (miles per sq. miles of territory)	0.01	0.01	0.01	0.07	0.07	0.08
18. Estimated per capita income ($U.S.)	95	236	315	$68	230	407
19. Percent contribution to GNP of:						
Agriculture, forestry, fishing	n.a.	53	43	55	36	28
Manufacturing, mining, construction	n.a.	38	46	13	29	42
Trade, services, other	n.a.	9	11	32	35	30

20. Distribution of foreign trade in percent:

	Albania 1939	Albania 1949	Albania 1961	Albania 1968	Bulgaria 1939	Bulgaria 1949	Bulgaria 1961	Bulgaria 1968
Western Eruope	57	1	5	12	77	10	8	17
Comecon (minus Soviet Union)	22	56	40	44	12	30	29	19
Soviet Union	1	42	36	0	1	55	52	55
Rest (including Yugoslavia)	22	1	19	44	10	5	11	9

(continued)

(APPENDIX TABLE A.1 continued)

	Greece			Romania			Yugoslavia		
	Prewar	1950's	1960's	Prewar	1950's	1960's	Prewar	1950's	1960's
	50,147	50,547	50,547	113,918	91,675	91,699	95,576	98,770	98,770
	7,222	8,100	8,800	19,852	17,500	19,721	15,596	17,886	20,000
	47.6	52.5	56.2	23.6	30.0	38.2	21.0	31.0	38.0
	11.0	11.7	10.3	10.4	15.9	18.6	11.1	15.5	10.4
	14.0	7.6	7.6	19.1	9.7	8.1	15.6	11.4	8.6
	25.0	19.3	17.9	29.5	25.6	26.7	26.7	26.9	19.0
	118.2	44.2	34.0	179.0	78.2	59.5	140.0	110.0	58.9
	40.8	23.6	17.8	45.0	11.0	10.0	50.0	25.0	18.0
	n.a.	3,727	6,337	5,500	17,100	21,742	2,594	9,400	15,875
	16	19	23	15	20	28	15	18	22
	50	54	47	75	64	54	70	62	53
	34	27	30	10	16	18	15	20	25
	19.9	26.6	29.9	42.5	40.7	41.3	33.5	32.8	32.3
	240	241	245	260	313	334	267	310	348
	8.0	33.0	65.0	0.2	5.0	21.5	0.6	12.0	32.9
	1,500	13,000	49,000	4,050	40,000	85,000	2,300	25,000	47,000
	n.a.	1.4	1.5	0.4	1.0	1.5	0.3	0.6	1.0
	0.195	0.397	0.614	n.a.	0.519	0.520	n.a.	0.494	0.523
	0.03	0.03	0.03	0.07	0.08	0.08	0.06	0.08	0.09
	80	326	566	95	180	353	100	220	466
	40	34	25	n.a.	34	22	49	33	22
	21	22	25	n.a.	26	44	29	30	41
	39	44	50	n.a.	40	34	22	37	37

	Greece				Romania				Yugoslavia			
	1939	1949	1961	1968	1939	1949	1961	1968	1939	1949	1961	1968
	62	36	56	76	58	25	25	32	64	39	48	52
	13	3	14	10	12	43	23	21	18	52	17	17
	1	0	4	4	1	24	41	31	1	8	6	16
	24	61	26	10	29	7	11	16	17	1	29	15

a Prewar = 1937–39.
b 1950s = 1957–59.
c 1960s = 1967–69.

Sources: National statistics; United Nations: Economic Survey of Europe, Demographic Yearbook, Statistical Yearbook.

Regional Summaries, Yugoslavia,
by Republics and Autonomous
Provinces

Indexes	Bosnia and Herzegovina	Croatia	Macedonia	Montenegro
Area in sq. miles	19,742	21,830	9,928	5,333
Population, 1971	3,742,852	4,422,564	1,647,104	530,361
Percent of total population, 1971	18.3	21.6	8.0	2.6
Population increase per 1,000 pop., 1961-1971	13.2	6.1	15.8	11.7
Infant mortality per 1,000, 1968	68.3	41.7	91.4	45.7
Birth rate per 1,000, 1968	23.1	15.2	25.6	20.7
Natural increase per 1,000, 1969	16.1	4.8	17.5	14.8
Illiteracy (age 10 yrs and over)				
1953-	39.7	15.1	33.8	29.0
1971-	22.7	8.9	18.0	17.2
Percent of urban population				
1961-	19.5	30.8	34.9	21.5
1971-	24.0	37.6	40.4	27.5
Percent of active population in				
Agriculture 1953-	68	60	69	67
1971	47	37.5	44.	44
Industry 1953-	15	24	14	14
1970	22	24	27	22
Services, etc. 1953-	17	16	17	15
1971	21	27	25	29
Regional per capita 1947-	82.9	107.3	62.0	70.8
1967-	67.3	124.5	65.6	76.3
Percent of social product, (GNP) 1970	11.7	26.6	5.6	1.9
Percent of total investments, 1969	10.9	23.1	9.0	2.4
Percent of industrial investments, 1969	12.1	17.3	9.1	3.1
Percent of total industrial output, 1969	12.7	29.1	4.3	1.5

(continued)

| | Serbia | | | | |
Slovenia	Serbia Proper	Vojvodina	Kosovo	Serbia Total	Yugoslavia *Total[a]
7,819	21,610	8,304	4,204	34,118	98,770
1,725,088	5,241,524	1,950,268	1,244,268	8,436,547	20,504,516
8.4	25.6	9.5	6.1	41.1	100.0
8.1	8.3	5.0	25.4	9.9	10.0
26.3	40.9	39.5	104.5	59.7	58.9
17.4	14.9	13.8	37.4	17.9	19.0
6.4	6.7	4.0	29.6	9.5	10.2
1.9	24.4	12.1	52.8	26.8	24.4
2.5	17.7	9.4	32.2	17.5	15.2
28.9		30.0	24.0	29.8	28.3
32.5	36.1	43.7	24.0	36.1	34.0
54	73	67	73	72	67
24	55	44	53	55	44.5
37	20	18	12	12	17
38	19	21	17	20	23
9	7	15	4	5	16
31	21	27	20	22	24
175.0	95.6	108.8	52.6		100.0
192.3	97.7	105.2	37.8	92.1	100.0
15.7	25.4	11.0	2.1	38.5	100.0
13.6	28.3	8.0	3.9	40.1	100.0
14.0	32.2	6.3	5.9	44.4	100.0
18.5	24.5	7.3	2.1	33.9	100.0

*aDue to rounding of figures total will not add up to 100.

Yugoslav censuses are for 1953, 1961, and 1971. 1971 figure estimates from Statistički Bilten.

Social Product (drustveni proizvod) excludes certain services such as government and professional services; it comprises material only. Generally estimated at 10 percent less than GNP as calculated in the US.

Sources: Statisticki Godisnjak Jugoslavije 1962-1971; Statisticki Bilten, Indeks, Jugoslavija 1945-64; Narodna Banka, annual reports, 1966-70.

Regional Structure of Investment and National Product, Yugoslavia[a]

Region	Percent of Investment		Percent of National Product	
	1965[b]	1969	1964	1969
Less developed	30. 1	26. 2	21. 3	22. 1
Bosnia and Hercegovina	12. 9	10. 9	12. 3	12. 8
Montenegro	3. 0	2. 4	1. 8	2. 1
Macedonia	10. 6	9. 0	5. 3	5. 1
Kosovo	3. 6	3. 9	1. 9	2. 1
Advanced	69. 8	73. 0	78. 6	77. 9
Slovenia	13. 6	13. 6	16. 1	16. 5
Croatia	23. 3	23. 1	26. 2	27. 3
Serbia proper	24. 1	28. 3	25. 2	24. 1
Vojvodina	8. 8	8. 0	11. 1	10. 0

[a]Data may not add to totals because of rounding.
[b]Data are not available for 1964 for Kosovo; therefore, 1965 was substituted.

Source: This summary table is taken from J. T. Crawford, "Yugoslavia's New Economic Strategy: A Progress" in Economic Developments in Countries of Eastern Europe, a compendium of papers submitted to the Subcommittee on Foreign Economic Policy of the Joint Economic Committee, Congress of the United States (Washington D. C. : Government Printing Office, 1970), p. 627. The author, commenting on this compilation, states, "The political goal of narrowing the gap between have and have-not regions appears to have taken a back seat since 1964. The less developed areas were generally hit hardest by the recession. Investment and output in Bosnia and Hercegovina, Montenegro, and Macedonia generally lagged behind the national growth rate during 1965-1969. Of the backward areas, only Kosovo, which is heavily supported by federal funds, was able to improve its share of total investment and national product."

Also see Statistički Godišnjak Jugoslavije 1970 and 1971.

APPENDIX TABLE A. 4

Participation of Republics in Total Yugoslav Manufacturing
Employment, 1960 and 1969
(in percent)

	1960	1969
Less developed	23. 0	22. 2
Bosnia and Herzegovina	14. 9	14. 0
Montenegro	1. 3	1. 6
Macedonia	5. 3	5. 2
Kosovo	1. 5	2. 4
Advanced	77. 0	76. 3
Serbia proper	22. 4	25. 7
Vojvodina	9. 8	8. 3
Croatia	27. 8	25. 4
Slovenia	17. 0	16. 9

Source: Statistički Godišnjak Jugoslavije 1961, 1970

APPENDIX TABLE A. 5

Regional Summaries, Bulgaria, by Okrugs
(1968 if not otherwise stated)

Indexes	Blagoevgrad	Bourgas	Varna	Veliko Turnovo	Vidin	Vratsa	Gabrovo	Kurdzhali	Kyustendil	Lovech	Mihailovgrad	Pazardzhik	Pernik	Pleven
1. Area in sq. mi.	2,503	2,917	1,505	1,808	1,197	1,604	794	1,560	1,173	1,598	1,386	1,677	921	1,596
2. Population in thousands	308	395	383	336	177	305	180	292	197	219	238	303	181	350
3. Percent of total total population	3.6	4.7	4.6	4.0	2.1	3.6	2.2	3.5	2.4	2.6	2.8	3.6	2.2	4.2
4. Infant mortality rate per 1000 live birth	36.4	31.1	29.3	22.3	21.1	26.2	14.5	39.8	23.3	24.1	25.0	22.9	23.1	26.1
5. Birth rate per 1000 population	21.9	18.8	17.5	13.4	13.1	15.5	12.7	28.0	15.9	13.6	13.6	19.3	14.6	14.8
6. Natural increase per 1,000	14.7	11.3	9.9	2.0	1.7	5.4	3.5	22.1	6.4	2.4	3.9	11.2	6.2	5.2
7. Percent urban population-1959 1968	28.8 39.9	36.2 54.3	39.9 61.0	26.0 38.8	20.0 38.9	23.6 37.5	45.3 61.6	13.6 20.2	29.2 46.7	23.7 42.6	20.6 39.0	34.0 48.5	43.9 53.0	25.8 42.5
8. Percent of total investments	1.9	9.1	7.1	4.1	3.9	2.4	2.4	0.9	1.7	2.4	1.9	2.8	1.2	6.3
9. Percent of industrial investments	1.9	11.9	6.7	3.8	6.1	1.8	3.1	0.8	2.1	3.0	1.3	2.5	1.3	3.8
10. Percent of industrial output, 1967	1.1	6.3	5.2	2.6	5.1	0.7	2.2	0.6	1.3	1.6	1.2	2.5	5.2	3.2

Indexes	Plovdiv	Razgrad	Rousse	Silistra	Silven	Smolyan	Sofia (City)	Sofia (District)	Starazagord	Tolboukhin	Turgovishte	Haskovo	Shoumen	Yambol	Bulgaria Totala
1. Area in sq. mi.	2,137	1,015	1,025	1,108	1,388	1,373	434	2,812	1,895	1,818	1,050	1,569	1,286	1,682	42,831
2. Population in thousands	654	199	282	172	231	172	941	316	365	238	177	291	248	220	8,370
3. Percent of total total population	7.8	2.4	3.4	2.1	2.8	2.1	11.2	3.8	4.4	2.8	2.1	3.5	3.0	2.6	100.0
4. Infant mortality rate per 1000 live birth	22.2	34.8	24.2	34.4	30.2	23.3	22.6	24.7	25.4	41.1	30.7	22.9	50.6	29.6	28.3
5. Birth rate per 1000 population	16.7	20.5	15.5	21.7	18.1	19.7	14.7	15.4	15.2	20.4	19.2	14.6	19.8	14.9	16.9
6. Natural increase per 1,000	8.4	11.3	7.0	13.1	9.8	13.8	7.6	5.8	5.4	12.2	9.5	6.0	10.9	5.6	8.3
7. Percent urban population –1959 / 1968	35.0 / 54.4	14.0 / 27.6	41.6 / 56.7	19.2 / 33.7	37.4 / 48.9	15.2 / 30.2	90.5 / 90.1	17.9 / 33.5	35.5 / 53.2	26.0 / 41.2	19.8 / 31.3	42.0 / 52.2	28.9 / 40.6	27.9 / 42.7	35.7 / 49.7
8. Percent of total investments	5.7	1.4	3.2	1.1	3.6	1.7	16.3	4.7	5.4	3.2	1.4	2.1	1.8	1.8	100.0
9. Percent of industrial investments	5.2	1.0	2.7	0.7	4.8	2.5	14.5	3.7	6.8	2.0	1.1	2.1	1.3	1.5	100.0
10. Percent of industrial output, 1967	7.4	0.6	3.5	0.3	1.9	3.3	18.5	3.8	12.5	0.7	0.5	4.6	1.5	1.2	100.0

aDue to rounding of figures, total will not add up to 100.

Source: Central Statistical Office, Statistical Yearbook of the People's Republic of Bulgaria, 1960–68.

293

APPENDIX TABLE A.6

Regional Summaries, Romania, by Judeteţe
(1969 if not otherwise stated)

Indexes	Alba	Arad	Argeș	Bacău	Bihor	Bistrița Năsăud	Botoșani	Brașov	Brăila	Buzău	Caraș-Severin	Cluj	Constanța
Area in sq. mi,	2,405	2,955	2,626	2,550	2,909	2,048	1,917	2,066	1,842	2,344	3,287	2,568	2,724
Population in thousands	389	490	560	638	602	279	470	468	357	499	365	658	506
Percent of total population	2.0	2.4	2.7	3.1	3.0	1.4	2.3	2.3	1.8	2.5	1.9	3.2	2.5
Infant mortality rate per 1,000 live birth	45.4	43.2	53.1	63.0	50.7	57.5	53.3	38.0	61.3	72.1	59.7	42.2	58.6
Birth rate per 1,000	23.6	19.3	28.2	33.0	23.3	26.5	30.8	28.8	24.9	27.7	19.6	23.6	28.7
Natural increase per 1,000	10.1	2.8	13.9	20.2	9.3	14.6	19.4	13.3	14.3	14.2	3.9	11.7	15.5
Percent urban population, 2,000 above	40.3	35.2	30.5	36.5	34.5	10.4	19.2	46.2	62.8	18.2	44.1	52.1	56.8
Regional percent of GNP	1.4	2.0	2.9	5.0	2.0	0.4	0.8	4.0	2.7	1.4	2.6	2.8	3.9
Percent of total invest- ment, 1966-70	1.0	1.3	4.8	3.0	2.4	0.3	0.6	3.3	2.2	1.5	1.4	2.7	5.0
Percent of industrial in- vestment	0.6	0.7	9.0	4.2	2.5	0.2	0.2	3.4	1.5	1.3	1.6	2.8	1.7
Percent of industrial output	1.5	2.5	2.1	3.7	2.4	0.3	0.6	6.1	2.2	1.1	2.9	3.6	2.2

Indexes	Covasna	Dîmbovița	Dolj	Galați	Gorj	Harghita	Hunedoara	Ialomita	Iasi	Ilfov	Maramures	Mehedinti	Mures	Neamt
Area in sq. mi,	1,431	1,443	2,858	1,708	2,178	2,552	2,742	2,553	2,112	3,176	2,370	1,892	2,584	2,274
Population in thousands	182	440	719	514	313	292	498	377	665	788	452	316	586	500
Percent of total population	0.9	2.2	3.6	2.5	1.5	1.4	2.5	1.8	3.3	4.0	2.2	1.0	2.9	2.5
Infant mortality rate per 1,000 live birth	40.0	57.0	63.4	51.5	63.3	34.7	58.3	73.9	56.7	62.2	48.2	59.9	41.2	66.8
Birth rate per 1,000	24.1	28.8	24.0	30.4	29.8	24.8	25.5	31.1	32.0	27.5	26.1	24.7	25.6	32.6
Natural increase per 1,000	12.4	13.5	9.0	17.3	15.1	13.4	11.9	17.3	21.2	12.4	14.3	8.6	13.8	19.4
Percent urban population, 2,000 above	38.9	38.2	35.1	46.5	27.3	33.0	66.1	24.8	37.4	12.8	45.4	30.6	36.6	28.8
Regional percent of GNP	0.6	2.3	3.2	3.3	1.8	0.8	6.0	1.8	1.7	2.9	1.6	0.9	3.3	2.9
Percent of total investment, 1966-70	0.5	1.0	4.3	5.8	2.2	0.9	4.2	2.6	2.4	2.6	1.1	2.2	2.2	1.5
Percent of industrial investment	0.4	1.6	4.1	8.0	2.9	0.8	6.1	1.2	2.5	1.8	1.3	2.7	2.4	1.7
Percent of industrial output	0.5	1.6	2.9	2.8	1.0	1.0	5.5	0.6	2.4	1.2	2.0	0.8	3.6	2.5

(continued)

APPENDIX TABLE A.6 (continued)

Indexes	Olt	Prahova	Satu Mare	Sălaj	Sibiu	Suceava	Teleorman	Timiș	Tulcea	Vaslui	Vîlcea	Vrancea	Municipiul București	Romania Total[a]
Area in sq. mi,	2,130	1,812	1,701	1,486	2,093	3,303	2,267	3,351	3,255	2,046	2,203	1,860	234	91,699
Population in thousands	494	743	370	266	435	607	536	631	246	454	384	367	1,555	20,010
Percent of total population	2.5	3.7	1.3	1.8	2.1	3.0	2.7	3.1	1.2	2.2	1.9	1.8	7.7	100.0
Infant mortality rate per 1,000 live birth	61.1	61.1	51.1	41.5	34.8	42.4	60.4	46.1	65.9	65.5	64.9	54.3	50.9	54.9
Birth rate per 1,000	28.2	29.6	25.4	25.1	25.1	29.5	24.3	20.5	28.7	33.8	29.6	28.9	21.8	26.7
Natural increase per 1,000	13.5	15.2	13.3	11.5	13.6	17.7	9.7	5.4	16.1	21.7	15.2	16.7	7.6	13.2
Percent urban population, 2,000 above	5.2	28.3	25.1	25.4	25.1	29.5	24.3	20.5	28.7	33.8	29.6	28.9	21.8	26.7
Regional percent of GNP	2.1	5.9	0.7	0.4	2.1	1.5	1.8	2.7	1.0	0.8	1.2	0.9	14.0	100.0
Percent of total investment, 1966-70	2.0	4.4	0.8	0.4	1.8	1.6	2.1	2.6	0.8	0.7	1.2	0.9	16.2	100.0
Percent of industrial investment	2.5	5.1	0.7	0.2	1.8	1.8	2.8	1.7	0.6	0.4	4.2	0.5	9.2	100.0
Percent of industrial output	1.1	6.7	0.2	1.2	3.7	1.9	0.9	3.7	0.5	0.7	0.7	0.8	17.7	100.0

[a]Due to rounding of figures, total will not add up to 100.

Source: Central Statistical office, _Anuarul Statistic Al Republicii Socialiste România_ for various years; statistical summaries from different publications.

APPENDIX TABLE A. 7

Regional Summaries, of Albania, by Rrethi

Indexes	Berat	Dibër	Durres	Elbasan	Fier	Gramsh	Gjirokastër	Ersekë (Kolonjë)	Korcë	Krujë	Kukës	Lezhë	Librazhd	Lushje
1. Area in sq. mi., 1958	411.5	605.7	332.4	581.0	459.8	269.9	438.9	312.4	842.0	236.3	603.8	182.2	391.1	274.9
2. Percent urban population, 1958	32.2	6.7	46.3	34.8	14.3	0	29.5	14.3	30.1	14.1	8.7	7.5	0	17.1
1966	35.8	9.7	51.4	37.6	19.4	8.1	31.7	23.5	33.6	24.2	8.1	13.7	8.2	21.5
3. Population in thousands, 1966	104.4	93.8	155.8	130.3	139.2	24.1	49.2	18.7	159.1	55.3	58.9	33.2	42.7	81.6
4. Percent of total population, 1966	5.3	4.8	7.9	6.6	7.0	1.2	2.5	1.0	8.1	2.8	3.0	1.7	2.2	4.2
1958	5.0	—	6.1	—	6.7	1.4	2.8	—	8.8	3.0	3.1	1.6	2.1	3.6
5. Birth rate per 1,000, 1967	39.2	43.5	33.6	37.9	39.3	40.0	25.4	26.7	28.2	42.4	45.3	40.8	41.3	38.1
6. Natural increase per 1,000, 1967	32.5	32.0	25.9	31.2	32.3	31.1	17.9	19.8	19.8	33.6	33.9	33.0	31.7	31.0
7. Percent of industrial output, 1958	5.1	—	12.9	—	9.6	0.1	3.3	—	10.7	0.5	0.4	0.3	0.4	1.0
1967	6.8	1.4	10.8	7.5	9.0	0.3	2.4	0.3	7.4	2.6	1.7	0.7	0.9	1.7

(continued)

(APPENDIX TABLE A. 7 continued)

Indexes	Mat	Mirditë	Përmet	Pogradec	Pukë	Sarandë	Skrapar	Shkodër	Tepelenë	Tiranë city	Tiranë District	Tropojë	Vlorë	Albania Total[a]
1. Area in sq. mi., 1958	396.9	269.5	366.8	279.9	374.1	423.5	271.0	977.9	315.4		446.3	402.7	621.2	11,101
2. Percent urban population, 1958	11.5	0	9.3	18.2	5.1	17.4	3.3	33.4	13.8	100.0	1.4	4.2	39.2	22.0
1966	9.5	16.0	18.3	22.7	13.9	24.7	9.4	33.1	25.1		19.6	9.5	48.1	33.3
3. Population in thousands, 1966	45.3	22.5	30.3	42.8	27.6	58.1	23.0	150.4	30.9	169.3	72.6	25.6	120.0	1,964.7
4. Percent of total population, 1966	2.3	1.1	1.5	2.2	1.4	3.0	1.2	7.7	1.6	8.6	3.7	1.3	1.6	100.0[a]
1958	3.0	1.1	1.8	2.2	1.3	2.7	1.5	8.1	1.7	7.9	3.6	1.3	6.2	100.0
5. Birth rate per 1,000, 1967	39.4	45.4	30.2	35.6	44.7	32.7	35.2	34.6	40.5		25.9	45.0	37.2	35.2
6. Natural increase per 1,000, 1967	29.1	35.6	23.6	26.9	30.9	26.4	27.6	26.7	33.1	19.6		31.0	31.1	26.9
7. Percent of industrial output, 1958	1.6	1.2	1.8	0.6	0.7	1.7	1.8	9.4	0.8	21.7		0.4	7.8	100.0[a]
1967	1.3	2.4	0.4	1.2	0.8	2.1	1.1	8.1	0.8	21.5		0.2	6.6	100.0

[a]Due to rounding of figures, total will not add up to 100.

Source: Vjetari Statistikor I Republikis Popullorë Të Shqitërisë for various years.

298

APPENDIX TABLE A.8

Regional Summaries, Greece, by Geographical Region

Indexes	Greater Athens	Central Greece and Euboea	Pelopon-nesos	Ionian Islands	Epirus	Thessaly	Macedonia	Thrace	Aegean Islands	Crete	Greece Total
Area in sq. mi., 1971	167	9,450	8,278	891	3,553	5,886	13,206	3,312	3,502	3,216	50,547
Population in thousands, 1971	2,530.2	991.7	985.6	183.6	309.6	659.2	1,883.2	329.3	416.5	456.2	8,745.1
Percent increase, 1961-1971	37	2	-10	-14	-12	-4	-1	-8	-13	-6	4.2
Percent of total population, 1971	28.9	11.3	11.3	2.1	3.5	7.5	21.7	3.8	4.8	5.2	100.0
Birth rate per 1,000, 1961	15.4	18.7	18.1	16.8	21.1	18.6	18.9	22.8	16.4	17.6	18.0
Natural increase in population per 1,000	8.1	11.4	10.0	6.9	14.4	12.1	11.5	14.4	6.4	9.8	10.3
Illiteracy (age 10 yrs. and over), 1961	10.1	21.8	19.5	26.6	22.4	21.7	16.9	29.5	18.7	18.4	17.8
Percent urban population in cities over 3,000 1961	94.9	20.6	24.3	23.8	18.6	26.8	36.4	24.9	20.3	26.8	42.1
1971	93.7	23.9	28.7	27.0	24.1	32.3	41.4	26.0	25.7	30.1	49.6
Percent of active population in agriculture, 1961	1.4	64.9	68.1	67.9	70.5	65.0	63.7	78.1	53.7	71.1	47.0
Percent urban population in industry, 1961	38.1	15.5	12.8	10.7	11.9	14.5	16.2	8.4	18.3	10.3	23.0
Percent urban population in services, 1961	52.2	17.0	15.7	17.9	14.4	17.1	16.5	12.0	24.0	16.3	30.0
Regional percent of GNP, 1968	37.2	10.9	11.2	1.4	2.3	6.0	20.5	2.9	3.8	3.8	100.0
Per capita productivity (in Drachmae), 1965	27,050	17,330	15,760	12,990	10,930	12,940	15,410	11,540	14,110	13,350	17,730
Percent permanent emigration, by origin, 1970	13.8	4.1	6.6	2.0	8.0	8.9	40.5	6.6	4.1	3.5	100.0

Sources: Commercial Bank of Greece, annual and quarterly reports; Ministry of Coordination, Economic Development Plan for Greece 1968-1972 (Athens, February, 1968); and Statistical Yearbook of Greece for various years.

APPENDIX TABLE A.9

Population Changes of Major Urban Concentrations,
Southeast Europe, 1939-71
(in thousands)

Country	1939	1955	1967
Albania			
Tiranë (capital)	25	108	169
Durrës	11	26	53
Elbasan	13	24	39
Korea	21	32	46
Shkodra	25	39	50
Vlorë	10	28	50
Bulgaria			1965
Sofia (capital)	329[a]	645[b]	811
Burgas	36	73	106
Plovdiv	100	162	223
Ruse	50	89	129
Sliven	49[a]	83	128
Stara Zagora	30[a]	55	88
Varna	70	120	180
Romania	1939	1950	1966
Bucharest (capital)	648	1,042	1,511
Brasov	59	83	240
Cluj	101	118	223
Constanta	59	79	200
Craiova	63	85	173
Galati	101	80	151
Iasi	103	94	195
Ploiesti	79	96	191
Timissoara	92	112	193

	1939	1951	1961	1971
Greece				
Athens (capital)[c]	499	565	628	
Greater Athens[d]	1,124	1,378	1,852	2,530
Piraeus[c]	205	186	184	
Nikea[c]	59	72	83	
Thessaloniki	192	218	251	
Greater Thessaloniki[d]		301	378	551
Larisa	33	43	56	
Pátrai	83	93	102	102[d]
Vólos	54	65	67	

	1939	1953	1961	1971
Yugoslavia				
Belgrade (capital)	385[c]	438	598	742
Zagreb	185	351	457	566
Skopje	64	119	172	312
Sarajevo	78	109	175	244
Ljubljana	79	113	157	173
Titograd	10[f]	15		54
Priština	20[f]	24		69
Niš	35	61	85	127
Novi Sad	63	77	111	142
Split	35	76	93	157

[a]1934.

[b]1950 figures are all for 1956.

[c]Athens, Piraeus, and Nikea for Greater Athens since 1961.

[d]The census of 1961 speaks of "urban agglomerations" as the largest population center of two neighboring municipalities or communes that were found to be situated not farther than 200 meters from each other, so that they could be considered as one built-up area.

[e]1937.

[f]1938.

Source: Official Statistical Yearbooks and census figures of individual countries.

THEORETICAL WORKS

Bićanić, Rudolf. <u>Problems of Planning - East and West</u>. The Hague: Mouton and Co.,1967.

Bobek, Hans, "Some Remarks on Basic Concepts in Economic Regionalization," <u>Economic Regionalization</u>. Proceedings of the 4th General Meeting of the Commission on Methods of Economic Regionalization of the International Geographical Union. Brno: September 7-12, 1968.

Darwent, D. F., "Growth Poles and Growth Centers in Regional Planning—A Review," <u>Environment and Planning</u>, I (1969), 5-32.

Dziewoński, Kazimierz, "Théories de la Région Économique," in M. Omer Tulippe, ed. <u>Mélanges de Géographie</u>. Gambloux: Editions J. Duculot, 1967.

Friedmann, John R. <u>Regional Development Policy</u>. Cambridge, Mass.: MIT Press, 1966.

Gauthier, Howard L. "Geography, Transportation, and Regional Development," <u>Economic Geography</u>, XVII (October, 1970), 612-19.

Gilbert, Alan. "Growth Poles—The Instant Solution to Regional Problems?" Colloquium on Regional Inequalities of Development, Commission on Regional Aspects of Economic Development, International Geographical Union. Brazil, 1971. Unpublished manuscript.

Ginsburg, Norton S. "On Geography and Economic Development," in Saul B. Cohen, ed. <u>Problems and Trends in American Geography</u>. New York: Basic Books, 1967.

Hamilton, F. E. Ian. "Aspects of Spatial Behavior in Planned Economies," <u>Regional Science Association</u>. Papers, XXV (1970), 83-105.

_____. "Models of Industrial Location," in Richard J. Chorley and Peter Haggett, eds. <u>Models in Geography</u>. London: Methuen Publishers, 1967.

305

Hansen, Niles M. "Development Pole Theory in a Regional Context," Kyklos, XX (1967), 709-27.

Hartshorne, Richard. "Geography and Economic Growth," in Norton Ginsburg, ed. Geography and Economic Development. Department of Geography, University of Chicago, Research Papers No. 62. Chicago, 1960.

_____. "The Role of the State in Economic Growth: Contents of the State Area," in Hugh G. J. Aitken, ed. The State and Economic Growth. New York: Social Science Research Council, 1959.

Hermansen, Tormond. Spatial Organization and Economic Development—The Scope and Task of Spatial Planning. UNRISD/69/C. 68. GE. 69-23863. Geneva: United Nations Research Institute for Social Development, July, 1969.

_____. et al. A Review of the Concepts and Theories of Growth Poles and Growth Centres. UNRISD/70/C.6. GE. 70-24266. Geneva: United Nations Research Institute for Social Development, November, 1970.

Higgins, Benjamin. "The Scope and Objectives of Planning for Underdeveloped Regions," Proceedings of the First Interamerican Seminar on the Definition of Regions for Development Planning. Rio de Janeiro: Comisión de Geografía, Instituto Panamericano de Geografía e Historià.

Hilhorst, J. "Regional Development Theory. An Attempt to Synthesize," in Multidisciplinary Aspects of Regional Development. Paris: Development Centre of the OECD 1968.

Hirschman, Albert O. The Strategy of Economic Development. New Haven, Conn.: Yale University Press, 1959.

Keeble, D. E. "Models of Economic Development," in Richard J. Chorley and Peter Haggett, eds. Models in Geography. London: Methuen, 1967.

Kuklinski, Antoni R. "Regional Development, Regional Policies and Regional Planning," Regional Studies, IV (October, 1970), 269-78.

_____. and Torsten Hägerstrand, eds. Information System for Regional Development. Lund Studies in Geography, Series B. Human Geography, No. 37, 1971.

Myrdal, Gunnar. Economic Theory in Underdeveloped Regions.
    London: Methuen Publishers, 1963.

Saarinen, Thomas F. Perception of Environment. Association of
    American Geographers, Commission on College Geography,
    Resource Paper No. 5, 1969.

Wilbur, Charles K. The Soviet Model and Underdeveloped Countries.
    Chapel Hill: The University of North Carolina Press, 1969.

Wilczynski, J. Socialist Economic Development and Reforms. New
    York: Praeger Publishers, 1972.

Wolpert, Julian. "The Decision Process in Spatial Context," Annals
    of the Association of American Geographers, LIV (December,
    1964), 537-58.

Wróbel, Andrzej, "Theories and Models of Regional Development:
    A Critical Examination," Colloquium on Regional Inequalities
    of Development, Commission on Regional Aspects of Economic
    Development, International Geographical Union. Brazil, 1971.
    manuscript.

BOOKS AND ARTICLES ON EAST-CENTRAL
AND SOUTHEAST EUROPE

Burks, Richard V. "The Communist Polities of Eastern Europe,"
    in James N. Rosenau, ed. Linkage Politics: Essays on the
    Convergence of National and International Systems. New York:
    The Free Press, 1969.

_____. "The Political Implications of Economic Reform,"paper
    presented for the Conference on Economic Reform in Eastern
    Europe, University of Michigan, November, 1970. Unpublished
    manuscript.

_____. Technological Innovation and Political Change in Communist
    Eastern Europe. Memorandum RM-6051-PR, 8-69. Santa
    Monica, Cal.: The Rand Corp., 1969.

Byrnes, Robert F., ed. The United States and Eastern Europe.
    Englewood Cliffs, N.J.: Prentice-Hall, 1967 (note especially
    the contributions by Burks and Spulber).

Christaller, Walter. "Das Grundgerüst der räumlichen Ordnung in Europa," Frankfurter Geographische Heft, XXIV (1950), 51-65.

Enyedi, György. "The Changing Face of Agriculture in Eastern Europe," Geographical Review, LVII (July, 1967), 358-72.

Ernst, Maurice. "Postwar Economic Growth in Eastern Europe, a Comparison with Western Europe," in Joint Economic Committee, Congress of the United States, New Directions in the Soviet Economy. Part IV: The World Outside. Washington, 1966.

Gamarnikow, Michael. Economic Reforms in Eastern Europe. Detroit: Wayne State University, 1968.

_____. "Wirtschaftsreform: Modelle, Realisierung und Bedeutung der Wirtschaftsreformen in den osteuropäischen Ländern," in Hermann Gross, ed. Osteuropa-Wirtschaftsreformen. Bonn: Atlantic Forum Edition, 1970.

Grossman, Gregory. "Economic Reform: The Interplay of Economics and Politics," in Richard V. Burks, ed., The Future of Communism in Europe. Detroit: Wayne State University, 1968.

Hertz, Frederick. The Economic Problem of the Danubian States: A Study in Economic Nationalism. London: Victor Gollancz, 1947.

Hoffman, George W. The Balkans in Transition. Searchlight Book No. 20. Princeton: D. Van Nostrand, 1963.

_____, ed. Eastern Europe: Essays in Geographical Problems. London and New York: Methuen and Praeger Publishers, 1971 (note especially the contributions by Jack C. Fisher, F. E. Ian Hamilton, Thomas M. Poulsen, Orme Wilson, Jr., and George W. Hoffman).

_____. "Thessaloniki: The Impact of a Changing Hinterland," East European Quarterly, II (March, 1968), 1-27.

Hungarian Academy of Sciences, Institute of Geography. Symposium on the Effect of Industrialization on the Agricultural Population in the European Socialist Countries. Budapest: October, 1967.

Jelavich, Charles and Barbara, eds. The Balkans in Transition. Berkeley and Los Angeles: University of California Press, 1963.

Kaser, Michael. Comecon, Integration Problems of the Planned
    Economies. London: Oxford University Press, 1967.

Kosiński, Leszek A. "Population Censuses in East-Central Europe
    in the Twentieth Century," East European Quarterly, V (1971),
    279-301.

McNeill, William H. Europe's Steppe Frontier 1500-1800. Chicago:
    The University of Chicago Press, 1964.

Mellor, R. E. H. Comecon: Challenge to the West. Searchlight
    Book No. 48. New York: Van Nostrand Reinhold Co., 1971.

Mihailović, Kosta. Regional Development in Eastern Europe: Ex-
    perience and Prospects. UNRISD/70/C.49. GE.70-18044.
    Geneva: United Nations Research Institute for Social Develop-
    ment, Programme IV—Regional Development, August, 1970.

Montias, John Michael. "Economic Nationalism in Eastern Europe:
    Forty Years of Continuity and Change," Journal of International
    Affairs, LXVI (1966), 45-71.

_____. "Types of Communist Economic Systems," in Chalmers
    Johnson, ed. Change in Communist Systems. Stanford, Cal.:
    Stanford University Press, 1970.

Moore, Wilbert E. Economic Demography of Eastern and Southern
    Europe. Geneva: League of Nations, 1945.

Pasvolsky, Leo. Economic Nationalism of the Danubian States.
    Washington, D.C.: The Brookings Institution, 1928.

Pounds, Norman J.G. Eastern Europe. London: Longmans Green,
    1969.

Roglić, Josip. "Die Gebirge als die Wiege des Geschichtlichen
    Geschehens in Südosteuropa," Colloquium Geographicum,
    Argumenta Geographica, Festzeitschrift Carl Troll, Band
    12. Bonn: Ferd. Dümmlers Verlag, 1970.

Ronneberger, Franz and Gerhard Teich, eds. Von der Agrar-zur
    Industriegesellschaft. Darmstadt: Hoppenstedt and Co.,
    1969.

Rosenstein-Rodan, Paul N. "Problems of Industrialisation of Eastern
    and South-Eastern Europe," The Economic Journal, LIII
    (June-September, 1943), 202-11.

Ruppert, Karl and Jörg Maier, eds. Der Tourismus und seine Per-
    spektiven für Südosteuropa. WGI-Berichte zur Regionalforschung,
    Heft 6. Munich: Eigenverlag der Südosteuropa Gesellschaft,
    1971.

Shaffer, Harry G. "East Europe: Varieties of Economic Management,"
    East Europe, XIX (1970), I-20-30; II-35-40.

Spulber, Nicolas. The Economics of Communist Eastern Europe.
    New York: John Wiley & Sons, 1957.

_____. The State and Economic Development in Eastern Europe.
    New York: Random House, 1966.

Stavrianos, L. S. The Balkans Since 1453. New York: Rinehart &
    Co., 1959.

Sugar, Peter F. "External and Domestic Roots of Eastern European
    Nationalism," in Peter F. Sugar and Ivo I. Lederer, eds.
    Nationalism in Eastern Europe, Vol. 1. Seattle: University of
    Washington, Far Eastern and Russian Institute Publications on
    Russia and Eastern Europe, 1969.

_____. "The Rise of Nationalism," in The Nationality Problem
    in the Habsburg Monarchy in the Nineteenth Century: A Critical
    Appraisal. Austrian History Yearbook, III (1967).

U.S. Congress, Joint Economic Committee. Economic Developments
    in Countries of Eastern Europe, A Compendium of Papers.
    Washington: Joint Economic Committee, 1970.

Yves-Pechoux, Pierre and Michel Sivignon, Les Balkans. Paris:
    Presses Universitaire de France, 1971.

COMPARATIVE CONTRIBUTIONS FOR THE
COUNTRIES OF SOUTHEAST EUROPE

Burks, Richard V. "The Politics of Economic Reform in Bulgaria
    and Romania," paper presented for the Conference on Economic
    Reform in Eastern Europe, University of Michigan, November,
    1970. Unpublished manuscript.

Hoffman, George W. "The Problem of the Underdeveloped Regions in Southeast Europe: A Comparative Analysis of Romania, Yugoslavia and Greece, " Annals of the Association of American Geographers, LVII (December, 1967), 637-66.

_____. "Regional Development Processes in Southeast Europe: A Comparative Analysis of Bulgaria and Greece, " in George W. Hoffman, ed. Eastern Europe: Essays in Geographical Problems. London and New York: Methuen and Praeger Publishers, 1971.

Marinov, Christo. Socialisticjeski mezhdunarodni kompleksi i raioni (Socialist International Complexes and Regions). Varna: D'rzhavno Idatelstvo, 1965.

Popov, Zoran. "Komparativna analiza privrednog razvoja SFR Jugoslavije i NR Bulgarske, " (Comparative Analysis of the Economic Development of Yugoslavia and Bulgaria), Ekonmist, XX (1967), 294-320.

Ward, Benjamin N. "Capitalism vs. Socialism: A Small Country Version, " in Gregory Grossman, ed. Essays in Socialism and Planning in Honor of Carl Landauer. Englewood Cliffs, N. J.: Prentice-Hall, 1970.

BOOKS AND ARTICLES ON THE
COUNTRIES OF SOUTHEAST EUROPE

Albania

Blanc, André. "Naissance et Evolution des Paysages agraires en Albanie, " Geografiska annaler, XIII (1961), 8-16.

Pano, Nicholas C. The People's Republic of Albania. Integration and Community Building in Eastern Europe. Baltimore: The Johns Hopkins Press, 1968.

Papajorgh, Harilla. The Development of Socialist Industry and its Prospects in the People's Republic of Albania. Tiranë: The State Publishing House, 1962.

Pernack, Hans Joachim. "Die albanishce Wirtschaftspolitik nach dem Zweiten Weltkrieg, " Estratto da "Shejzat, " XIII (1969), 1-21.

Bulgaria

Bernard, Philippe. Growth Poles and Growth Centres as Instruments of Regional Development and Modernization with Special Reference to Bulgaria and France. UNRISD/70/C.25. GE.70-14470. Geneva: United Nations Research Institute for Social Development, Programme IV—Regional Development, Volume III, 1970.

Beshkov, A. S. and Valev, E. B., eds. Geografiya Na Bŭlgariya, Vol. 2, Ikonomičheska Geografiya (Geography of Bulgaria, Vol. 2: Economic Geography). Sofia: Bulgarian Academy of Sciences, 1961.

Brown, John F. Bulgaria under Communist Rule. New York: Praeger Publishers, 1970.

Dellin, L. A. D. "Bulgarian Economic Reform—Advance and Retreat, " Problems of Communism XX (1970), 44-52.

Hoffman, George W. "Transformation of Rural Settlements in Bulgaria, " Geographical Review, LIV (1964), 45-64.

Jacolin, Henry. "Transports et développement économique en Bulgarie, " Revue de géographie de Lyon, XVL (1970), 405-31.

Marinov, Christo. Osnovni vuprosi na geografskoto razpredelenie na proizvodstvoto i ikonomicheskoto rayonirane (Fundamental problems in the geographical distribution of production and economic regionalization). Varna: D'rzhavno Idatelstvo, 1963.

Zachariew, Iwan. "Regionalizacja ekonomiczna w Bulgarskiej Republice Ludowej, " (Economic Regionalization in the Bulgarian People's Republic) Przeglad geograficzny, XXXVIII (1966), 611-18.

Greece

Campbell, John and Phillip Sherrard. Modern Greece. Nations of Modern World Series. New York: Praeger Publishers, 1968.

Candilis, Wray O. The Economy of Greece 1944-1966: Efforts for Stability and Development. New York: Praeger 1968.

Coutsoumaris, George. The Morphology of Greek Industry. Athens:
    Research Monograph Series, Center of Economic Research No.
    6, 1963.

Kayser, Bernard et al. Exodue Rural et Attraction Urbaine en Grèce.
    Athens: Centre National de Recherches Sociales, 1971.

_____. Géographie Humaine de la Grèce. Paris: Presses Uni-
    versitaires de France, 1964.

_____. "La Grèce Modern: 1. La peninsula hellenique," in
    l'Encyclopaedia Universalis, (1971).

Maddison, Angus et al. Technical Assistance and Greek Development.
    Paris: Development Centre Studies 6, October, 1965.

McNeill, William Hardy. Greece: American Aid in Action 1947-1956.
    New York: The Twentieth Century Fund, 1957.

Papandreou, Andreas G. A Strategy for Greek Economic Development.
    Athens: Center of Economic Research, Research Monograph
    Series, No. 1, 1962.

Pepelasis, Adamantios, "Greece," in Adamantios Pepelasis et al.,
    eds. Economic Development. New York: Harper & Bros.,
    1961.

Sanders, Irwin T. "Greek Society in Transition," Balkan Studies,
    VIII (1967), 317-32.

The Economist (London). A Survey: The Two Faces of Greece, July
    31, 1971.

Ward, Benjamin. Greek Regional Development. Athens: Center
    for Economic Research, Research Monograph Series, No. 4,
    1962.

                            Romania

Academiei RPR, Institutul de Cercetari Economice. Dezvoltarea
    Economica a Rominiei 1944-1964 (Economic Development of
    Romania 1944-1964). Bucharest: Editura Academiei RPR,
    1964.

Blakovici, Petre, "Cerinte noi în organizarea teritorială şi sistem-
atizarea rurală, " (New requirements in territorial organization
and in rural systematization), Probleme Economice, XX (November, 1967), 3-18.

Brown, John F. "Rumania Today: I. Towards Integration, " Problems
of Communism, XVIII (January-February, 1969), 8-17.

_____. "Rumania Today: II. The Strategy of Defiance," Problems
of Communism, XVIII (March-April, 1969), 32-28.

Dobrescu, Emilian. The Structure of Romanian Economy. Bucharest:
Meridiane Publishing House, 1968.

Iancu, Aurel. "Îmbunătătirea repartizării teritoriale a industriei,"
(Improving the territorial distribution of industry), Lupta de
casa, XLVI (October, 1966), 11-23.

Mareş, D. "Industrializarea socialistă şi dezvoltarea legăturilor
economice dintre regiunile ţării, " (Socialist industrialization
and the development of economic relations among the regions
of Romania), Probleme Economice, XIX (September, 1966),
16-30.

Matley, Ian M. Romania: A Profile. New York: Praeger Publishers,
1970.

Mihăilescu, Vintilă et al. "Der geographische Aspekt in der funk-
tionalen Klassifizierung der Stadte, " Petermanns Geographische
Mitteilungen, 112 (1968) 275-83

_____. "Die Wirtschaftsregionen Rumäniens, " Revue Roumaine
de Géologie, Géophysique et Géographie. Série de Géographie,
XIV (1970), 197-207.

Moldovan, Roman. "Dezvoltarea economica a regiunilor in trecut
inapoiate, " (Economic development of the formerly backward
regions), Probleme Economice, XIV (1961), 76-95.

_____. "Die Ökonomische Entwicklung Rumäniens in den Jahren
des sozialistischen Aufbaues, " Österreichische Osthefte, XII
(September, 1970), 1-18(Beilage).

Montias, John Michael. Economic Development in Communist Rumania.
Cambridge, Mass.: MIT Press, 1967.

Morariu, Tiberiu et al. The Geography of Romania. 2nd ed. Bucharest: Meridiane Publishing House, 1969.

Rohleder, Claus D. "Wirtschaftsreformen: Rumanien," in Hermann
Gross, ed. Osteuropa-Wirtschaftsreformen. Bonn: Atlantic
Forum Edition, 1970.

Stan, Christache. "Industrialisation et Urbanisation en Roumaine,"
Revue Roumaine de Géologie, Géophysique et Géographie.
Série de Géographie, XIII (1969), 129-43.

Turnock, David. "The pattern of industrialization in Romania,"
Annals of the Association of American Geographers, LX
(September, 1970), 540-59.

                              Yugoslavia

Bajt, Aleksander. "Decentralized Decision Making Structure in the
Yugoslav Economy," Economics of Planning, VII (1967), 73-85.

Bićanić, Rudolf. "Economics of Socialism in a Developed Country,"
Foreign Affairs, XIVL (July, 1966), 633-50.

_____. "Problematika jedinstva privreda u Jugoslaviji," (Problems
of the unity of the economy of Yugoslavia), Zbornik pravnog
fakulteta u Zagrebu, "Spomenica prof. Rudolfu Bićaniću, XIX
(1969), 302-16.

Blăsković, Vladimir. Ekonomska Geografiya Jugoslavije. 3rd ed.
(Economic Geography of Yugoslavia). Zagreb: Novinsko/Izdavaći
i Birotehnički Zavod, 1970.

Bombelles, Joseph T. Economic Development of Communist Yugoslavia 1947-1964. Stanford, Cal.: The Hoover Institute on
War, Revolution and Peace, 1968.

Crawford, J. T. "Yugoslavia's New Economic Strategy: A Progress
Report," in U.S. Congress, Joint Economic Committee. Economic Developments in Countries of Eastern Europe, A Compendium of Papers. Washington D.C.: Joint Economic Committee, 1970.

Dzeba, K. and M. Beslac. Privredna reforma, što i zašto se mijenja. (Economic reforms, why and what is changing). Zagreb:
Novinsko izdavacka kuca Stvarnost, 1965.

Fisher, Jack C. Yugoslavia—A Multinational State. San Francisco: Chandler Publishing Co., 1966.

Hamilton, F. E. Ian. Yugoslavia: Patterns of Economic Activity. New York: Frederick A. Praeger, 1968.

Hočevar, Toussaint. The Structure of the Slowenian Economy 1848-1963. New York: Studia Slovenica, 1965.

Hoffman, George W. and Fred Warner Neal. Yugoslavia and the New Communism. New York: The Twentieth Century Fund, 1962.

Horvat, Branko. "Nationalismus und Nation," Translated from Serbo-Croatian in Gledišta, 5-6 (1971), Wissenschaftlicher Dienst-Südosteuropa, 8-9 (August-September, 1971), 136-46.

Mihailović, Kosta. Nerazvijena područja Jugoslavije. 2nd ed., (Underdeveloped Regions of Yugoslavia). Belgrade: Economic Institute, 1970.

_____. "Regionalni aspekt privrednog razvoja," (Regional aspects of economic development) in Problemi regionalnog privrednog razvoja. Belgrade: Ekonomska Biblioteka No. 18, 1962.

Roglić, Josip. "The Yugoslav Littoral," in J. M. Houston, The Western Mediterranean. London: Longmans, 1964.

Shoup, Paul. Communism and the Yugoslav National Question. New York: Columbia University Press, 1968.

Sichert, Pavle. "Regional Aspects of Yugoslav Economic Development and Planning," in Multidisciplinary Aspects of Regional Development. Paris: OECD Development Centre, 1968.

Simitčiev, Asen. Development of the economically underdeveloped regions of Yugoslavia. Studies No. 35. Belgrade: Medunarodna Politika, 1970.

Štajner, Rikard. "The System of Planning," Yugoslav Survey, XII (February, 1971), 15-30.

Sukijasović, Miodrag. Yugoslav Foreign Investment Legislation at Work: Experiences so far. Belgrade and New York: The Institute of International Politics and Economics and Oceana Publications, Inc., 1970.

The Economist (London). Another Way. A Survey of Yugoslavia,
      August 21, 1971.

Tomasevich, Jozo. Peasants, Politics, and Economic Change in
      Yugoslavia. Stanford, Cal.: Stanford University Press,
      1955.

Vrišer, Igor. "Centralna naselja v Jugoslaviji," (Central Places in
      Yugoslavia), Ekonomska revija, 4 (1968), 395-430.

Vucinich, Wayne S., ed. Contemporary Yugoslavia. Berkeley: Uni-
      versity of California Press, 1969 (note especially the con-
      tributions by Joel M. Halpern, George Macesich, Wayne S.
      Vucinich, and M. George Zaninovich).

Wilkinson, H. R. "Perspective on Some Fundamental Regional
      Divisions in Yugoslavia Illyria," in R. W. Steel and R. Lawton,
      eds., Liverpool Essays in Geography. London: University of
      Liverpool Press, 1967.

Zaninovich, M. George. The Development of Socialist Yugoslavia.
      Baltimore: The Johns Hopkins Press, 1968.

SPECIAL PUBLICATIONS

Attention is drawn to the following organizations and their
valuable research publications:

American Universities Field Staff: Reports on Southeast Europe,
      including Yugoslavia by Dennison I. Rusinow

Radio Free Europe, Research reports on the countries of Southeast
      Europe

United Nations: Development Programme (UNDP), Economic Com-
      mission of Europe (Survey and Economic Bulletin), Research
      Institute for Social Development, Programme IV—Regional
      Development (all published between 1969-71), Industrial Develop-
      ment Corporation

OECD: Economic Surveys for Greece and Yugoslavia, Mediterranean
      Regional Project (Development Project), Special OECD studies

The Economist Intelligence Unit, Ltd.: quarterly and annual reports
      on Romania, Bulgaria, Albania, and Yugoslavia

Adaptive approach, 188
Adaptive location decisions, 188
Administrative regions, 175

Balanced growth, 81, 83, 151, 199
Balkan Mountains, Balkan, 8, 9, 12, 25, 29
Bulgaria, 9, 11

Carpathians, 8, 10
Chiflicks, 29-30, 42
Comecon, 89, 131
Command economy, 87, 94
Complexes, 175, 192
Congested, 148

Danubian Plateau, 9
Depression of 1930s, 47, 61
Development approaches, 79, 80
Development, economic, 145, 192
Development planning, 146, 147, 191
Development strategy
  Albania, 43, 44, 45, 56
  Bulgaria, 42, 45, 52, 54, 202, 222, 224-25, 233
  Greece, 41, 45, 53-56, 63, 221
  Romania, 50, 53, 61, 205, 222, 233
  Yugoslavia, 45, 63, 209, 216, 227, 239
Dinaric Ranges, 5, 8, 15, 16
Dobruja, 9, 11, 12

Economic reform, 106, 113, 116, 120
Economic regions, 175
Economic space, 153
Epirus, 5, 22

Equality-inequality, 69, 70, 83
Evenness in growth of equalization, 151, 189, 198, 199

Foreign capital in Yugoslavia, 52
Foreign investments, 123
Foreign workers
  Bulgaria, 129, 198
  Greece, 106, 197, 230
  Yugoslavia, 122, 197, 206
Fund for the Development of
  Underdeveloped Regions, 173, 185, 218

Great Alfold, 10
Growth center, growth areas, 152, 201, 204, 211
Growth pole, 151, 153, 155, 193, 201

Hungary, 3, 164

Industrial centrals, 160, 167, 222
International division of labor, 69

Joint partnership or mixed
  cooperation, 81

Land reforms, 49
Location decisions, 75, 159, 185

Macedonian-Thracian Massif, 5, 8, 9, 12, 14, 19
Maize, 27, 39
Maritsa Basin, 8, 9, 14
Moldavian Tablelands, 9, 10, 11
Morava-Vardar depression, 8, 14, 18

Old Romania, Moldavia, Walachia,
  5, 28

Pannonian Basin, 9, 11
Pindus Mountains, 5, 8, 22
Planning instruments, 183
Planning, regional; regional
  development, 145, 158, 181, 192, 214
Polarization effect, 151, 154, 201
Postwar boundary changes, 73-74

Region, 147
Regional cooperation, 231-32
Regionalism, 170-71
Regional policy, 147, 148, 149, 150, 157,
  158, 182
Rumelian Basin, 8

Serbia, 42
Social product, 99
Southeast Europe, 12
Soviet model, 70, 75-76, 88

Spatial activity sphere, 188
Spread and backwash effect, 151, 152
Sredna Gora, 8
Stara Planina, 8
Surplus population, 50, 60

Thracian Basin, 8
Transhumance, 10, 39
Transylvanian Basin, Transylvania, 9,
  10, 12, 43
Trickling-down effects, 151, 152, 201

Unbalanced growth, 80, 151
Underdeveloped regions, 83, 172, 184,
  192, 203, 217, 220
Urban plan, 227

Vlasia, Vlachs, 11, 26
Vojvodina, 17, 26, 192

Walachian Plain, 9, 10, 11
Workers' management, 87, 217

GEORGE W. HOFFMAN, Professor of Geography at the University of Texas, has written for many years in the field of economic and political geography. He has traveled widely in Europe and, specifically, in most of the socialist countries of East Central and Southeast Europe.

Dr. Hoffman is editor of Eastern Europe: Essays in Geographical Problems (Methuen and Praeger Publishers, 1971) and A Geography of Europe; co-author of Yugoslavia and the New Communism; and author of Balkans in Transition. He has written nearly one hundred scholarly articles and extended reviews. In addition he is editor of Praeger's European Profile Series and of Van Nostrand Reinhold's Searchlight Books and is on the editorial board of the East European Quarterly.

Professor Hoffman was a Fulbright Professor in Munich in 1962 and in Heidelberg in 1972. He studied at the University of Vienna, American University, and Harvard University and received a Ph.D. in Geography from the University of Michigan.